Welcome to

ALL ABOUT
HISTORY
Book of
KINGS
& QUEENS

Throughout history, monarchs have had a huge impact on the world, whether uniting nations or tearing them apart. Some have inherited great power, while others have fought to take what they saw as rightfully theirs. There have been kings that instigated wars to demonstrate their strength and conquer the world, and queens who helped shape the future of their nations. In this book we take a look at some of the most iconic and influential monarchs the world has ever seen, from Herod and Cleopatra to Henry VIII and Louis XIV. We'll also take a look at the 30 kings and queens who changed the world, the ten kings who can lay claim to the bloodiest reign, the royal warriors who did battle to claim their thrones, and how the British monarchy was born.

KINGS & QUEENS

Imagine Publishing Ltd
Richmond House
33 Richmond Hill
Bournemouth
Dorset BH2 6EZ
☎ +44 (0) 1202 586200
Website: www.imagine-publishing.co.uk

Head of Publishing
Aaron Asadi

Head of Design
Ross Andrews

Editor-in-Chief
Dave Harfield

Senior Art Editor
Helen Harris
Greg Whitaker

Design
Lauren Debano-Elliot

Photographer
James Sheppard

Printed by
William Gibbons, 26 Planetary Road, Willenhall, West Midlands, WV13 3XT

Distributed in the UK & Eire by
Imagine Publishing Ltd, www.imagineshop.co.uk. Tel 01202 586200

Distributed in Australia by
Gordon & Gotch, Equinox Centre, 18 Rodborough Road, Frenchs Forest,
NSW 2086. Tel + 61 2 9972 8800

Distributed in the Rest of the World by
Marketforce, Blue Fin Building, 110 Southwark Street, London, SE1 0SU

Part of the

ALL ABOUT HISTORY

bookazine series

IMAGINE PUBLISHING

Contents

80

76

Contents

30
Kings and Queens who changed history

Monarchs have ruled kingdoms the world over for centuries, but only these few have changed the course of history during their reigns

Elizabeth I

**Defeated the Spanish Armada
- 18 August 1588**

The Virgin Queen who reigned over a golden age, paving the way for the British Empire

She was known by several names - the Virgin Queen, Good Queen Bess, Gloriana - and the legacies of Queen Elizabeth I are many, but of all the ways that she changed the world, there is one episode of her life in particular that stands out. It was the summer of 1588, and having been angered by his 'heretic', 'illegitimate' sister-in-law Elizabeth I, the Protestant ruler who succeeded the English throne at 25 years old after his wife Mary I died, the Catholic King Philip II of Spain invaded England with a great fleet of 22 galleons and over a hundred armed merchant ships.

The attack of the Spanish Armada marked the beginning of an unofficial war between England and Spain that had been brewing for years. Releasing England from the Catholic Church re-imposed on it by Philip II and his late Queen Consort, Elizabeth I had not only resurrected the Protestantism that the Spanish rulers sought to quash, she had gone on the year before to formalise treaties with Protestant rebels in the Netherlands. For a King who wanted to remove all trace of Henry VIII's assault on Catholicism, it was galling to see his daughter Elizabeth solidify Protestant power in Europe.

Meanwhile, pioneers of her realm like Sir Francis Drake were undertaking expeditions of exploration, making enemies of the Spanish as they did so. Philip II was said to have put a price of 20,000 ducats (around £4/$6.5 million) on Drake's head for his piracy against Spanish vessels. Spanish animosity had built to breaking point while Elizabeth I was building the beginnings of what would later become the British Empire, all while supporting artists, thinkers and writers like William Shakespeare and Christopher Marlowe at home, and leading a golden age for the arts and sciences.

Highly intelligent and very well educated, Elizabeth I surrounded herself with people she could trust and built strong relations with her people that fostered a sense of solidarity. As the Church was breaking apart in Europe and monarchs wrestled for power, Elizabeth I stood for Protestantism while still honouring English Catholics by preserving some of their practises. She gave a sense of identity to England at the point preceding its global dominance.

And on 18 August 1588, about a week after her navy routed the Spanish Armada at the Battle of Gravelines, chasing it up to the Scottish coast, Elizabeth I gave one of the world's most famous speeches to the troops at Tilbury, a force of 4,000 who were standing by ready to defend the Thames Estuary against any attempt to take London. She promised to take up arms herself against any prince of Europe, and declared: "I know I have the body of a weak and feeble woman, but I have the heart and stomach of a King."

REIGN 1588-1603

COUNTRY ENGLAND AND IRELAND

LEGACY

DEFEATED THE SPANISH ARMADA, RETURNED ENGLAND TO A PROTESTANT RULE AND LED A GOLDEN AGE OF EXPLORATION, THE ARTS AND SCIENCES

Elizabeth I was both highly intelligent and well loved by her people, nurturing and defending England and its culture while transforming it into a global power

Victoria

**Grandmother of Europe becomes
Empress of India – 1 May 1876**

The Queen who led the Industrial Revolution, and ruled the largest ever empire

After her husband Prince Albert died, Queen Victoria began wearing black mourning clothes on a regular basis, and continued to do so throughout her life

Queen Victoria's reign was a time of transition towards new technologies and infrastructures, and at the Great Exhibition in 1851 she saw new machines like the camera, talking and printing telegraphs, microscopes, locomotives and more. But one of Victoria's many lasting legacies was her expansion of the British Empire on a massive scale. Until the death of her husband Prince Albert, after which she descended into a period of depression and mourning that overshadowed her later years, Queen Victoria was a vibrant presence who represented the spirit of the times.

Her 63-year reign - the longest in British history - saw the British Empire encompass a quarter of the world's land, with Britain's colonies spanning the globe and its navy ruling the seas. In 1857, however, a series of mutinies began in the armies of the East India Company, with sepoys who had been working for the Company beginning to rebel against the occupation of their lands. One of the turning points in the struggle for independence was the moment when a soldier was asked to bite open one of the cartridges for his rifle, which were usually made using animal fat forbidden to the Sikh and Muslim sepoys. It sparked an uprising that, the following year, led to the dissolution of the East India Company.

The rule of the East India Company, which had been governing Indian lands with private armies, passed to Victoria, and this began the period of British Raj rule that lasted until India declared independence in 1947. During this period, Victoria oversaw the construction of vast rail networks at home, where she became the first British monarch to travel by train, and saw the first passenger line in North India opened in 1859. In 1876, Victoria was proclaimed Empress of India, and marked the height of British colonialism.

The far and fervent reach of British colonialism had an unmistakable impact on global history, and Victoria was the face of it. Her standards, morality and decisions shaped the face of the world, and tied British culture to that of dozens of other countries. There are few Queens who gave their names to an age, but Victoria was one of them. Not only that, she earned the name 'grandmother of Europe' by raising nine children who married into nobility across the continent, tying together its aristocracies just as she knitted together her global empire and brought Britain to the peak of its rule.

REIGN 1837-1901

COUNTRY
GREAT BRITAIN

LEGACY
EXTENDED THE BRITISH EMPIRE ACROSS THE WORLD AND BECAME THE EMPRESS OF INDIA, WHILE PRESIDING OVER A NEW INDUSTRIAL AGE

Henry VIII

Created the Church of England - November 1534

Starting the Protestant Reformation to wed Anne Boleyn, Henry VIII shaped modern Christianity

A dashing man in his youth who grew morbidly obese in later years, Henry VIII nonetheless took six wives between 1509 and 1547

One of England's lustier Kings, Henry VIII defied Rome and changed the course of Christianity in both Britain and Europe through his desire to divorce his first wife, Catherine of Aragon, and marry Anne Boleyn. By 1526, Catherine, daughter of Isabella of Castile and Ferdinand II, was over 40 years old and had failed to produce a male heir for Henry. After multiple miscarriages she no longer appealed to the King, and he became infatuated with the younger, prettier Anne Boleyn.

When he married Catherine in 1509, he first had to get the Pope to grant a dispensation accepting that her earlier marriage to Henry's brother Arthur had never been consummated. Now, in order to annul his marriage to Catherine, Henry needed the Pope to agree that the opposite was true; that her marriage to Arthur *had* been consummated. This looked unlikely, so Henry took matters into his own hands. It was around 1527 when he began openly consorting with Anne Boleyn, and 1529 when he began attacking the church through his government, changing legislation and levying new taxes. It culminated in Henry's abrupt disappearance with Anne, and subsequent banishing of Catherine and her daughter from London after they returned a month later. Henry was threatened with excommunication unless he 'cast off the concubine, Anne.' His response was to enact a bill to remove almost all of Rome's subsidies from English churches.

Eventually, in 1534, Henry passed the Act of Supremacy that declared him 'the only supreme head on earth of the Church of England', removing papal authority from Britain and making himself the head of state and religious affairs. By this time, Anne had already given birth to a girl, and was surrounded by rumours of infidelity. Henry beheaded her for these crimes, executing her for treason, adultery and incest, and went on to marry Jane Seymour in May 1536.

Pope Paul III excommunicated Henry, and the Church of England seceded from Roman Catholic rule. Protestant reformers didn't gain much ground in the years immediately following the end of Catholic rule, but it did pave the way for future change. Henry began the Reformation, and his son (with Jane Seymour), was the first English monarch to be raised a Protestant.

REIGN 1509-1547

COUNTRY ENGLAND

LEGACY

DEFIED THE POPE AND CATHOLICISM BY DIVORCING TO REMARRY, AND CREATED THE PROTESTANT CHURCH IN ORDER TO DO SO

Charlemagne

United western Europe in the Carolingian empire - 800 CE

Charlemagne ruled the continent for the first time since the Romans and led a Renaissance

Charlemagne ruled almost all of western Europe and brought in systems of weights, writing and currency

REIGN 768-814 CE

COUNTRY FRANCE AND GERMANY

LEGACY

CHARLEMAGNE ENDED THE DARK AGES IN EUROPE AND MADE THE FIRST MEDIEVAL RENAISSANCE POSSIBLE

King Charles the Great, or Charlemagne, was King of the Franks, Italy and later became the 'Emperor of the Romans' in a move that divided the vestiges of the old Roman empire forever. His coronation by Pope Leo III on Christmas Day 800 CE had circumvented the claim of Empress Irene of Constantinople. What Leo had done was legitimise a second claim to the imperial authority that dated back to the first Roman emperors, and so started centuries of competing claims of sovereignty.

Long before then, though, young Charlemagne became King of the Franks. Initially, he shared the rule of the kingdom with his brother Carloman, but his death in 771 left Charlemagne the sole ruler of the entire Kingdom. He went on from there to conquer the Lombards and become King of Italy in 774, and the expanded Frankish state he created eventually went on to become known as the Carolingian Empire, after Charlemagne's family name. Charlemagne's rule saw the Carolingian Renaissance, the first of three that were to sweep medieval Europe between the 8th and 9th Centuries, and during this time there was a marked increase in literature and architecture, the arts, legal and religious studies and more.

Some of Charlemagne's own writings, like the Admonitio Generalis, opened up discussions of rational ideas across Europe, and during his reign he introduced administrative reforms throughout the land. He has since been called the 'father of Europe', and both the French and German monarchies consider Charlemagne to be a part of their history. Not only did he oversee this Renaissance, he took part in it. Charlemagne standardised weights, measures and coins, devising systems of pounds, feet, livre, shillings and pence, and he even tried to standardise Christianity throughout his empire. Charlemagne instilled his love of learning in the monastic schools that he developed during his reign. He saw an end to the Dark Ages following the death of Rome.

Isabella I of Castile

Sent Columbus to the New World – 17 April 1492

Isabella of Castile united the Spanish Kingdoms and funded the discovery of the century

REIGN 1474-1504

COUNTRY SPAIN

LEGACY
GAVE PROTECTION AND FINANCE TO CHRISTOPHER COLUMBUS, GIVING SPAIN A STRONGHOLD IN THE AMERICAS THAT STILL HAS A POWERFUL LEGACY TODAY

Remembered as the 'Mother of the Americas' by some, to others, Queen Isabella I of Castile will always be remembered as the architect of the Spanish Inquisition that ravaged Europe during her reign and for decades afterwards. She and her husband Ferdinand II, King of Aragon, Naples, Sicily and Valencia, united the old Spanish Kingdoms under their rule and modernised their collective Kingdom, freeing it of debt and restructuring its politics. It was the beginning of Spain as we know it, and Isabella and Ferdinand made a powerful team.

When Christopher Columbus came to them seeking protection and finance for a voyage to discover the New World, they assisted him. On 17 April 1492, Isabella and Ferdinand signed a commission making him admiral of a funded fleet, and with that support planted Spain and its culture firmly in the Americas.

Financed Christopher Columbus' journey to discover the New World and raised the Spanish Inquisition to power with her husband Ferdinand II

Despite her ultimate defeat, Boudica became a powerful symbol of rebellion and the leader of the Celtic tribes who attempted to overthrow the occupation

REIGN 60-61 CE

COUNTRY BRITAIN

LEGACY
REVOLTED AGAINST THE ROMAN EMPIRE IN BRITAIN AND, ALTHOUGH SHE ALMOST SUCCEEDED, ENDED UP SECURING BRITAIN FOR THE ENEMY

Boudica

Lost the last battle for resistance to the Romans – 60/61 CE

Queen Boudica led the southern Celtic tribes in revolt against Roman rule

Queen of the Iceni tribe in what is now known as Norfolk, England, Boudica repelled the Romans from Londinium, the capital, before eventually falling to the governor Gaius Suetonius Paulinus. Though ultimately unsuccessful, she almost threw the invaders out of Britain for good, and left an indelible cultural mark that led Queen Victoria to claim her as her namesake centuries later.

When Boudica's husband, King Prasutagus of the Iceni, died in 60 or 61 AD, the Romans were quick to capitalise on this opportunity. They flogged Boudica, raped her daughters, and called in their debts from the tribesmen. Boudica fought through these terrible trials and went on to lead 100,00 Iceni and other old East Anglian tribes in revolt against the Ninth Spanish Legion and the capital of the Roman lands, Londinium. The later defeat of Boudica, however, ensured Roman rule in the south of Britain for generations to come.

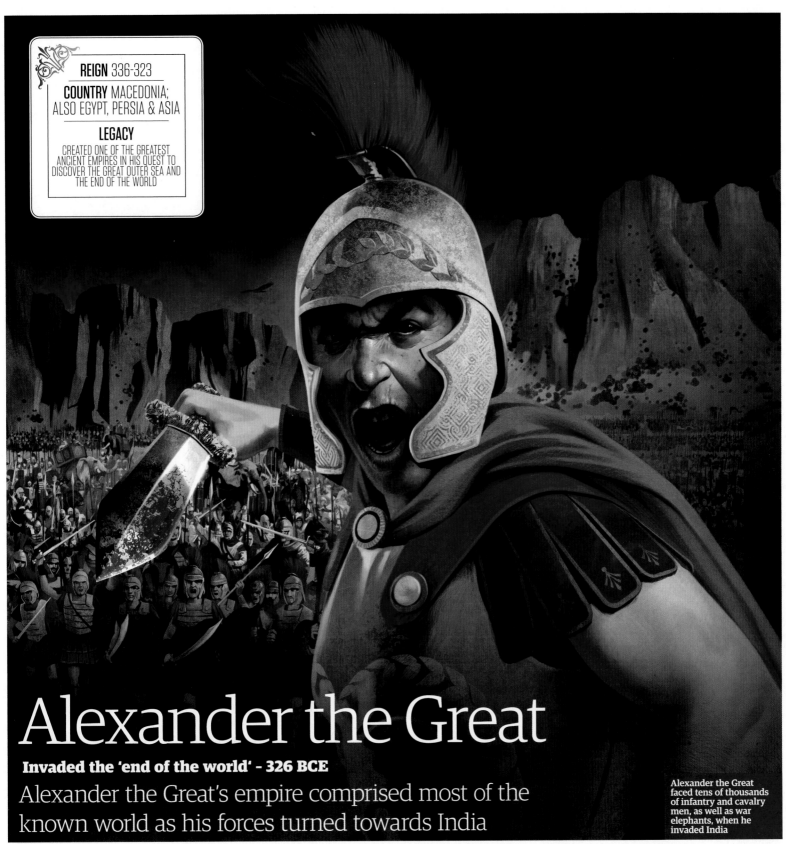

REIGN 336-323

COUNTRY MACEDONIA; ALSO EGYPT, PERSIA & ASIA

LEGACY
CREATED ONE OF THE GREATEST ANCIENT EMPIRES IN HIS QUEST TO DISCOVER THE GREAT OUTER SEA AND THE END OF THE WORLD

Alexander the Great

Invaded the 'end of the world' - 326 BCE

Alexander the Great's empire comprised most of the known world as his forces turned towards India

Alexander the Great faced tens of thousands of infantry and cavalry men, as well as war elephants, when he invaded India

King Alexander of Macedonia came to power after his father, King Phillip II of Macedon, was assassinated in 336 BCE, and he inherited both a strong kingdom and a capable army. He put them both to work quickly, proving himself a ruthless leader who was changing the world with his vision.

Continuing to establish himself as an extremely capable military tactician, his armies defeated the Achaemenid and Persian empires, leaving Alexander to rule Persia and Asia Minor, and then swept on towards India, which was the edge of the known world at the time. Alexander sought to rule over the Aegean as Athens had done before,

and as he marched he left great cities in his wake, naming each one Alexandria. By 326 BCE he had made it deep into India, where his army now struggled against the jungle, harsh climes and ferocious warriors. He was eventually turned back, but he spread Greek culture deep into the east and ushered in the Hellenistic period.

Louis XIV

The Sun King chosen by God

Declared he was chosen by God to rule, and ensured that no one could challenge him

After inheriting the French throne at the age of four, Louis XIV spent a lifetime reaffirming his status as his nation's supreme ruler. By the time he died at the age of 76, he had ruled longer than any monarch in European history.

During the early years of his reign, the country was run by Louis' mother and his minister Cardinal Mazarin, during which time he saw the French people revolt against their rule, and the family was forced to flee Paris more than once. As the King, Louis promoted the idea of divine right and referred to himself as the 'Sun King'. He left Paris to build an enormous palace for himself at Versailles, which he encouraged the nobility to inhabit to avoid dissent. He revolutionised France's infrastructure, making the country more prosperous and easier to control. However, he spent much of his rule at war, and the final 30 years of his 72-year reign were spent in costly and unsuccessful conflict.

REIGN 1643-1715

COUNTRY FRANCE

LEGACY

PROMOTED THE NOTION OF THE DIVINE RIGHT TO RULE AND THE ABSOLUTE POWER OF THE MONARCHY, PAVING THE WAY FOR THE FRENCH REVOLUTION

Louis build the great Palace at Versailles, a symbol of royal power and opulence

The Gunpowder plot put paid to any concerns that James I had Catholic sympathies, whether they were correct or not

James I

First King of Great Britain

United England and Scotland, and believed that he had the Divine Right to do so

By the time James VI of Scotland took the throne of England, he had already been a monarch for 36 years. He was named King of Scotland at the age of one, and believed so firmly in the Divine Right of Kings that he wrote a book on the subject. When he came to England after the death of Elizabeth, I he had himself proclaimed the first king of Great Britain. Believing he knew exactly what he was doing, James would argue endlessly with Parliament over trivial matters, refusing to back down and lose face.

While many worried that James was too lenient on Catholics, his reaction to the Gunpowder Plot of 1605 proved otherwise. He had authorised work on the King James Bible, the good book translated and altered to conform to the Church of England's beliefs. His extravagant spending angered politicians, while he lacked his predecessor Elizabeth's love for the people. By the time of his death, the seeds of the Civil War had already been sown.

REIGN 1567/1603-1625

COUNTRY GREAT BRITAIN

LEGACY

BROUGHT THE CONCEPT OF DIVINE RIGHT TO ENGLAND, AND WAS THE FIRST KING OF GREAT BRITAIN

Nebuchadnezzar II

Warrior king of the Babylonian Empire

Created the Babylonian Empire, forming a state whose legend survives to this day

REIGN 605-562 BCE
COUNTRY BABYLON
LEGACY
TURNED BABYLON INTO AN EMPIRE AND WAS RESPONSIBLE FOR THE EXILE OF THE JEWS

Ancient Babylon had at last found stability under the rule of Nabopolassar. With his son Nebuchadnezzar II, it would find glory. When the young man took power, he asked the gods that he be "satiated with splendour," and spent the rest of his reign making sure that this would be the case.

His father had secured independence from Assyria. Nebuchadnezzar fought the Egyptians, Palestinians and Syrians to create a Babylonian Empire. He built the Hanging Gardens of Babylon and took control of the Mesopotamian trade routes to the Mediterranean, using the fortunes gained from his efforts to turn his city into a true wonder of the world. The walls had his name inscribed on them, while chariot races took place along their tops.

To many, Nebuchadnezzar will forever be remembered as the man who destroyed the Temple in Jerusalem and deported many prominent Jews to Babylon. He is remembered in the Bible as an enemy of God.

Nebuchadnezzar funnelled the majority of the fortune he made through trade and war into turning the city of Babylon into a true wonder of the world

Louis XVI

The French king who lost his head

The last in a line of profligate monarchs, Louis was executed for treason in the French Revolution

REIGN 1774-92
COUNTRY FRANCE
LEGACY
HIS FAMILY'S LEGACY OF SPENDING AND BELIEF IN DIVINE RIGHT LED TO THE FRENCH REVOLUTION

Louis XVI was the object of the Revolution's wrath, and he could not escape the executioner's scaffold

Louis XVI's reign was doomed from the start. After a succession of out-of-touch French kings who believed that they were chosen by God and an ever-worsening financial crisis, his attempts to continue that legacy led to revolution and his death.

His marriage to Marie Antoinette was a political victory, but the (incorrect) image of her as an uncaring, ever-spending snob meant that she was unpopular with the populace. Careless spending and supporting the American War of Independence meant that France was on the verge of bankruptcy. In desperation, Louis called the 'States General' to raise taxes without giving Parliament any power. The political factions united in opposition, and the people supported them, storming the Bastille in 1789 and forcing the royal family to leave Versailles for Paris. When Louis and his family were caught trying to escape, a new constitutional monarchy was established in retaliation, but it wasn't long before France was declared a republic in September 1792. On 21 January 1793, Louis was executed for treason.

Henry V

The Shakespearean hero who put France to the sword

William Shakespeare wrote of a wayward prince who found his way, but Henry was always a committed politician and soldier. He argued with his father about how to rule but, on becoming king, he led two hugely successful military campaigns in France that would never be matched. His finest hour was at the Battle of Agincourt in 1415, but he died after just nine years on the throne.

> **REIGN** 1413-1422
> **COUNTRY** ENGLAND
> **LEGACY**
> HIS MILITARY SUCCESSES IN FRANCE INSPIRED GENERATIONS OF ENGLISH KINGS TO TRY AND REPEAT THEM

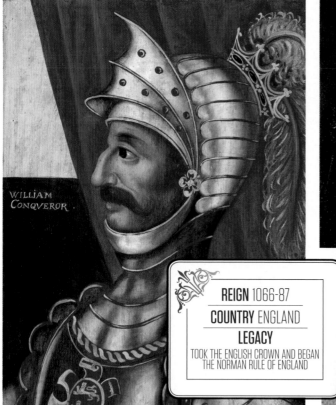

> **REIGN** 1066-87
> **COUNTRY** ENGLAND
> **LEGACY**
> TOOK THE ENGLISH CROWN AND BEGAN THE NORMAN RULE OF ENGLAND

William The Conqueror

The King who invaded England

The Duke of Normandy invaded England in 1066, and waited to face the recently crowned Harold at Hastings, stating that the crown had been promised to him. After a decisive victory, William took the English throne, secured borders and treaties with the Scottish and the Welsh, and ordered the creation of the *Domesday Book*. He brought England stability and a new royal line.

Alfred The Great

Turned the tide against the Viking invasion

When Alfred became King of Wessex, England was the victim of persistent attack from Danish Vikings, who struck further and further south. He used guerrilla warfare against their troops, in the process forcing them to consider a treaty. By creating a strong base and defences, promoting literacy and justice, and creating a partition treaty in 886 CE, Alfred brought peace and prosperity.

> **REIGN** 871-899 CE
> **COUNTRY** WESSEX
> **LEGACY**
> BROUGHT PEACE AND PROGRESS TO ENGLAND

Gustav II Adolf Of Sweden

The saviour of Sweden

Gustav had inherited three international wars when he took the throne at the age of 16, but after a series of campaigns he made peace with Denmark, Poland and Russia and found a way to resolve the internal conflicts that beset Sweden. With the country at peace, he developed an infrastructure and bureaucracy that stabilised the nation, before entering the 30 Years War to claim territory in the Baltic.

REIGN 1740-86

COUNTRY PRUSSIA

LEGACY

TURNED PRUSSIA INTO THE GREATEST MILITARY POWER IN EUROPE

Frederick II Of Prussia

Frederick turned Prussia into a military superpower

After an abusive childhood at the hands of his father, Frederick II went on to unite the disparate territories of the Prussian territories, using his military might and cunning to create one of Europe's great powers, even after defeat in the Seven Years' War. As significant as his military accomplishments were, his commitment to enlightened absolutism is just as important, with a rationalistic approach to religion and justice.

REIGN 1611-32

COUNTRY SWEDEN

LEGACY

TURNED A SWEDEN IN CHAOS INTO A STABLE, PROSPEROUS NATION

John III Sobieski Of Poland-Lithuania

The soldier who became a king

Before he was king, John III was already a hero after leading the Polish military against the Swedes, Tartars and Cossacks. When the Ottomans advanced on Europe, he joined with Pope Leopold and led the glorious campaign to relieve the Holy Roman Empire's forces at the Battle of Vienna in 1683. He would never recapture that glory, but his victory against overwhelming odds was legendary.

REIGN 1674-96

COUNTRY POLAND-LITHUANIA

LEGACY

HELD BACK THE OTTOMAN EMPIRE

Edward I
United England by any means necessary

Edward was determined to create a unified England that recognised him as its ruler. When he returned from the Crusades after his father's death, he invaded Wales twice to subdue rebel forces and brought it under English rule, creating new legal and trade systems to ensure funds for his brutal campaigns. His final years were spent fighting the Scottish uprisings with shockingly brutal methods.

REIGN 1274-1307

COUNTRY ENGLAND

LEGACY
A LEGACY OF BRUTAL CONFLICT IN WALES AND SCOTLAND

Cnut The Great
The king who made England part of a bigger world

The Viking king who told the tide to turn back understood that the power of a king is fleeting. However, he amassed plenty in his lifetime, having invaded England and taken the crown in 1017. He divided the country into kingdoms to ensure peace, and sent his Danish soldiers back home, finally creating a huge empire by conquering Norway in 1025.

REIGN 1516-56

COUNTRY SPAIN

LEGACY
FOUGHT OFF THE OTTOMAN INVASION, BUT SAW HIS EMPIRE CRUMBLE

Charles V
Faced the end of an empire

Charles became Holy Roman Emperor while the Protestant Reformation was taking place in 1519. For the majority of his reign he allowed religious freedom, provided Protestants fought with him against France and the rising Ottoman threat in the East. Riches found in the Americas weren't enough to keep his campaigns going, however, and much of his empire in Europe was lost. He finally abdicated in favour of his son.

REIGN 1016-35

COUNTRY ENGLAND, DENMARK, NORWAY

LEGACY
CREATED AN ENGLISH-SCANDINAVIAN EMPIRE

Mbande Nzinga

The African queen who held off the Portuguese

Mbande Nzinga was born into conflict with the Portuguese, who were raiding the Ndongo territory for slaves. When her cruel brother asked for help while negotiating with them, she secured a treaty and had him killed. Having taken power, she cancelled the treaty when it became clear that the Portuguese had broken it. Between 1639 and 1648 she held back her enemies, finally agreeing to a treaty that kept her in power.

> **REIGN** 1623-63
>
> **COUNTRY** THE NDONGO (ANGOLA)
>
> **LEGACY**
> FOUGHT OFF PORTUGUESE SLAVE TRADERS AGAINST OVERWHELMING ODDS

> **REIGN** 1154-1204
>
> **COUNTRY** ENGLAND
>
> **LEGACY**
> SURVIVED HER HUSBAND TO BE A CRUCIAL PART OF HER SONS' RULE

Eleanor Of Aquitaine

The queen who defied her king to bring stability

The ambitious Eleanor made Henry of Anjou her second husband, who became the King of England. She assisted her children with a rebellion attempt in 1173, and ensured that her favourite son Richard's throne was kept safe during his time in the Crusades. She kept his kingdom running smoothly, negotiating his wedding and release from prison, and assisted her son John when he became king.

> **REIGN** 1560-89
>
> **COUNTRY** FRANCE
>
> **LEGACY**
> BRUTALLY ATTEMPTED TO CRUSH THE WARS OF RELIGION TO KEEP HER SONS ON THE THRONE

Catherine De' Medici

France's regent during the Wars of Religion

Catherine stepped into power in 1560 when her husband Henry II of France - and her eldest son Francis - died in quick succession. As regent for her ten-year-old son Charles, she kept power grabs at bay from the nobility and used increasingly violent methods to quell the French Wars of Religion, which culminated in her involvement in the St Bartholomew's Day Massacre. Her influence continued throughout the reign of her son Henry.

Charles II
The Restoration King

After Parliament's rule following the Civil War, Charles II was invited to return to power in 1660. He encouraged tolerance (after punishing those who had executed his father) and promoted peace with France and international trade in America and India. He ruled during the Great Fire and the Great Plague, but is better known for his mistresses, his belief in Catholicism and conflicts with Parliament.

REIGN 1660-85

COUNTRY ENGLAND

LEGACY
RESTORED ENGLAND TO A MONARCHY AND RETURNED THE MONARCHY TO ITS OLD WAYS

REIGN 1936-52

COUNTRY ENGLAND

LEGACY
PROVIDING THE VOICE OF LEADERSHIP DURING CONFLICT

George VI
Refused to leave London during World War II

Following his brother's abdication, the shy, awkward George VI took the crown shortly before World War II broke out. He remained in Buckingham Palace during the Blitz and visited bombed homes, as well as meeting the troops at home and abroad after D-Day. Ever conscious of the military's efforts, he created the George Cross and the George Medal.

Charles IV
The Holy Roman politician

When Charles was born, the kingdom he stood to inherit was that of Luxembourg and Bohemia. When he died, he was the Holy Roman Emperor, with Italy, Germany and Lombardy owing fealty to him. He preferred to use his skills as a politician to gain power, promoting the arts, sciences, charities and church building, as well as amassing a staggering empire in a (mostly) peaceful manner.

REIGN 1346-78

COUNTRY
HOLY ROMAN EMPIRE

LEGACY
USED TREATIES AND NEGOTIATIONS TO GAIN POWER OVER THE HOLY ROMAN EMPIRE

REIGN 1696-1725
COUNTRY RUSSIA
LEGACY
FORCED RUSSIA TO BECOME
A MODERN STATE

REIGN 1902-53
COUNTRY SAUDI ARABIA
LEGACY
CREATED SAUDI ARABIA AND BEGAN
THEIR OIL INDUSTRY

REIGN 1849-78
COUNTRY ITALY
LEGACY
CREATED THE FIRST UNITED
KINGDOM OF ITALY

Peter I
The Russian reformer

Peter took control of a Russia in tatters and began a period of modernisation. He promoted education and the sciences to improve industry and looked to Western methods to strengthen his Navy and bring Russian territories together, as well as bringing the church under his control and modernising the alphabet. He was cruel and unpopular, but dragged Russia into the modern age.

Ibn Saud
The father of Saudi Arabia

Ibn Saud began his journey to power by reclaiming his father's territory in central Arabia in a bloody coup. He fought off Turkish forces and encouraged religious fanaticism to support his rule as he expanded his territory through conquest of his Arab rivals. He founded the Kingdom of Saudi Arabia and brokered the first oil deals of the region, changing its fortunes forever.

Victor Emmanuel II
The Sardinian who united Italy

After inheriting a failed war with Austria, Victor paid his way out of the conflict and turned the kingdom of Sardinia-Piedmont into something much greater. With the help of Count Cavour and Garibaldi, the Piedmontese army took territory from Prussia and France to create the first united Italy.

REIGN 522-486 BCE
COUNTRY PERSIA
LEGACY
EXPANDED AND CONSOLIDATED THE
PERSIAN EMPIRE AND TURNED IT
INTO A GREAT, ENLIGHTENED AND
PROSPEROUS KINGDOM

King Darius The Great
The Persian architect

Darius took power through violence and cunning. Once on the throne, it was largely through this second attribute that he turned Persia into a true empire. He divided his kingdom into 'satrapies', ordered the construction of roads, promoted trade, ordered a single currency and official language and encouraged religious tolerance. Under his guidance the Persian Empire became a shining beacon of prosperity and enlightenment.

10
Murderous Kings

A blood-curdling countdown of
history's deadliest monarchs

I n this day and age it's quite difficult to imagine the sheer power that kings and queens once wielded over their subjects. In many ways these monarchs were more similar to modern dictators than the rulers that we know today. Murder was often a means to a political end, while crimes of passion would rarely be met with any immediate consequences.

Although the kings had ultimate power, it was a power they were forced to fight for - often using fear, war and murder, among other methods, to stay at the top. The position of king was a precarious one and, driven by this fact and an unhealthy dose of paranoia, certain monarchs left a bloody trail through history.

But beyond paranoia, what drove them to such bloodshed? Several of these kings earned their place on this list with their military campaigns. War was a show of strength, a display of dominance. With an almost-constant state of conflict, territories were lost and won with great frequency, which, of course, meant that they had to be reclaimed. The glory of a kingdom was not just determined by its size necessarily, but by a king's unwavering belief that the lands at stake belonged by right to the throne. Look at Edward I's brutal campaigns

in Wales and Scotland, or Charles II of Navarre's ludicrous notions of what belonged to him - both of whom feature in this roundup of deadly royals.

Murder was often the simplest way to ensure that anyone plotting against the king was removed. Even with the introduction of the Magna Carta in England in 1215 and the emergence of Parliament, the monarch's essentially free rein to end the lives of their subjects remained. Flimsy evidence could be put forward to prove a case for treason and conspiring against the monarch, as Henry VIII demonstrated on several occasions. Meanwhile, with the whole country watching, any hint of rebellion would have to be squashed quickly and brutally, as Louis I of Aquitaine did to great effect.

In other cases, the reason behind a king's bloodthirsty nature would now be attributed to some form of mental illness. Purity of the bloodline comes with a price, as lineages would abruptly end with offspring suffering from deformities, congenital illnesses and insanity.

Whether through violent fits of rage or cold calculation, these ten kings ensured that the pages of history books dedicated to them were written in blood, but which of them takes the crown as the deadliest?

The Massacre of St Brice's Day in 1002 led to all Danes in England being put to the sword

"He issued an order that all Danes in England should be executed, calling it 'a most just extermination'"

REIGN 978-1016

COUNTRY ENGLAND

WORST CRIME
MASSACRED ALL DANES IN ENGLAND

10 Aethelred II

Aethelred's tenure as king of England led to the inglorious epithet of Aethelred the Unready. However, a better translation of the moniker would be 'ill-advised', as it is generally agreed that the counsel Aethelred received was little and poor.

Although he was too young to have been complicit in the murder of his older brother (Edward the Martyr), who was killed after having been on the throne for only two and a half years, the crime was carried out by those loyal to him in order that the younger sibling would take his place. This meant that there was a lot of mistrust surrounding the young monarch and, as the reputation of the murdered boy grew after his

death, it would become increasingly difficult for Aethelred to unite his subjects.

And the necessity for a united British army was urgent with a renewed threat from the north. The Danes had recommenced raids along England's coast, breaking the treaty they had made with Aethelred's father, Edgar. After the English suffered a serious defeat at the Battle of Maldon in 991, Aethelred began paying tribute to the Danes in return for peace. However, the Danes were hard to appease and had restarted hostilities by 997.

Finally, in 1002, Aethelred reached breaking point and took drastic action. On 13 November he issued an order that all Danes in England should

be executed, calling it "a most just extermination". It was an indiscriminate attempt at a show of strength that claimed the life of Danish leader Sweyn's sister, Gunhilde, and Sweyn invaded in retaliation, leading to Aethelred's downfall.

WARMONGERING	★★★★★
INSANITY	★★★★★
POLITICAL MURDERS	★★★★★
PERSONAL MURDERS	★★★★★

09 Louis I

Louis the Pious was, in many ways, as sensible a leader as his nickname would suggest. His father, Charlemagne, appointed him King of Aquitaine at the tender age of three. He became King of the Franks and Emperor of Rome upon his father's death in 814 and decided that, in order to avoid any diplomatic issues, any of his unmarried sisters would be packed off to nunneries.

When Louis nearly died in an accident in 817, he decided to ensure that, should he suddenly expire, there would be a neat plan of succession to set out who ruled what in the Frankish empire. He confirmed that his nephew Bernard would remain the king of Italy, but the will described his son Lothair's position as 'overlord', implying that Italy would be submissive to him. Needless to say, the wording of this document did not please Bernard

REIGN 814-840
COUNTRY AQUITAINE
WORST CRIME
HAD HIS NEPHEW KILLED

and, spurred on by rumours that Lothair was to invade, he set about preparing a rebellion. However, word quickly reached Louis I of Bernard's plan and the king immediately took an army to confront his errant nephew. Bernard was shocked by the speed of the king's reaction and went to try and negotiate, before being forced into surrender. It's here that Louis' place in this list of murderous kings is assured...

He sentenced his nephew to death, before deciding that he should be blinded instead – a punishment that was apparently merciful. However, the procedure was not entirely successful. As a result, while Bernard was indeed blinded, he spent two days in unbearable pain before dying anyway. Three civil wars would follow but the legacy of this killing would haunt the deeply religious ruler for the rest of his life.

WARMONGERING	★★★★★
INSANITY	★★★★★
POLITICAL MURDERS	★★★★★
PERSONAL MURDERS	★★★★★

08 Charles II (SPAIN)

The reason for Charles II's reputation as a bloodthirsty king is very much rooted in his heritage. He was the last of the Habsburg line – a lineage that was so devoted to preserving the purity of its bloodline through inbreeding that it eventually led to a man like Charles. Disfigured, infertile and cursed to spend his life suffering from various illnesses, the king was in a similar amount of mental anguish.

Charles II's condition was no secret among the European court. He was just three years old when the throne became his and his mother, Mariana, became queen regent, designating much of the work of governing the country to advisors.

His mother remained regent long after Charles could have taken kingship himself, but it was decided that such a move would be unwise. A struggle for power began when Mariana was exiled, and Don Juan José (Charles's half-brother) took responsibility for the country and the king.

Charles's illness was grotesquely misunderstood at the time - interpreted as a sign that the king was probably bewitched; he would even undergo an exorcism in the final years of his life.

His worst crime was the 1680 auto-de-fe (display of public penance and executions) in Madrid, during which many heretics were burned. Charles II attended the trial and burnings, though the executions were probably ordered by someone else. A blood-soaked reign, but a misunderstood one.

Heretics being trialled at an auto-de-fe in Madrid in the 1680s

REIGN 1665-1700
COUNTRY SPAIN
WORST CRIME
BURNED HERETICS AT THE STAKE

WARMONGERING	★★★★★
INSANITY	★★★★★
POLITICAL MURDERS	★★★★★
PERSONAL MURDERS	★★★★★

07 Charles II
(NAVARRE)

Charles II believed that the kingdom of Navarre was far too small for a man with such a noble lineage as his and spent his life trying to wheedle his way to a more important status. He ordered the assassination of the Constable of France in 1354 and made a deal with the English, forcing the French King John II to make peace.

John grew tired of his treachery and finally arrested him in 1356, only for Charles to be broken out in 1357. When John II agreed to a peace treaty with the English, Charles II freed all the prisoners in Paris. With the city on the verge of revolution, Charles U-turned and took the opportunity to lead the aristocracy at the Battle of Mello and the subsequent massacre of the rebels.

He blindly swore patriotism and honour while consistently reaching out to the opposition in the hope of a better deal. His meddling in the war between Castile and Aragon proved disastrous and he staged being captured to avoid having to participate. Towards the end of his life he tried to convince English king Edward III to invade and overthrow Charles V, as well as being involved in two attempts on Charles's life. When his scheming with Gascony against Castile went wrong, Navarre was invaded in 1378 and he was forced to agree to an alliance with Castile and France. He burned to death in 1387, allegedly when the sackcloth filled with brandy he was bathing in caught fire.

REIGN 1349-1387

COUNTRY NAVARRE (SPAIN/FRANCE)

WORST CRIME
MURDER, TREACHERY AND COWARDICE

Charles II the Bad having the leaders of the Jacquerie executed

WARMONGERING ★★★★★
INSANITY ★★★★★
POLITICAL MURDERS ★★★★★
PERSONAL MURDERS ★★★★★

06 Herod I

"He ordered that his wife be executed if he didn't return from an expedition"

There are many who would claim that King Herod committed his most heinous deed with the Massacre of the Innocents. However, the story of the slaughter of all boys in Bethlehem under the age of two is only found in the Bible; there are no historical records from the time detailing such an atrocity. Herod's more frequently documented crimes were much more personal.

In fact, Herod was an excellent ruler of Judaea. Having obtained the position after being forced to flee Galilee when the Palestinians had reclaimed their land, he strengthened his kingship when he divorced in order to marry Mariamne, which pacified a leading sect of Jewish priests (the Hasmoneans). However, as time went by, it became clear that Herod was not well.

REIGN 37-4 BCE

COUNTRY JUDAEA

WORST CRIME
KILLED HIS WIFE AND CHILDREN

He was prone to fits of mental instability, which made his fierce love for his wife all the more dangerous. At one point, before leaving for a political expedition, he ordered that Mariamne should be executed if he didn't return from this expedition because he couldn't face the idea of her being with another man. His jealousy was exploited by his sister, Salome - who despised Mariamne - to convince Herod that his wife was plotting against him. Mariamne was executed in 29 BCE, and Herod - believing that their two sons, Alexandros and Aristobulus, would try to take revenge for their mother - had both their children killed in 7 BCE. Two years later, Antipater - Herod's only son by his first wife - was also executed for the same reason.

Massacre of the Innocents

WARMONGERING ★★★★★
INSANITY ★★★★★
POLITICAL MURDERS ★★★★★
PERSONAL MURDERS ★★★★★

05 Richard I

The man dubbed 'Lionheart' spent most of his life fighting. He first took up arms against his father, Henry II, in 1173 and continued to aggressively pursue the throne until Henry's death in 1189, when some quite reasonably suggested that Richard had driven the king to his grave.

Blood was spilled on the same day that Richard took the crown, when the barring of Jewish figures from the coronation was misinterpreted as an order to instigate violence against all of London's Jews. Richard ordered the executions of those who took part, but the instances of copycat 'Christian' violence would set the tone for a king who was desperate to join the Crusades.

Together with Phillip II of France, who had assisted Richard in his fight for the throne, England joined the Third Crusade. Spending the bulk of his father's treasure chest to raise a new army, Richard set off for the Holy Lands in 1190. He blazed a bloody trail through Sicily and Cyprus before arriving at Acre, Israel, in 1191.

Following the successful siege of the city, he ordered the execution of 2,700 Muslim prisoners. The crusade eventually ground to a halt and Richard was forced to retreat in 1192, only to be captured in Vienna by Leopold V. Once ransomed, he discovered that his brother, John, had given Normandy back to King Phillip in his absence.

In 1196, Richard built castles in Normandy to fortify his presence. He continued his war against Phillip until 1199, when he was struck by an arrow from the nearly undefended Châlus-Chabrol chateau. The wound turned fatally gangrenous - an undignified end for the warrior king.

REIGN 1189-1199
COUNTRY ENGLAND
WORST CRIME
WAR CRIMES OF THE CRUSADES

WARMONGERING	★★★★★
INSANITY	★★★★★
POLITICAL MURDERS	★★★★★
PERSONAL MURDERS	★★★★★

04 Edward I

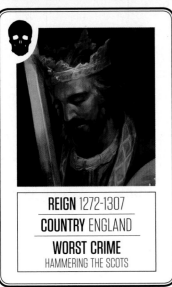

REIGN 1272-1307
COUNTRY ENGLAND
WORST CRIME
HAMMERING THE SCOTS

When Edward I came to the throne he had a very clear goal in mind: to take back what he saw as English land which had been stolen. Upon Henry III's death, Edward returned to England from the Crusades and started planning a military campaign in Wales. Beginning with a successful invasion in 1277 he executed the Welsh leader, Llewelyn, in 1282 and Llewelyn's brother, David, a year later in response to rebellions.

The war in Wales had a devastating effect on the nation's finances. This was compounded when Edward responded violently to French King Philip reclaiming the territory of Gascony by sailing to attack in 1297, later returning to quell the Scottish rebellion. Edward intervened to such an extent that the Scots allied with the French and attacked Carlisle. Edward invaded in retaliation, beginning a brutal and lengthy conflict that earned him his nickname, Hammer of the Scots.

WARMONGERING	★★★★★
INSANITY	★★★★★
POLITICAL MURDERS	★★★★★
PERSONAL MURDERS	★★★★★

03 Erik XIV

While many kings can lay claim to ordering the deaths of hundreds - even thousands - during the course of their reign, not many can say they committed murder with their own hands. The king of Sweden Erik XIV suffered from mental instability, but not to an extent that made him incapable of ruling. He strengthened Sweden's position in northern Europe by claiming territory in Estonia, leading to the Seven Years' War of the North between 1563 and 1570. Although his military campaigns were successful Erik's mental state was rapidly deteriorating and evidence points towards schizophrenia.

He became paranoid, eager to believe rumours of treason. He even executed two guards for 'making fun of the king'.

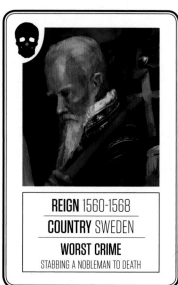

REIGN 1560-1568

COUNTRY SWEDEN

WORST CRIME
STABBING A NOBLEMAN TO DEATH

But it would be the Sture murders that would break him. Believing that the noble family would make a play for the throne, Erik began persecuting the Stures - specifically Nils Sture. In 1567, one of Sture's pages was tortured until he told Erik what he wanted to hear. Following a trial, death sentences began to be issued but the king was indecisive. Finally, he visited them at the castle in Uppsala (north of Stockholm) where they were imprisoned and told them that they were forgiven. When Erik left he discovered that a rebellion was underway, led by his brother, John. It was only a few hours later that Erik returned and stabbed Nils Sture before ordering the execution of the others.

WARMONGERING	★★★★★
INSANITY	★★★★★
POLITICAL MURDERS	★★★★★
PERSONAL MURDERS	★★★★★

02 Henry VIII

English king Henry VIII's voracious nature and hot temper have become the stuff of legend. He is renowned for being a man of ferocious appetites - in all aspects of life - and he was prepared to use any means necessary to quell his opposition.

Shortly after ascending to the throne, Henry married Catherine of Aragon, as his father, Henry VII, had wanted to secure an alliance with Spain. At the time he executed Edmund Dudley and Richard Empson - two of his father's advisors - on the grounds of treason. This was to become something of a pattern for Henry. From Thomas More to Thomas Cromwell, anyone who Henry perceived as either a threat to the throne or to his secession from the Catholic church was liable to find themselves with their head on the block.

However, he's most notorious for his list of spouses, driven by his desperation for a male heir and straightforward lust. The annulment of his

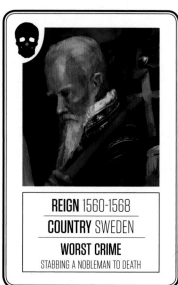

REIGN 1509-1547

COUNTRY ENGLAND

WORST CRIME
EXECUTING ALL WHO OPPOSED HIM

marriage to Catherine of Aragon was prompted by a combination of the two as Anne Boleyn had already caught his eye. As we all know, Anne Boleyn did not last long before facing the executioner's axe - having been dubiously accused of infidelity, treachery and incest. Anne was followed by Jane Seymour, who died in childbirth; Anne of Cleves, who Henry soon separated from; and then the unfortunate Catherine Howard. Henry accused Catherine of being unfaithful with her secretary, Francis Dereham, while she claimed that Dereham had raped her. Despite her protests, she was sent to her death. Fortunately for his last wife, Catherine Parr, he died before she too could fall out of his favour.

The exact number of executions ordered by Henry VIII has not been conclusively agreed upon, but it is generally believed to be between 57,000 and 72,000. As a gruesome aside, he also made 'death by boiling' a legitimate form of execution.

Anne Boleyn in the Tower of London portrayed just before her execution under the orders of Henry VIII

WARMONGERING	★★★★★
INSANITY	★★★★★
POLITICAL MURDERS	★★★★★
PERSONAL MURDERS	★★★★★

"Anyone perceived as a threat was liable to find themselves on the block"

01 Leopold II

Desperate to establish a colony overseas, Belgian king Leopold II turned to Africa and the potential riches of the Congo. To circumvent his own parliament, he created a dummy organisation called the International African Association, which he claimed would act in the interests of philanthropy and scientific research with a view to converting the citizens to Christianity. It was all completely legal and it gave the monarch the freedom to act however he wanted in the land under his control.

Its stated aim could not have been further from the truth. What had attracted Leopold to the Congo, in addition to the notion of creating an empire, was the tremendous supply of rubber in the area. He would spare nothing in order to get what he wanted. Despite having promised that he would protect the people of the Congo from slavers, Leopold promptly and brutally turned the country into a slave state.

The treatment of the workers was savage and uncompromising. Leopold allowed some missionaries into the Congo in order to allay the fears of foreign powers who believed he might be doing exactly what he was doing, and reports began to reach Europe about the maiming and executions of the men and women working on the plantations, as well as of the mass dumping of corpses.

It's impossible to know exactly how many people died during Leopold's rule of the Congo but the estimated figure is in the millions. The atrocities led to the establishment of the first human rights movement and Leopold was finally compelled to give up the Congo to the Belgian parliament in 1908.

REIGN 1865-1909

COUNTRY BELGIUM

WORST CRIME
FORMING A SLAVE COLONY IN AFRICA

WARMONGERING ★★★★★
INSANITY ★★★★★
POLITICAL MURDERS ★★★★★
PERSONAL MURDERS ★★★★★

10 Royal Warriors

From blood-drenched warlords to military reformers,
we count down the ten greatest warrior kings in world history

10 William I, The Conqueror
King of England (1066-1087)

A descendant of Vikings given land in Northern France, William's upbringing prepared him for a life of war. The illegitimate heir of the Duke of Normandy, he inherited the title aged seven where he was soon seen as an easy target for challengers. Leading men into battle since his teens, he claimed the throne of England in 1066.

Arms And Armour

The Norman broadsword - similar to the Viking broadsword - was a brutal slashing weapon designed to be wielded on horseback, and the Normans made great use of cavalry with their kite-shaped shield designed to protect the left side of the body, and wore a coned helmet to deflect blows to the head and hauberk chain-mail, which covered the thighs and arms to provide extra protection.

Enemies

William's bloody beginnings - one of his guardians was murdered in the William's bedchamber while he slept - was evidence of a legion of foes, from nobles like Guy of Burgundy to French king Henry I. After the death of the English king Edward I,

William claimed he had been named successor, making an enemy of Harold Godwinson, the powerful Earl of Wessex, who took the throne claiming the exact same thing.

Strategy

His background in the fractious Norman politics made him an expert at retaining power more than seizing it - rewarding allies and punishing rivals, centralising government and building fearsome castles. Prior to invasion he used Harold's own spies to spread disinformation prior to his invasion and attacked Harold's lands to try and goad the king into rushing into battle.

Definitive Battle

Though William's army had been waiting to sail for months, the threat of Harold's force on the coast put him off invasion. Only when the Norwegian king Harald Hardrada launched a similar attempt on the throne in the North, did William cross the channel and confront the English on 14 October 1066, 11 miles north west of Hastings in Kent.

The Battle of Hastings, as portrayed by Philip James de Loutherbourg

Despite larger English numbers and high ground, in the Battle of Hastings the Normans had a tactical advantage - a mixed force two parts infantry, one part cavalry and one part archers, while the English force was made up mainly of infantry - including the fearsome huscarls which were the backbone of his army. A relic of the Viking age, these professional warriors carried long-handled axes with a swing big enough to cleave a knight from horse to helmet.

After failing to break the English lines, which held up an impenetrable shield-wall on the slope, William began to feign retreat, hoping to draw out the English in pursuit so that gaps might be left in their defences. Harold's tactics were limited by his inflexible army and wearied from their march south after fighting off Harald Hardrada. Somewhere in the fighting - the arrow to the eye, though unproven, remains the most compelling myth - Harold Godwinson fell, and the army began to crumble. Only his loyal huscarls remained, forming a defensive ring around their king's body, they fought to the end.

Storming of Seringapatam under General Baird and death of Tipu Sultan, May 4, 1799, in the Third Anglo-Mysore War

09 Tipu Sultan

Sultan Of Mysore (1782 - 1799)

As Sultan of India's last truly independent kingdom, Tipu held the British Empire at bay with deadly rockets and a highly skilled army, described as the finest fighting force in the world by one of the British officers to fight him - the future Duke of Wellington.

Arms And Armour

The Tipu Sultan's armoury contained dozens of elaborately embossed (many with gold tigers inset or snarling tiger heads on the pommel) curved shamshir and talwar swords - the radical curves, much greater than that of a European sabre, were capable of a devastatingly downward slash. Trained by French officers, he could fight with a pair of flintlock pistols, a devastating flintlock blunderbuss and used a flintlock rifle with murderous accuracy at the Siege Of Seringapatam.

Enemies

Though he took arms against rival Indian monarchs, Tipu's chief opponent was Britain's rapacious East India Company, which saw Mysore as the last obstacle to a British-dominated India. The Sultan owned a ghoulish tiger automaton

which savaged a British redcoat at the turn of a handle. The symbolism wasn't lost on the British and following his death at the Siege Of Seringapatam the East India Company issued a medal showing a lion besting a tiger in combat.

Strategy

Tipu's father Hyder Ali pioneered the use of rockets in battle - swapping bamboo tubes for iron which could contain a greater explosive charge - and Tipu Sultan added a wheeled rocket launcher, which could fire between five and ten rockets. After fighting alongside his father's French allies in the first Anglo-Mysore War, Tipu Sultan rearranged his army along European lines.

Definitive Battle

Having succeeded his father as the ruler of Mysore part-way through the Second Anglo-Mysore War, Tipu Sultan wasted no time. As one of his father's

commanders, Tipu's expertly drilled soldiers had devastated the East India Company forces - reliant on poorly trained Indian 'sepoys' - with guerilla assaults, inducing panic with a rain of rocket artillery, and he was hungry to drive victory home.

The Siege Of Mangalore began on the 18 May 1873, and the 250 soldiers of the 2/42nd Royal Highland Regiment and the 1,500 Indian sepoys found themselves surrounded by an estimated 140,000 troops under Tipu's command, including 400 French soldiers and artillery. This was the Sultan's entire army and the region's principal seaport was effectively Britain's last toehold on the coast of India. Under constant bombardment from rockets and cannons, and running low on supplies, the defenders held out valiantly but had no choice but to capitulate, signing the Treaty Of Mangalore in 11 March 1784 which limited East India Company interference. Shares plummeted along with prestige - this was the last treaty the East India Company signed in India to their detriment.

"Described as the finest fighting force in the world by one of the officers to fight him - the future Duke of Wellington"

08 Somdet Phra Naresuan Maharat

The Great King Of Siam (1590 – 1605)

Raised as a hostage, Thai prince Naresuan buried his hatred and studied under Burma's generals and martial artists. Returning to Siam - now Thailand - as king, this daring monarch declared his country's independence and fought off five separate invasions, killing the Burmese crown prince in an elephant duel.

Arms And Armour

Naresuan was an expert shot with the (often inaccurate and unreliable) Portuguese musket that could shatter bone with its lead ball at 80 to 100 meters and a ferocious hand-to-hand fighter, using a curved sword called a krabi up close and a lance-like Ngaw while mounted on his elephant. His armour, though elaborately decorated in Thai style, was Portuguese plate armour, capable of deflecting sword swipes and even musket fire.

Enemies

Raised alongside King Bayinnaung's grandson prince Minchit Sra, the two became fierce rivals from childhood. After Naresuan returned to Siam, Burma's new monarch (and Bayinnaung's son) King Nanda Bayin began to doubt his loyalty and ordered his son and heir, Minchit Sra, to kill him. Sra suffered a crushing defeat that restored Siam's independence and six years later the two would meet for a final face-off.

Strategy

Adopting Portuguese and Burmese tactics, Naresuan added 21 new rules of combat to Siam's Treatise On Victorious Warfare - a sort of Thai *Art Of War*. In the field his most celebrated manoeuvre was to feign retreat and draw the enemy into pursuit where elephant cavalry would then charge to decimate the enemy.

Definitive Battle

After seeing off two previous Burmese invasion forces, dispatched more to intimidate Siam back into line than to decapitate Naresuan's reign, the third - and largest - one came in early 1593 led by the king's childhood nemesis Minchit Sra.

Naresuan met them in the central province of Suphan Buri on 18 January 1593 for the Battle Of Nong Sarai. Arranging his army into a 'lotus array' formation - a small force at the front, with a larger force behind supported by significant flanking troops - his initial reconnaissance quickly crumbled before the larger attackers, and rather than come to their aid Naresuan held firm.

Believing that the Thai army was in retreat, Minchit Sra's forces crashed through the jungle in pursuit suddenly colliding with the bulk of the army in fierce close-quarter fighting.

Spotting Minchit Sra on his own elephant, Naresuan rode forward and issued a challenge to single combat. Striking first with a glancing blow to the king's cheek from his vicious war scythe, Minchit Sra was suddenly vulnerable from the wide swing and Naresuan slashed him with fatal blow with his lance.

With the heir to the throne dead, his army retreated in confusion and for the next decade Burma would find itself on the defensive in the war with Siam.

07 Shaka Kasenzangakhona

King Of The Zulu (1816 - 1828)

Better known as the deadly Shaka Zulu, this illegitimate son of an African chief turned a loose alliance of tribes into the powerful Zulu Kingdom, revolutionising his army with new tactics and weapons that left them unbeaten until the coming of the British Empire in the 19th Century.

Arms And Armour

Shaka phased out the assegai throwing spear as the Zulu's primary weapon in favour of a shorter iklwa that allowed a flurry of savage close-quarter kills. The assegai was still used for softening up the enemy at range, prior to a deadly charge and Shaka was often pictured with one. Shaka also deployed a heavier cowhide shield that could deflect incoming blows.

Enemies

The brutality of the Zulu expansion - known today as the Mfecane, which means 'crushing' or 'scattering' - made Shaka many enemies, like Zwide kaLanga - rival of Shaka's father and ambitious king of the Ndwandwe. The pair's dreams of domination were fundamentally incompatible, leading to the two-year Ndwandwe-Zulu War.

Strategy

That Shaka forced his men to discard their sandals to toughen them up is fiercely disputed, but it underlines the emphasis the leader placed on a finely drilled and determined force. Supported by six-year old 'apprentices' carrying supplies and driving cattle with them as self-transporting rations, the Zulu were a fast-moving force despite their size, using a 'buffalo horn' pincer-type encirclement to overrun their foes.

Definitive Battle

With the Zulu Kingdom hoovering up smaller tribes, absorbing or driving away those Shaka defeated, their northernmost neighbours the Ndwandwe knew conflict was inevitable. In May 1818, the Ndwandwe king Zwide gathered his warriors and marched south to confront his rising rival. Outnumbered by 8,000-10,000 Ndwandwe to 4,000 Zulus, Shaka took up defensive positions on the rocky outcrop that gives the Battle Of Gqokli Hill its name.

With numbers against him, Shaka's buffalo horns formation would have stretched his forces too thinly and he instead formed them in the defensive ring around the top of Gqokli Hill, with reinforcements hidden from view in a depression.

With spear bombardment ineffective, the Ndwandwe were forced to charge upwards where the Zulu's savage close combat skills gave them the edge, launching vicious counter-attack after counter-attack against the aggressors. With the Ndwandwe beginning to wear down, Zwide made one last push - sending 1,000 reserves round the south side of the hill, he formed up his soldiers into a tight column which through sheer force of numbers could punch through the Zulu on the north side and force them down onto his waiting spears. Shaka finally deployed his buffalo horn, sending Zulu either side down the Ndwandwe column to attack from the side - severing Zwide's army at its narrowest point.

Zulu warriors being forced by Shaka to dance on thorny ground

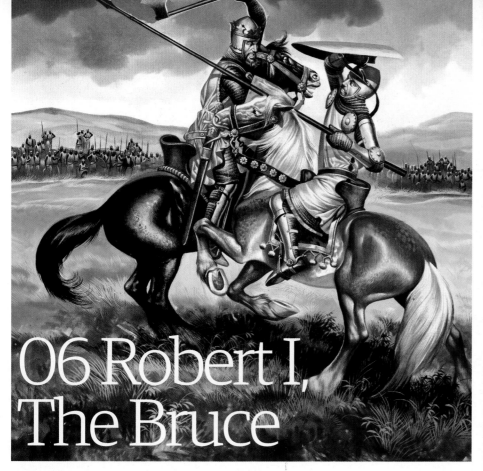

06 Robert I, The Bruce

King Of Scots (1306 - 1329)

One of the many claimants of the Scottish throne, Robert the Bruce fought alongside William Wallace in a bitter guerilla war to end English rule. After defeating the larger English army at the Battle Of Bannockburn, he turned the tables on the occupiers and took the war to Northern England and Ireland.

Arms And Armour

Though they'd fallen out of favour as a cavalry weapon, Robert the Bruce fought with a battle-axe which could hammer through armour plate and tear up chain-mail like confetti. Often lightly armoured, Robert rode a palfrey - a nimble riding horse - allowing him greater manoeuvrability than the average English knight on his heavy chargers.

Enemies

While Robert's chief rival for the Scottish crown was John Balliol - crowned in 1292, he abdicated in 1296, humiliated by English interference - his most implacable foes were Edward I, the Hammer of the Scots, and his son Edward II. Edward I had been invited to mediate over the contest for the Scottish throne and had used it as an open invitation to rule, a tradition Edward II continued when he ascended the throne in 1307.

Strategy

Becoming a capable guerilla fighter, Robert the Bruce expanded on the hit and run tactics of William Wallace and used lightly armoured and mobile skirmishers to attack by surprise. His raids across the border into Yorkshire and Lancashire became so successful he was able to extort protection money and buy better weapons and armour.

Definitive Battle

Scottish tactics had been traditionally to steer clear of pitched battles, but the English garrison at Stirling Castle had agreed to surrender if reinforcements hadn't arrived by midsummer. This was a victory that Edward II couldn't afford to hand Robert the Bruce.

The Scottish forces, mainly archers and infantry armed with long spears that formed into prickly circles of death called schiltrons, numbered around 5,000-10,000, while the English mustered 13,700-25,000 men - the largest army to ever invade Scotland. In order to deny the English the only flat ground in which they could deploy their devastating cavalry charge, the Scots dug pits which forced them onto the marshy Carse of Stirling. While English nobles squabbled over tactics, a young noble riding ahead spotted the Scottish king and charged, nimbly skirting aside on his lighter horse Robert brought down his axe so hard that he split the knight's helmet - and head - in two.

Over the two-day battle the English forces became increasingly disorganised and divided. With panic taking over, Edward II and his bodyguards fled leaving his army in complete ruins and Scotland in the hands of the Scottish.

05 Cyrus II The Great

King Of Persia (559 - 530 BC)

'King of the world' and the first monarch to be immortalised as 'The Great', master diplomat and strategist Cyrus II overthrew the Median Empire and turned his native Persia from a minor state into a superpower that stretched from Turkey in the west to Pakistan in the east.

Arms And Armour

Cyrus II fought alongside his elite bodyguard, the Persian Immortals, clad in a lightweight breastplate made from leather and quilted flax and covered with overlapping iron scales. It was dense enough to turn a fatal spear lunge into a flesh wound, while his wickedly sharp acinaces short sword could unleash a flurry of deadly stabbing attacks.

Enemies

Cyrus II took on many of the ancient world's most feared powers, from the Babylonian Empire to the warlike Scythians, but he finally met his match with the nomadic Massagetae, led by the warrior queen Tomyris. After Cyrus II captured her son Spargagises by getting him and his men drunk, Tomyris defeated the Persian king in a fierce battle, chopped off his head and crucified his body.

Strategy

Where other kings assembled tribesmen for battle, Cyrus II formed a professional army. An enthusiastic adapter of new technology and resources as his empire expanded, he later added powerful composite bows and a navy. Cyrus II also developed modern tactics, being the first general on record to arrange his men in formations.

Definitive Battle

Babylonia was the last major power in Asia Minor that still stood before the Persian war machine - now ring-fenced in the north, east and west by Cyrus II's empire, the king began to soften up his opponent with a propaganda campaign that promised freedom in contrast to religious persecutions. Routing the Babylonian army at Opis, north of Babylon in October 539 BC, the vast walled city itself seemed impregnable. Cyrus II divided his army into two, one force waited where the Euphrates river entered the city, while the other he led to a basin where further upriver where they began to dig. With the river now shallow, the army left by the city walls stormed across the river bed. The Babylonians were taken by surprise, and Cyrus II seized the city almost bloodlessly.

04 John III Sobieski, The Lion Of Poland

King Of Poland (1674-1699)

Trained for war from an early age, Polish noble John Sobieski climbed the ranks to become Grand Hetman – supreme commander – of the armies of the Polish-Lithuanian Commonwealth. Elected King by the council of nobles, he reformed the military and at the head of the fearsome Winged Hussars lifted the Turkish siege of Vienna.

Arms And Armour

As a keen hunter and lifelong commander John Sobieski was an expert fighter and a skilled horseman; he would ride into battle with Poland's terrifying hussars, their feathered pennants streaming as they charged. Like his hussars, John III wore armour of iron scales riveted to leather and came armed with a sleek and deadly lance that could impale effortlessly, an array of deadly blades and at least two loaded wheellock pistols.

Enemies

The Ottoman Turks called him "the Lion of Lechistan" (Lechia being an archaic name for Poland), while his campaigns as Grant Hetman against the warlike Cossacks and Tartars of Ukraine saw him branded "Scourge of the Tartars", and he fought both the nigh-on unstoppable Ottoman Empire and the brutal Tartar Khanate for much of his life, famously driving the former out of Central Europe entirely.

Strategy

John III transformed the army from a feudal-style system reliant on the nobles to a professional army. He phased out pike infantry in favour of berdiche – a terrifying looking poleaxe that could double as a musket-rest – and expanded the use of light cavalry, using the heavily armed Winged Hussars as the army's elite shock troops. His new army specialised in quick, decisive action, often using terrain that slowed less mobile armies.

Definitive Battle

With the Turkish Ottoman Empire sweeping across Eastern Europe, they lay siege to Vienna, one of the great cities of the Holy Roman Empire and key to the Mediterranean-German trade routes. Reluctant to destroy Vienna, one of the richest cities of Europe, the Turks tried to starve the defenders into surrender, buying the time John Sobieski needed to bring his army – a force so large that Poland and Lithuania were left virtually undefended – the vast distance.

On 12 September, 1683, two months into the Siege of Vienna, the Polish-Lithuanian army and German reinforcements were close enough to spook Ottoman general, Mustafa Pasha, and he launched a last attack on the city. Not expecting an attack to come from the Wienerwald forest – too dense for any conventional army – he'd left his flank largely undefended and with Sobieski at their head the Winged Hussars poured out into the unprepared Ottomans. A counter-attack was beaten back, and Vienna's defenders emerged from their heavily fortified gates to join the fray. "We came, we saw, and God conquered," wrote Sobieski to Pope Innocent XI as the Turkish advance into Europe was finally checked. From hereon, the Ottoman Empire began a slow decline that lasted just over 200 years.

> "As a keen hunter and lifelong commander John Sobieski was an expert fighter and a skilled horseman"

Winged Hussars charge into the Battle of Vienna in this painting from 1925

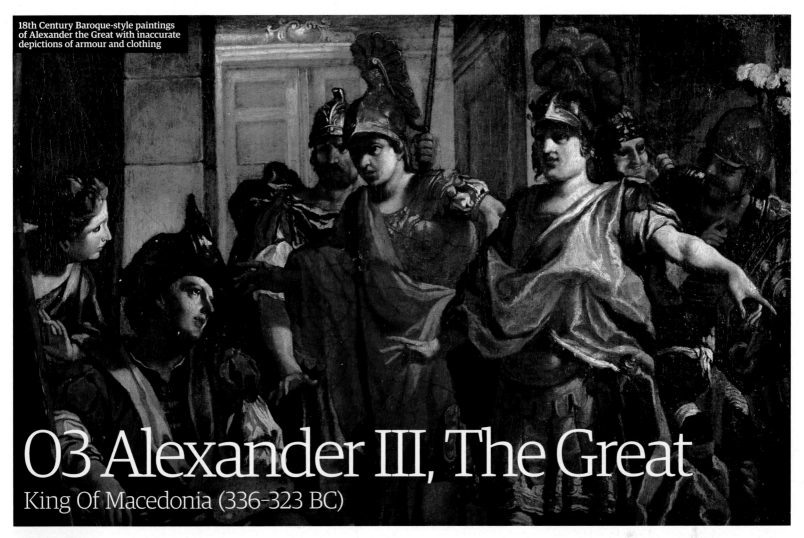

18th Century Baroque-style paintings of Alexander the Great with inaccurate depictions of armour and clothing

03 Alexander III, The Great
King Of Macedonia (336-323 BC)

Inheriting a strong army and his father's ambitions, Alexander III of the northern Greek state of Macedon created one of the ancient world's largest empires by the time he was 30. Undefeated in battle, he triumphed against overwhelming odds with his tightly drilled 'phalanx' of spearmen and strategy.

Arms And Armour

Leading his force from the front line, Alexander the Great wore laminated linen armour glued together with rabbit skin and flax seeds, which while flexible, could resist sword blows. In combat he wielded a kopis, a sharply curved sword that benefited from the downward swing of a mounted warrior and if that wasn't enough, he also practiced the Ancient Greek martial art of pankration, which focused on punches and grappling.

★★★★★

Enemies

With much of the Ancient World falling under Alexander III's sandals, his enemies were legion, but as a Greek he always saw the Persian Empire as their ultimate foe and his first wars were against the Persian Achaemenid Empire founded by Cyrus the Great. Persian king Darius III faced Alexander in battle three times, and ran away in every one.

★★★★★

Strategy

The core of Alexander III's strategy was the phalanx, a block of infantry armed with 18 foot-long sarissa spears so long that the first five rows were effective in combat. In the field, he was a quick-thinking strategist who would do what it took to ensure victory – noticing the turning circle of scythed Persian chariots was poor, he arranged his men into a U-shape, so that their dead would choke them to a standstill.

★★★★★

Definitive Battle

After defeating Persia, Alexander III had to subdue the kingdom of King Porus in what is now the Punjab region of Pakistan in order to continue his eastward expansion. At the dawn of the Battle of the Hydaspes in May 326 BC, Porus arranged his army of 20,000-50,000 infantry, 2,000-4,000 cavalry and 130 war elephants across the Jhelum River to repel any attempt at crossing the fast-moving, monsoon-swollen waters at the Haranpur ford. Taking half his army of 11,000 and crossing the river upstream, Alexander's main force under the command of Craterus launched feints across the water to keep the Indian king distracted. Realising the gambit, Porus turned his main force toward Alexander, who weakened the Indian left cavalry with horse archers before charging the weakened flank with his own cavalry.

Turning his main force toward the assault on his flank, Porus suddenly found Craterus' larger host crashing into his rearguard. With the larger force confused and the war elephants panicking, the Macedonians encircled the Indians completely. To Porus' credit, he defeated Alexander in single combat, impressing the Greek so much that he was allowed to retain his kingdom in exchange for recognising Alexander the Great as his superior.

★★★★★

"In the field, he was a quick-thinking strategist who would do what it took to ensure victory"

02 Gustav II Adolf

King Of Sweden (1611 - 1632)

Considered one of the greatest generals of all time by Napoleon Bonaparte. Though the Scandinavian monarch more widely known by the Latin name Gustavus Adolphus didn't survive the Thirty Years War, his innovations turned Sweden into the Baltic's dominant superpower for a hundred years and kick-started the modern age of warfare.

Arms And Armour

Though the cuirass - a Roman-style breastplate - was the protection de jour for the 17th Century, Gustavus Adolphus refused to wear it because it irritated an old war wound - a musket shot to the neck. Gustavus Adolphus led from the front, charging into battle on horseback armed with a rapier - a sleek thrusting sword which could easily deliver a mortal wound with one smooth motion.

Enemies

A zealous defender of the Protestant Reformation in Germany, his enemies effectively included the monarchs of Spain, Austria, Hungary, the Holy Roman Empire and their allies. If any one figure deserves a mention it was the general of the Holy Roman Empire's army Johann Tserclaes, Count of Tilly who massacred 25,000 of the 30,000-strong population of Frankfurt. Until Sweden joined the war, Tilly had never known defeat.

Strategy

At the core of Gustavus Adolphus's military reforms were flexibility, equipment and training. In an age of large blocks of infantry supported by distant cannon, the Swedes used lighter artillery that could be constantly redeployed to where it was needed and shallower lines of infantry that could shield cavalry and support their charges with gunfire.

★ ★ ★ ★ ★

Definitive Battle

With the Swedes landing in northern Germany and the Count of Tilly bringing his army up from northern Italy to meet him, only the Electorate of Saxony stood in their way. So far untouched by war, the Elector, John George I denied transit to Tilly's army - so Tilly invaded and John George I allied with Gustav.

The combined Swedish and Saxon army collided with the Catholic forces near to Leipzig on 17 September 1631 for the Battle of Breitenfeld, though both sides were evenly matched in arms and troop numbers, the more flexible Swedish quickly gained the upper hand. Opening with artillery volleys from both sides, the smaller Swedish canons with their impeccably drilled crews were able to fire three to five times for every one from the Imperial lines. Then the first Imperial charge was met with a counter-charge led by Gustavus Adolphus himself, allowing the Swedes to capture the Imperial artillery on Tilly's left flank.

The artillery was then turned against their former masters by the Swedes who had been trained in multiple disciplines. The Imperial line collapsed and 80 per cent of their forces were killed. In the aftermath, more German city states allied themselves with Sweden and the Holy Roman Empire was forced to rebuild its army from scratch.

★ ★ ★ ★ ★

"His innovations turned Sweden into the Baltic's dominant superpower"

Gustavus Adolphus at the Battle of Breitenfeld

01 Richard I, The Lionheart

King Of England (1189 - 1199)

Though his coat of arms adorns the English football strip, Richard the Lionheart doesn't live up to his patriotic image. This merciless warrior king spoke only French and spent more of his reign at war on the Third Crusade to retake Jerusalem from the Islamic Fatimid Caliphate than he did in England.

Arms And Armour

Richard I wore chain-mail over a padded undergarment designed to absorb the force of any blow, but often threw himself into battle unprotected. Charging on horseback, his couched lance could punch a hole through armour and scatter terrified infantry, while his perfectly balanced great sword - wielded one or two-handed - put strength and momentum behind sharp steel, taking it clean through flesh and bone.

★★★★★

Enemies

Saladin - the powerful Sultan of the Fatimid Caliphate - is the Lionheart's classic nemesis, but the two had a mutual respect with Saladin sending fruit when Richard fell ill. Ultimately it was Richard's fellow Crusader, Philip II of France, who became his most embittered opponent, making a play for Normandy while the English army was in the Middle East.

★★★★★

Strategy

While savagery was his calling card - his reputation alone caused Philip II to flee the battlefield - the Lionheart was a logistical genius and a quick-thinking pragmatist, famously tethering boats together to create a floating bridge across the river Rhone in France. Richard knew how far to push his army and never marched his army out of reach of their supplies.

★★★★★

Definitive Battle

Following the recapture of the vital port of Acre, Richard I took sole command of the Third Crusade. Marching to Arsuf - 15 kilometres north from what is now Tel Aviv in Israel - from where they planned to strike inland to Jerusalem, the Crusaders were met by Saladin's forces on 7 September 1191 at the Battle of Arsuf.

Both armies were roughly equal in size, though Saladin's forces were more equally divided. Richard wanted to keep his forces with their backs to the coast where they could be supplied by ship, while Saladin wanted to draw them out and sever their supply lines. Using his flexible horse archers and skirmishers, Saladin harassed the Crusader flanks with growing intensity - trying to goad them into charging, where the divided Crusaders could be crushed. Richard's iron discipline only went so far and the knights on the flank began to charge after hours of needling. With split-second thinking, the king committed the entire army into this impulsive charge taking the unprepared Fatimids by surprise. Christian chroniclers claimed the Fatimid dead to be 7,000 while the Crusaders lost only 700 - even taking into account the propaganda factor it was a decisive victory.

★★★★★

Richard the Lionheart arriving at Acre

Queen Victoria's Age of invention

Discover how Victoria's reign inspired innovation that would shape the modern world

T he air was heavy with the smog of the Industrial Revolution as Britain chugged and clinked with new-fangled machinery. It marked a period where major technological developments hugely enhanced the standard of living and set the groundwork for today's somewhat sleeker gadgetry.

By the 1830s, first-world countries were powered by steam and built with iron; there were engines, bridges and trains in drains. Elsewhere, advances in medicine were coming thick and fast. There were tablets that would ease pain and ether that would remove it entirely. A surgical operation was no longer something to consider committing suicide over. Mortality rates fell and Europe's population doubled during the 19th Century to 400 million.

Among the life-saving qnventions were those that enabled communication, via phone and radio, and home improvements that made life a little easier. Here you'll find the best of the best, as well as the stories of how they came to life in what was a fascinating time in history.

VICTORIA
British Empire 1837-1901

Brief Bio
Reigning during the height of the Industrial Revolution, which had begun under her 18th Century predecessors, Victoria presided over an age of technological innovation that can only be rivalled by the engineering wonders of the ancient world and the fierce march of progress during the 20th and 21st Centuries. It was influenced by the former, and gave us the latter.

Medicine

Anaesthetic

Before anaesthetic, the ancient Greeks would use herbal concoctions in a bid to reduce the stress. The word itself is Greek, meaning 'without sensation', but this wasn't coined until 1846 when poet and physician Oliver Wendell Holmes referred to a new technique he'd witnessed, where a patient was given ether before having a tumour painlessly removed.

Ether had existed for hundreds of years, but no one had thought to use it as an anaesthetic until former dental student William Morton began experimenting in secret on small animals and even himself until the time came to give a public demonstration. Until then, students had been inhaling ether fumes for fun, dubbed 'ether frolics', where people would lose control of their motor functions and incur cuts and bruises without feeling any pain.

Gone were the days of plying patients with alcohol and opium, commanding several men to pin them down as the scalpel made contact with flesh. Deaths were reduced and surgeons were able to take more time operating and in return, make more medical discoveries.

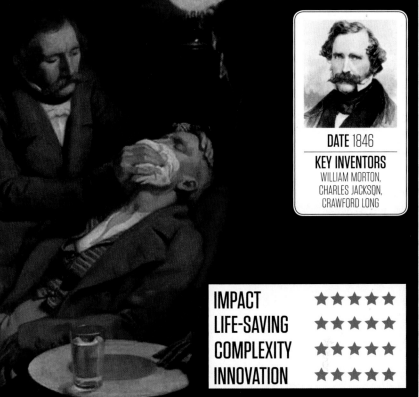

DATE 1846
KEY INVENTORS
WILLIAM MORTON,
CHARLES JACKSON,
CRAWFORD LONG

IMPACT	★★★★★
LIFE-SAVING	★★★★★
COMPLEXITY	★★★★★
INNOVATION	★★★★★

Aspirin

Aspirin is one of the most successful over-the-counter pain remedies of all time, with new benefits constantly being uncovered. It was one of the first drugs to be made available in tablet form, which isn't surprising when you consider that the natural form of aspirin is found in plants such as willow and myrtle and had been used for easing pain for centuries. In 400 BCE, Greek physicians were serving women willow leaf tea during childbirth and in 1763 a reverend in England was dishing out dried willow bark to sufferers of rheumatic fever.

But it wasn't until the Victorian era that it went beyond a herbal folk medicine, as salicylic acid was made from the active ingredient in willow by French scientists. Further tweaking was needed, though, since it left many upset stomachs in its wake. German scientists created a more stable and palatable form in 1897 and aspirin was launched two years later. It took thousands of minds from across the world to develop this natural remedy and refine it into a potentially life-saving preventive tablet.

DATE 1899
KEY INVENTORS
CHARLES FREDRIC,
FELIX HOFFMANN

IMPACT	★★★★★
LIFE-SAVING	★★★★☆
COMPLEXITY	★★★★★
INNOVATION	★★★☆☆

X-ray

DATE 1895
KEY INVENTORS
WILHELM RÖNTGEN

Ever wondered what the 'X' in X-ray stands for? You might be disappointed to learn that even its inventor, German physicist Wilhelm Röntgen, didn't know. While experimenting with passing electrical currents through a cathode tube filled with a special gas, he discovered the tube produced a glow. It seemed he had discovered an invisible light that he didn't fully understand, so he called it 'X-radiation', because in maths, 'X' means unknown.

Röntgen didn't stop there, even drafting in his wife and producing the first X-ray photo of her hand. News travelled fast throughout the world and scientists were able to replicate and refine X-ray images, as Röntgen's belief that scientific discoveries belonged to the world kept him from patenting his invention.

The medical community embraced his discovery, making fractures, bullets and foreign bodies bared for all to see. Röntgen shied away from his newfound fame, but his breakthrough was celebrated the world over and he was eventually awarded the first Nobel Prize in Physics.

IMPACT	★★★★★
LIFE-SAVING	★★★★☆
COMPLEXITY	★★★☆☆
INNOVATION	★★★★★

Industrial

Sewing machine

Clothing was stitched by hand in the early 1800s and tailors' businesses were booming, continuing a tradition over 20,000 years old. When the first sewing machine was invented by French tailor Barthelemy Thimonnier in 1830, a riot broke out and a group of his fellow tailors set fire to his factory, fearing unemployment. This machine never came into general use and almost a decade later American machinist Elias Howe would improve on the design by creating a lockstitch that linked together two threads and wouldn't come undone. His machine was faster than anything that came before it at a rate of 250 stitches a minute, yet Howe struggled to persuade clothing manufacturers to pay for his pricey invention. In 1846 he left America for London where corset-maker William Frederick Thomas would invest to protect the Howe machine from being copied. Howe's invention wound up making Thomas a very wealthy man and Howe was left with nothing.

DATE 1846

KEY INVENTORS
BARTHELEMY THIMONNIER,
ELIAS HOWE

IMPACT	★★★★☆
LIFE-SAVING	★★★★★
COMPLEXITY	★★★★★
INNOVATION	★★★★★

Suspension bridge

The famous inventor, designer and engineer Isambard Kingdom Brunel was a huge part of Britain's Industrial Revolution, building bridges, tunnels, railways, docks and ships. He changed the way people could travel and many of his designs still stand today, such as London's Paddington Station (1854) and the Clifton Suspension Bridge in Bristol.

The latter was a wrought-iron marvel, linking Clifton in Bristol to Leigh Woods in North Somerset, England. It also marked Brunel's first commission. It was the earliest of its kind, high enough so that tall ships could sail beneath it and sturdy enough to provide safe passage for pedestrians and horse-drawn carriages. Unfortunately, due to the Bristol riots, the bridge wasn't built until after his death but this distinctive landmark served as a fitting memorial to the great man.

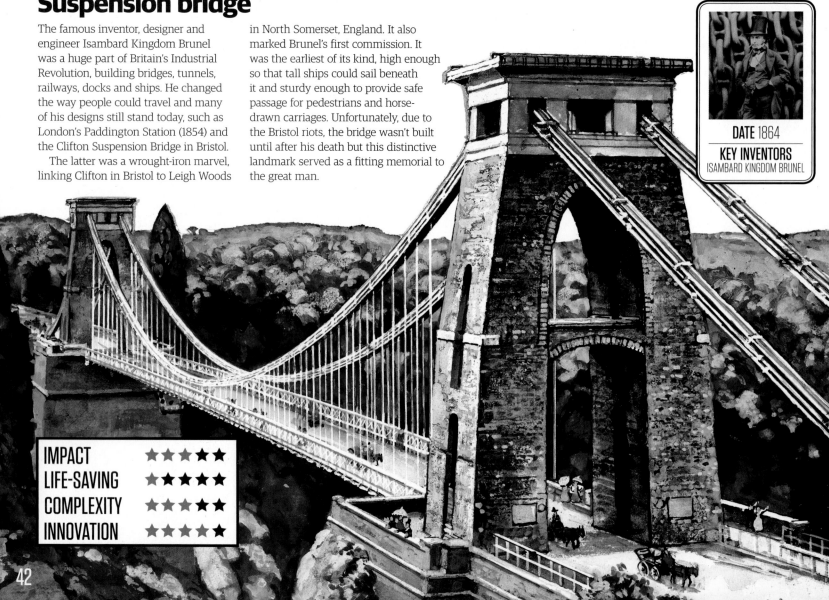

DATE 1864

KEY INVENTORS
ISAMBARD KINGDOM BRUNEL

IMPACT	★★★★☆
LIFE-SAVING	★★★★★
COMPLEXITY	★★★★☆
INNOVATION	★★★★☆

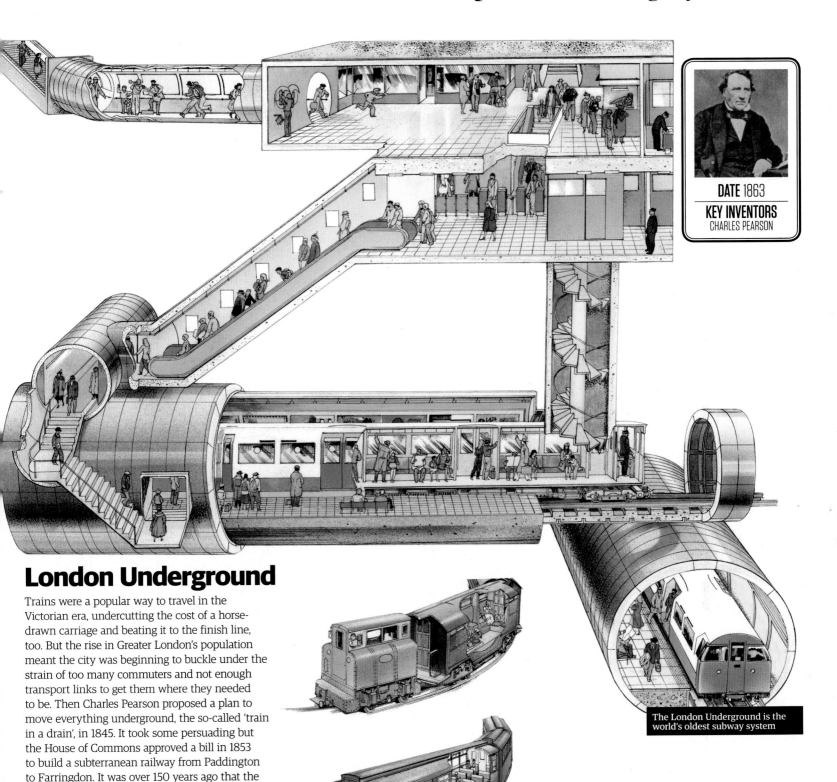

DATE 1863
KEY INVENTORS
CHARLES PEARSON

London Underground

Trains were a popular way to travel in the Victorian era, undercutting the cost of a horse-drawn carriage and beating it to the finish line, too. But the rise in Greater London's population meant the city was beginning to buckle under the strain of too many commuters and not enough transport links to get them where they needed to be. Then Charles Pearson proposed a plan to move everything underground, the so-called 'train in a drain', in 1845. It took some persuading but the House of Commons approved a bill in 1853 to build a subterranean railway from Paddington to Farringdon. It was over 150 years ago that the world's first underground train made its debut journey, with passengers anxious to experience it.

The Metropolitan was a huge success and 26,000 people hopped aboard each day in the first six months. However, it wasn't just the gap they had to mind, as commuters were enveloped in clouds of smoke from the steam trains and other passengers (smoking wasn't banned until after the King's Cross fire in 1987). The Underground continued to grow, reaching out to the then sleepy villages of Hammersmith and Morden and the transport links caused their modest populations to boom. Charles Pearson never lived to see his vision completed, having died a year before the Underground opened, but his legacy is everlasting.

The London Underground is the world's oldest subway system

IMPACT ★★★★★
LIFE-SAVING ★★★★★
COMPLEXITY ★★★★★
INNOVATION ★★★★★

Communication

Radio

Italian inventor Guglielmo Marconi had heard about the existence of so-called radio waves that travel through the air and it made him wonder whether sound could travel the same way, via air waves.

He built two machines, one that could transmit messages and another that could receive them and managed to make a bell ring across the room using this method. Excited by his initial success, he worked on increasing the distance but no one wanted to invest to help him develop his machines, so he moved to Britain where his technology was welcomed by the army and the Post Office. He registered for a patent in 1901, then set about making a radio wave transmitter and a receiver to convert the waves into electricity, which then turned into sound. The first signals he was able to send were in Morse code, but this vital discovery would later develop the ability to transmit speech across long distances.

> "This vital discovery would later develop the ability to transmit speech"

DATE 1900

KEY INVENTORS
GUGLIELMO MARCONI

Marconi sent the first radio signal across the Atlantic Ocean in 1901

IMPACT	★★★★★
LIFE-SAVING	★★★★★
COMPLEXITY	★★★★★
INNOVATION	★★★★★

Victoria was the first British monarch to be photographed

DATE 1884
KEY INVENTORS
GEORGE EASTMAN

Photographic film

The Victorians enjoyed taking photographs of their loved ones, whether alive or even post-mortem. The technology quickly developed from the earliest camera in 1826 and Queen Victoria became the first British monarch to have her photograph taken. For a long time it was an expensive and laborious process but one man set out to make the camera "as convenient as the pencil".

American entrepreneur and keen photographer George Eastman invented paper-based photographic film and a roll holder, which made it possible for people to capture candid photos quickly. By 1901 he had founded the Eastman Kodak Company and developed the Kodak Brownie, a camera that everyday people could afford to own. This film helped develop the motion picture industry and it was the first company to produce photography kits for the masses. Kodak still exists today, but sadly it has shifted its focus from cameras to printers.

IMPACT	★★★★★
LIFE-SAVING	★★★★★
COMPLEXITY	★★★★★
INNOVATION	★★★★★

Telephone

Some of the greatest inventions known to man were made completely by accident and Alexander Graham Bell's breakthrough was no different. While experimenting with electro-audio stimulation, he used two springs connected by a long piece of wire. He gave one end to his assistant, Thomas Watson, and he held the other in a different room.

The idea was that when one spring was moved, the other would too, but actually what happened was that the sound of the spring moving travelled down the wire and was heard at the other end. This device struggled to carry the sound of their voices, but Bell knew he had something, so quickly registered for a patent to stop others from using the same idea. Only two hours after Bell had submitted his request, another inventor had tried to register the same patent but was too late and the fame would forever belong to Bell.

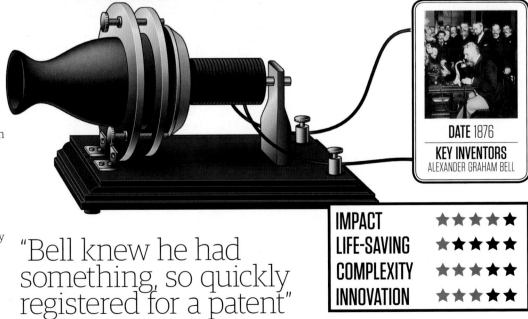

DATE 1876
KEY INVENTORS
ALEXANDER GRAHAM BELL

"Bell knew he had something, so quickly registered for a patent"

IMPACT	★★★★★
LIFE-SAVING	★★★★★
COMPLEXITY	★★★★★
INNOVATION	★★★★★

Home improvements

Electric lamp

Thomas Edison didn't invent the light bulb, but he's often mistaken for doing so. The incandescent light bulb was in fact the brainchild of Joseph Swan, a British physicist, in 1878 but early incarnations were impractical due to their short life span and high cost to manufacture. Edison, however, was the first to come up with the commercial light. He perfected the formula by using a coiled carbon filament and the first test lasted 13.5 hours.

During his first demonstration, the inventor declared: "We will make electricity so cheap that only the rich will burn candles." Edison had registered patents in his native America but they came under dispute for being based on other inventors' works. To avoid a potential legal battle with Swan, whose British patent had been awarded a year before, the pair became business partners instead, forming Ediswan in 1883 and together they fulfilled Edison's vision of providing cheaper bulbs.

DATE 1878
KEY INVENTORS
THOMAS EDISON, JOSEPH SWAN

IMPACT	★★★★★
LIFE-SAVING	★★★★★
COMPLEXITY	★★★★★
INNOVATION	★★★★★

Vacuum cleaner

Hubert Booth's light bulb moment came when he observed an American's new cleaning invention that blew out air. He thought it would be far more efficient if the contraption sucked in air instead and the idea evolved into the vacuum cleaner, a device that almost every household in the modern world couldn't be without. What made Booth believe that he was really onto something was when demonstrating to friends at a posh London restaurant. He placed his handkerchief on the velvet seat of his chair and inhaled as hard as he could, before coughing and spluttering because of all the dust that had come out of the cushion. The handkerchief didn't fare so well either, as Booth and his friends discovered that it was now filthy.

An invention was born, but far from the slender pieces of equipment we have nowadays, this vacuum cleaner was so cumbersome it had to be drawn by a horse and cart. This was because most Victorian houses didn't have electricity so Booth's machine got its power from coal or oil. It would park outside a house and an extra-long hose would snake in through the windows, ridding homes of years and years of accumulated dust.

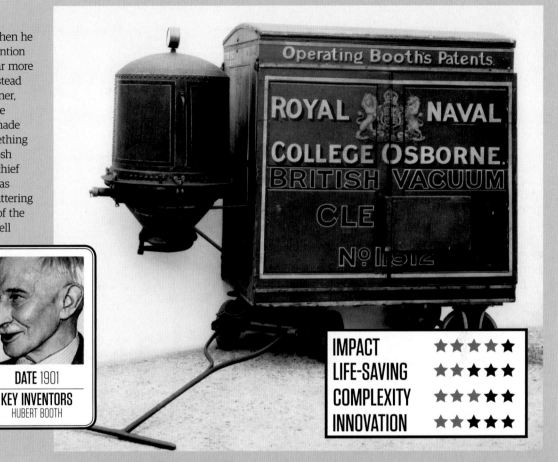

DATE 1901
KEY INVENTORS
HUBERT BOOTH

IMPACT ★★★★★
LIFE-SAVING ★★★★★
COMPLEXITY ★★★★★
INNOVATION ★★★★★

Flushing toilet system

Many inventions are born out of a need to fix a problem and using an earth closet was enough to drive several inventors to work on a solution. This primitive lavatory, or 'privy', was simply a wooden bench with a hole cut out and a bucket underneath, where dry earth was used to cover waste. Naturally, they were pretty whiffy and most privies could be found at the bottom of the garden for this very reason, while chamber pots were used in the house for any night-time emergencies. It was hardly fit for a queen, but Queen Victoria did indeed use an earth closet at Windsor Castle.

In 1852, a successful, state-of-the-art loo arrived when pottery manufacturer Thomas Twyford invented the first flushing toilet. It was made of china instead of wood or metal, but the design wasn't entirely original having been based on the attempts of inventor JG Jennings, yet Twyford was hailed as a pioneer in hygiene.

DATE 1852
KEY INVENTORS
THOMAS TWYFORD

"Queen Victoria did indeed use an earth closet at Windsor Castle"

IMPACT ★★★★★
LIFE-SAVING ★★★★★
COMPLEXITY ★★★★★
INNOVATION ★★★★★

The birth of the British monarchy

Discover how the union of England and Scotland shaped the line of succession and the modern British monarchy

The United Kingdom of Great Britain has not always been united, or known as Great Britain for that matter. Prior to 1707, this seemingly small island in the North Atlantic had been divided for centuries. England (including Wales) and Scotland were in fact two independent countries, and it wasn't until the passing of the Treaty of Union through both Parliaments in 1707 that the two kingdoms united, officially marking the birth of Great Britain, and as a result, its monarchy.

The first sovereign to rule over Great Britain was Queen Anne. Officially she had reigned as queen of both countries for five years prior to the Treaty, as both the Kingdom of England and the Kingdom of Scotland had shared a monarch since 1603, when King James VI of Scotland inherited the English throne from Queen Elizabeth I through relation. This was known officially as the Union of Crowns. It was the Treaty of Union, however, that united the monarchy under one crown, and then eventually one government.

Due to the treaty, Queen Anne was the first and last monarch from the House of Stuart dynasty to rule over the United Kingdom of Great Britain. Six years prior to 1707, in 1701, it had been decided

through the Act of Settlement that Catholics were to be prohibited from inheriting the throne, and so Sophia of Hanover, a Protestant and the granddaughter of James VI and I, would become Queen Anne's heir. Although Anne had many direct Catholic descendants, she had no surviving children. Sophia of Hanover was her closest protestant relative, which meant in 1714, when Queen Anne died, the House of Stuart dynasty came to an end as the House of Hanover succeeded the throne.

By this time, however, Sophia of Hanover had died aged 83, and so her eldest son George inherited the crown and became King George I of Great Britain. George's succession was controversial, as many people hadn't agreed with the protestant succession that had been outlined in the Act of Settlement, and as a result riots were documented across England in opposition to his coronation. Despite the initial hostility, George I reigned as king up until his death in 1727. During his reign, Britain began to modernise and a cabinet government was formed, which meant that the monarchy held less power over political affairs.

George's son and heir George II succeeded to the throne in October 1727 after his father's death.

Queen Elizabeth II, the current monarch of Great Britain, leaving Westminster Abbey as part of a procession after her coronation on 3 June 1953

Treaty of Union

How England and Scotland united to form Great Britain and the British monarchy

The United Kingdom of Great Britain was officially formed in 1707, when the Parliaments of England and Scotland passed the Treaty of Union agreement. Prior to this date, England (including Wales) and Scotland were independent countries that had two separate governments. The Treaty of Union was designed to merge the Kingdoms of England and Scotland together, creating the United Kingdom of Great Britain.

Negotiations to unite the countries began in 1705 under the reign of the English and Scottish monarch Queen Anne, although there had been several failed tempts prior to this date. 31 commissioners were appointed by each Parliament to negotiate the terms, and talks began on 16 April 1706 at the Cockpit-in-Court in London. After a few days, the Treaty was finalised on 22 July 1706, and two separate acts of union were to be passed through each government before it was put into effect. The first act of union, known as the Union with Scotland Act, was passed by the Parliament of England in 1706, with the second, the Union with England Act, being passed by the Parliament of Scotland shortly after in 1707.

The treaty itself consisted of 25 articles, with two stating that one monarch was to rule over Great Britain and a single unified Parliament of Great Britain was to be formed. In addition to this, agreements regarding trading between England and Scotland were set, alongside the decision to introduce a common currency. On 1 May 1707, England and Scotland officially united.

The union between Great Britain and Ireland, however, did not occur for another 93 years. It was during the reign of King George III that in 1800, Great Britain and the Kingdom of Ireland united to form what is now known as the United Kingdom of Great Britain and Ireland. To signify the union, the Union Flag incorporated the St Patrick's Cross.

The official copy of the Treaty of Union, ratified by the parliaments of England and Scotland in 1907

George II's own son and heir apparent, Frederick Louis, Prince of Wales, was next in line to become king. Frederick, however, died unexpectedly in 1751. This mean that in 1760, after King George II's death, Frederick's eldest son George III inherited the crown.

It was during George III's reign that Great Britain and Ireland united, changing his official title to King George III of the United Kingdom of Great Britain and Ireland. George III was also the first monarch of Great Britain since its formation in 1707 to be born and raised in the country he ruled. While sovereign, George saw Britain through many military conflicts, including the Battle of Waterloo in 1815. His early reign was considered successful. However, he is often remembered through history for the mental illness that plagued him in later life, which as a result earned him his nickname 'Mad George'. During his illness, his son and heir apparent, George the Prince of Wales, served as Prince Regent – a position that enabled him to exercise full power as king while his father was incapacitated. This period is known as the Regency in British history, and Regent's Park, as well as Regent Street in London, was named after him. Upon George III's death in 1820, his son, the Prince of Wales, inherited the throne and was titled King George IV of the United Kingdom of Great Britain and Ireland.

George IV reigned as king for ten years, and upon his own passing, had no legitimate issue to inherit the throne. His younger brother, William IV, who was third in line to the throne during George III's reign, became King. William himself reigned for a relatively short period of time (1830-1837), and also had no surviving legitimate children at the time of his death. He was succeeded by his young niece Victoria, Prince Edward, Duke of Kent and Strathearn's daughter, who was only 18 at the time.

Royal coat of arms
How the Royal coat of arms represents the United Kingdom of Great Britain and its monarchy

Crowned golden lion
Tying the Royal coat of arms altogether at the top is the royal helm, crest and mantling, which appear directly above the shield. A crowned golden lion faces sideways, looking out, at the very top.

The shield
The central shield represents the different parts of the United Kingdom. The two opposite quarters that bear three lions stand for England. The second quarter, which features a roaring red lion, details the arms of Scotland. And the third, which features a golden harp, represents the arms of Ireland.

Arms of Dominion
The Royal coat of arms is officially known as the Arms of Dominion, and is used to identify the current British monarch. It reflects the history of the country and the monarchy it represents.

The supporters
The English lion that appears on the left-hand side of the shield is known as the Dexter supporter, while the Scottish unicorn on the right is known as the Sinister supporter. Both stand on top of the green compartment, which shows the Scottish thistle, Irish shamrock and English rose.

Mottos
Below the compartment appears the sovereign's motto 'Dieu et mon droit', which stands for 'God and my right'. And around the shield, along the blue belt reads, 'Honi Soit qui mal y pense' ('Evil to him who evil thinks'), which symbolises the ancient Knighthood, the Order of the Garter.

DIEU ET MON DROIT

Scottish Royal coat of arms

Scotland has its own version of the Royal coat of arms. This features two representations of Scotland as apposed to one, and the unicorn appears as the Dexter holding the Scottish flag, while the lion is the Sinister holding the English flag. A red lion, as opposed to a gold one, appears on top holding a banner that reads 'In Defens' ('In defence'). The motto of the Order of the Thistle sits along the compartment and reads 'Nemo me immune lacessit' ('No attacks me with impunity').

Defining moment
Monarch 1 1707
Regnal name: **Queen Anne**
Name: **Anne**
Birth/death: **6 February 1665 – 1 August 1714**
Reign: **1 May 1707 – 1 August 1714**
Dynasty: **House of Stewart**
Queen Anne had reigned as Queen of England and Scotland since 1702. However, the signing of the Treaty of Union in 1707 meant she became the first monarch of the United Kingdom of Great Britain.

Defining moment
Monarch 4 1760
Regnal name: **King George III**
Name: **George William Frederick**
Birth/death: **4 June 1738 – 29 January 1820**
Reign: **25 October 1760 – 29 January 1820**
Dynasty: **House of Hanover**
George III became King of Great Britain in 1760, after inheriting the throne from his grandfather King George II. During his reign, Great Britain and Ireland united to officially form the United Kingdom of Great Britain and Ireland, and in 1815, Britain defeated Napoleon at the Battle of Waterloo.

● Monarch 6
Regnal name: **King William IV**
Name: **William Henry**
Birth/death: **21 August 1765 – 20 June 1837**
Reign: **26 June 1830 – 20 June 1837**
Dynasty: **House of Hanover**
King William IV was the third son of King George III; he inherited the throne from his eldest brother King George IV, who had no legitimate issue at the time of death. Upon William's death in 1837, his 18-year-old niece Victoria inherited the throne.

Timeline

1707

● Monarch 2
Regnal name: **King George 1**
Name: **George Louis**
Birth/death: **28 May 1660 – 11 June 1727**
Reign: **1 August 1714 – 11 June 1727**
Dynasty: **House of Hanover**
King George I was the first monarch from the House of Hanover. He inherited the throne from Queen Anne, due to the Act of Settlement in 1707, which stated only Protestants could reign. By the time of Queen Anne's passing in 1714, George I was her closest protestant relative.

● Monarch 3
Regnal name: **King George II**
Name: **George Augustus**
Birth/death: **30 October 1683 – 25 October 1760**
Reign: **11 June 1727 – 25 October 1760**
Dynasty: **House of Hanover**
George II was the last British monarch to be born outside of Great Britain. He ascended the throne upon the death of his father George I. His eldest son and heir apparent Frederick died, leading to his grandson George III inheriting the throne.

● Monarch 5
Regnal name: **King George IV**
Name: **George Augustus Frederick**
Birth/death: **12 August 1762 – 26 June 1830**
Reign: **29 January 1820 – 26 June 1830**
Dynasty: **House of Hanover**
King George IV inherited the throne from his father George III after serving as Prince Regen for nine years previously, due to his father's mental illness. George IV's only legitimate issue, Princess Charlotte of Wales, died in 181

A portrait of King George III. He reigned from 1760-1820, but suffered from mental illness, resulting in a regency being established in 1811

William the Conqueror

William the Conqueror was the first Norman King of England and is often referred to as William I of England. After successfully invading the country in 1066, he reigned as sovereign up until his death in 1087.

Prior to this, William's cousin, Edward the Confessor, ruled as one of the last Anglo-Saxon kings of England from 1042 until his death in 1066. Although Edward was married, he had taken a vow of celibacy, which meant he had no heirs to the throne. On his deathbed, Edward declared that the English earl Harold Godwinson was to succeed him. William, however, refuted Harold's claim to the throne, and so in 1066, he gathered a fleet and invaded England, famously killing King Harold during the Battle of Hastings. Upon William's own death in 1087, his lands were divided among his sons. His second son, William II, inherited the throne.

The modern British monarchy we know today descends from William the Conqueror. In fact, he is Queen Elizabeth II's 22nd great grandfather. Since William I's death in 1087, most reigning monarchs of England, and later Great Britain, come from the same line of senior descent. Only 23 ruling monarchs have not been direct descendants of William I, including sovereigns from the House of Lancaster, Tudor and Stuart.

Defining moment
Monarch 7 1837
Regnal name: **Queen Victoria**
Name: **Alexandrina Victoria**
Birth/death: **24 May 1819 – 22 January 1901**
Reign: **20 June 1837 – 22 January 1901**
Dynasty: **House of Hanover**
Queen Victoria is currently the longest reigning monarch in British history, reigning for over 63 years up until her death in 1901.

Defining moment
Monarch 10 1936
Regnal name: **King Edward VIII**
Name: **Edward Albert Christian George Andrew Patrick David**
Birth/death: **23 June 1894 – 28 May 1972**
Reign: **20 January 1936 – 11 December 1936**
Dynasty: **House of Windsor**
Edward VII was the only British monarch to abdicate, after Parliament opposed his intent to marry Wallis Simpson.

Monarch 11
Regnal name: **King George VI**
Name: **Albert, Frederick Arthur George**
Birth/death: **14 December 1895 – 6 February 1952**
Reign: **11 December 1936 – 6 February 1952**
Dynasty: **House of Windsor**
George VI reigned as King of Great Britain until his death in 1947. During his reign, Great Britain went to war with Nazi Germany, Ireland declared itself a republic, and the British Empire transitioned into the Commonwealth of Nations.

1926

Monarch 8
Regnal name: **King Edward VII**
Name: **Albert Edward**
Birth/death: **9 November 1841 – 6 May 1910**
Reign: **22 January 1901 – 6 May 1910**
Dynasty: **House of Saxe-Coburg and Gotha**
Queen Victoria's eldest son and heir inherited the throne after her death, becoming King Edward VII. Due to his mother's long reign, he was the longest serving heir apparent in British history, until 2011 when Charles, Prince of Wales, surpassed it.

Monarch 9
Regnal name: **King George V**
Name: **George Frederick Ernest Albert**
Birth/death: **3rd June 1865 – 20th January 1936**
Reign: **6th May 1910 – 20th January 1936**
Dynasty: **House of Windsor**
During George V's reign, the First World War broke out. While other empires fell, he was able to expand the British one. In 1917, due to ill feeling as a result of the war, he changed the German House of Saxe-Coburg Gotha to House of Windsor.

Monarch 12
Regnal name: **Queen Elizabeth II**
Name: **Elizabeth Alexandra Mary**
Birth/death: **21 April 1926 – present day**
Reign: **1952 – present day**
Dynasty: **House of Windsor**
Queen Elizabeth II is the current monarch of Great Britain and Head of the Commonwealth. She is now the second longest reigning monarch of the United Kingdom, after 61 years on the throne.

The House of Windsor

Why did the monarchy change its Royal house name to Windsor?

Historically, monarchs do not have surnames; they are known by the countries they rule over and the Royal house name that they inherit from their fathers when they succeed the throne.

Queen Victoria was the last British monarch to reign under the House of Hanover dynasty. Her successor and heir apparent Edward VII inherited the throne after her death in 1901, under his father's Royal house name the House of Saxe-Coburg and Gotha. Edward was the first and last monarch of Great Britain to reign under this name, as upon his death in 1910, his son George V inherited the throne and subsequently changed the name to the House of Windsor in 1917.

George's decision to change the German dynastic name was a result of World War I, which occurred between 1914-1918. Due to anti-German sentiment at the time, the English name Windsor was adopted and was to be used as both the new Royal house name and as a family surname. This officially marked the start of the House of Windsor dynasty.

Following George V's death in 195, his eldest daughter and the current monarch of Great Britain, Elizabeth II, inherited the throne, continuing the House of Windsor line. Queen Elizabeth II still reigns under this Royal house name, as will her direct heirs and descendants. In 1960, however, under an Order in Council, Elizabeth II adapted the personal Windsor surname to incorporate her husband's heritage (Philip Mountbatten). The new surname, Mountbatten-Windsor, can be used by some of her descendants who do not carry the styles 'Royal Highness', 'Prince' or 'Princess'.

Although the surname has changed, the official Royal house name of Windsor remains the same. As of today, many British Royals use the Mountbatten-Windsor surname for official documents, including those that have styles.

The official Royal portrait of Prince George's Christening. (Back row, L-R) Prince Phillip, the Duke Of Edinburgh, Charles, Prince of Wales, Camilla the Duchess of Cornwall, Prince Harry of Wales, Pippa Middleton, James Middleton, Carole Middleton and Michael Middleton; (Front row, L-R) Queen Elizabeth II, Catherine, Duchess of Cambridge carrying Prince George Alexander Louis of Cambridge and Prince William, Duke of Cambridge

Queen Victoria is currently the longest reigning monarch of Great Britain. After inheriting the throne in 1837, she reigned for 63 years until her death in 1901. As a result, she is one of the most famous British monarchs in history. During her reign, also known as the Victorian era, Great Britain modernised, thanks to the industrial revolution and changes to politics, the military, science and culture. Victoria was also the last monarch to reign from the Royal House of Hanover. Her son and successor King Edward VII reigned (1901-1910) customarily under his father's dynastic name, the House of Saxe-Coburg and Gotha. In 1917, however,

Queen Elizabeth II and her husband Prince Philip, Duke of Edinburgh, stand side by side on her coronation day in 1953

seven years after Edward VII's son George V inherited the throne, the Royal house name was changed to Windsor as result of World War I (1914-1918) and anti-German sentiment at that time.

The current British monarchy still reign under the House of Windsor name today, and it was first inherited by George V's son and successor, Edward VIII, in 1936. As the only monarch since the union of Great Britain in 1707 to abdicate the throne, Edward VIII reigned under the House of Windsor for less than a year. His decision to abdicate was a result of his wish to marry the divorced American socialite, Wallis Simpson, which at the time would

"Edward VIII's wish to marry a divorced American socialite caused outcry across Britain"

have caused outcry across Britain and conflicted with his role as the Head of the Church of England. Upon Edward's abdication, his brother Albert ascended to the throne, and was formally styled King George VI.

Due to George VI's succession, his eldest daughter Elizabeth became heir apparent to the throne. And in 1953, she officially became Queen Elizabeth II upon her father's death. Elizabeth II is the current monarch of Great Britain and is also the second longest reigning sovereign in British history. In 2012 she celebrated her Diamond Jubilee, which marked her 60 years as reigning monarch.

Darius is said to have ascended the throne by winning a contest that involved nobles sitting on their horses until one of them neighed

DARIUS I
Persia, 550-486 BCE

Brief Bio

Rising from an unimportant place in the royal dynasty of Persia and an also-ran role as a spearman during the Persian campaign against Egypt, Darius eventually took the throne of Persia after becoming involved in a plot to kill the usurper Bardiya. His loyal army ensured that the rocky early days of his reign rapidly smoothed out as a series of conquests brought Persia wealth and empire.

550 – 486 BCE

King Darius I

Ruling the vast Persian Achaemenid Empire at its height, Darius I became world-renowned for his unstoppable military might, impressive construction prowess and an astute ability to manage his realm's finances

What would you do if you inherited one of the largest and most powerful empires the world had ever seen? Well, if you were Darius I, the third king of the mighty Persian Empire, you would spend your reign making it even better, transforming its economy and embarking on a series of military campaigns that would lead you to earn the title of Darius the Great.

However, Darius the Great didn't begin his life as a figure destined for greatness, being merely the eldest of five sons of Hystaspes, a member of the Persian royal house that served under King Cyrus and King Cambyses II. According to the account of Herodotus, the titular Father of History who details the Persian Empire in his *Histories*, Darius was a youth 'of no consequence at the time' and ended up nothing more than spearman in the army of Cambyses II during the Empire's Egyptian conquest. Later Darius would rise to become the personal lancer of Cambyses II and there it would seem his role in history could have ended, a mere footnote in an epic age.

All this would change in a radical series of events that, oddly enough, would begin with a dream. Following Cambyses being made King of Persia by his father Cyrus, and Darius ascending to Cambyses' side as his personal lancer, Cyrus suddenly had a dream while he was away at war in which a vision of Darius equipped with wings stood astride Europe and Asia. Upon waking, Cyrus decided that the dream was a warning that he and his son's empire was in danger and that Darius was forming plans to overthrow Cambyses. Fearing for his son's life, Cyrus sent Darius' father Hystaspes back to court to watch over his son strictly until he returned.

Returning to court, Hystaspes could not find any treasonable intentions in Darius during the time Cambyses remained king. Cambyses II's reign was indeed cut short, but rather than by Darius, a man who may or may not have been his brother, Bardiya, seized the throne for himself. According to the accounts of Darius' life, Cambyses attempted to march against Bardiya, but ended up committing suicide. Other accounts state that Cambyses died from a stab wound that turned gangrenous. Either way, Cyrus's fears had become reality, with Cambyses falling from power and the Persian Empire temporarily falling into chaos.

Darius, now freed from his role as lance-bearer to Cambyses, joined with various other noblemen from Persia who were against the usurper's rule and in September 522 BCE succeeded in a plot to kill the new king in the fortress of Sikayauvati. While the death of the usurper king ended months of chaos and uncertainty, the throne of the world's greatest empire was now vacant and with no obvious successor. What happens next is debated greatly among historians, with various different accounts describing the how Darius ascended the throne - some more bizarre than others. However, what all the accounts agree on is that the following morning Darius was King of Persia.

Darius was soon crowned at Pasargadae and afterwards he moved to Ecbatana to begin the rule of his vast empire. Just as soon as he arrived, however, he learned of numerous revolts against his leadership in Elam and Babylonia. He moved and crushed these quickly, but soon more revolts sprung up in Media, Parthia, Assyria and Egypt - now large swathes of his empire were openly at war with him. Just when things looked like they would end poorly for Darius, his substantial and overly loyal army came to his rescue, proceeding

on a brutal campaign across Persia, smashing each revolt and executing its leaders. Within a single year every revolt was quelled and Darius was now unopposed as King of Persia.

> Darius began many projects during his reign, including two canals linking the Red Sea to the River Nile

From this point on Darius' reign went, in general, from strength to strength. He undertook many military campaigns in central Asia, Aria and Scythia, radically transforming the empire's economy and adding to its infrastructure greatly with new roads, canals and civic structures. The Achaemenid Empire was vast and now under Darius' astute management and delegation it became the world's most wealthy and powerful realm, expanding rapidly and even gaining the support of some of the powerful Greek city states, which had either been won over through force of arms or by trade. Darius was now effectively untouchable - his will was law and he was without doubt the most powerful man in the entire world.

There was one problem, though. One issue that, as Darius' reign progressed, not only became more apparent but could not be quelled or conquered. It was the fact that much of mainland Greece was - openly or not - hostile to the Persian Empire and kept expressing this by interfering in his captured territory of Ionia and Lydia in Asia Minor. Small skirmishes became larger fights, trade slowed and influence weakened, with tensions between Greeks

and Persians escalating as a result. After almost a decade in which Darius' forces invaded Thrace and many cities of the northern Aegean, these tensions finally boiled over into open war, with the Greeks sending an army to burn Sardis, which is located in modern-day Turkey.

Darius responded to this by sanctioning not only the recapture of the region, which included many of the Ionian islands, but also a full-scale invasion of the Greek mainland, with Athens and Eretria - both key players in the burning of the city of Sardis - targeted for punishment. Assembling an army of over 20,000 men and placing them at the command of his most trusted of commanders,

"Darius was now effectively untouchable, his will was law and he was the most powerful man in the entire world"

● **Simple spearman**
According to historical reports, prior to seizing power, Darius was a simple spearman in the army of King Cambyses II of Persia, fighting much in the Egyptian campaign of 528-525
528 BCE

Timeline

550 BCE

● **The five Hystaspes sons**
Darius I is born as the eldest of five sons to Hystaspes and Rhodugune. His father is an officer in King Cyrus II of Persia's army and a noble in his court.
550 BCE

● **Power grabbed**
After an elevation to King Cambyses II's personal lancer, as well as the leader's death by his own hand – or maybe by assassination – Darius fights off rivals for the throne and quickly takes it for himself.
522 BCE

● **Indus Valley**
Darius I, now King of Persia, begins a campaign of conquest into the Indus Valley. A year later he wins control of the valley from Gandhara to modem-day Karachi and appoints the Greek Scylax of Caryanda to explore the Indian Ocean.
516 BCE

● **Scythian failure**
Darius leads a campaign against the Scythian people of eastern Europe. The Scythian army retreats deep into its territory and refuses to engage in combat with the Persians, outmanoeuvring Darius and forcing him to withdraw.
513 BCE

● **Asian minor submits**
By 510 BCE Darius I expands his empire to include Asia minor and some of the Greek islands. The rest of Greece resists the Persian expansion, leading to an increase in tensions between the two rival powers.
510 BCE

Mardonius, Darius proceeded to take Thrace and Macedon. However, before he could advance any further his fleet was wrecked in a storm off the coast of Mount Athos, stopping his conquest of Greece dead. Battered by the storm and harried by the Greek army, Darius' men were forced to withdraw, returning to Persia.

Not used to failure, Darius immediately directed his empire's vast resources to instigate another invasion, assembling a second army of 20,000 men and sending them back to Greece under the command of his nephew Artaphernes and his most trusted admiral Datis. This time Darius' army wasn't hindered in its passing and upon landing in Greece in 490 BCE it besieged, captured and burnt Eretria before quickly advancing towards the city of Marathon.

At this point, victory for Darius seemed all but certain, however outside of Marathon his army was met with a Greek one that, despite being half its number, pulled off one of the most remarkable military victories in history, defeating the Persians in mortal combat and forcing the remnants to retreat for a second time back to Persia.

This defeat at Marathon marked the end of the first Persian invasion of Greece and, despite him proceeding to live a few more years, the end of Darius I too, with the great king's health rapidly deteriorating over the next four years. Darius the Great died in Persia in 486 BCE, where his body was embalmed and then placed in a gigantic tomb. His kingdom was passed on to his son, Xerxes, who would himself would go on to famously launch the second Persian invasion of Greece. Unfortunately for him, just like his father, the might of the Persian Empire, by far one of the largest military forces in the world up to that point, would not be enough to deliver victory.

Modern-day views on Darius the Great's tenure as king are mixed, tending to differ from ancient sources in that they take a wider perspective on his reign, rather than merely his substantial conquests. The Persian Empire was

> Darius organised his empire by dividing it into provinces, with each overseen by a satrap, which was a type of governor

> Darius was succeeded by his son, Xerxes, who had to contest the succession with his elder half-brother

indeed expanded by Darius and he recorded some notable military victories, however his inability to defeat the Scythians and Greeks caused his military record to be tarnished. If you look at his reign more from a cultural and financial perspective, it's arguably very positive. Darius can be credited for making the Archaemenid Empire the capital of trade, wealth and technological innovation, with many of his advances still being relevant today.

Darius I the Great, 549-486 BCE, with a parasol bearer in a reconstruction of a relief

An economical leadership

How did Darius help make the Persian Empire the wealthiest in the world?

During his time as King of Persia, Darius I conducted an introduction of a universal currency, the daric. This was introduced shortly before 500 BCE and was applied across the empire's constituent countries as a way to regulate trade and commerce. This move was so successful that the daric even became recognised beyond the Persian Empire, into central and eastern Europe.

There were two types of daric, a gold coin and a silver coin. Only Darius himself could order the minting of gold darics, while silver darics could be minted by important generals and satraps (regional governors). The introduction of both of these coins and their widespread adoption created a boom in international trade for the Persian Empire, with textiles, tools, carpets and metal objects sold en masse. To further aid this trade boost, Darius also created a royal highway, a type of postal and commercial shipping system.

Reportedly, the daric also improved the Persian Empire's governmental revenues also, with new daric-specific taxes on land, livestock and markets created. This increased revenue helped maintain and improve the empire's infrastructure and directly funded Darius' numerous construction projects, including roads, canals and temples.

486 BCE

● **First Persian invasion**
Darius I springs an invasion of mainland Greece, with his general Mardonius taking Thrace and Macedon. Unfortunately, Mardonius' fleet is wrecked in a storm off the coast of Mount Athos, stopping the conquest in its tracks.
492 BCE

● **Round two**
Darius I launches a second campaign against the Greeks two years later under the command of military generals Datis and Artaphernes. While they make some progress, the Persian army suffers a massive defeat at the Battle of Marathon.
490 BCE

● **Furious in defeat**
Darius is angered greatly by the failure of the Greek conquest and after the remnants of his force returns to Persia, he immediately starts preparations for another. Internal strife and power struggles in Persia delay it.
488 BCE

Darius dies ●
After years of preparation for another invasion of Greece, a revolt against Persian rule breaks out in Egypt, with the toll worsening Darius' health markedly. He dies shortly after and is entombed in a rock-cut sepulchre tomb.
486 BCE

73/74 – 4 BCE

Herod I, King of Judea

Cruel, paranoid and held in the grips of madness, Herod I ruled the ancient kingdom of Judea with an iron fist, brutally slaying any who opposed him

During his reign, Herod commissioned a number of building projects, including a huge temple in Jerusalem

H erod of Idumea was born into one of the most volatile regions of the ancient world. He quickly learned to fear rivals, suspect betrayal and watch his own back. The Romans had taken over much of his homeland, and solidified their grip on the area through unpopular puppet kings. Rebellion was in the air, and from a young age Herod was forced to pick sides - work with the invaders or fight for an independent homeland. His father was a high-ranking official of King Hyrcanus II and had the ear of the Roman senate, so used this prestigious position to grant Herod a governorship in 49 BCE in the province of Galilee. Herod knew this position came from powerful Roman patronage, and he made sure the Romans knew he would continue supporting them if they supported him by instigating a brutal regime in Galilee for the glory of Rome.

Unfortunately for Herod, not everyone shared his astute sense of accommodation when it came to the Romans. In 40 BCE, the puppet king Hyrcanus died and was replaced by Antigonus, who quickly set about ejecting the Roman garrisons from Judea and exterminating any native that had conspired with them against their own people. For Herod

Herod was known to suffer hallucinations of his dead wife and slip into psychotic states when he was being threatened

this meant he lost his power and position. He was forced to flee into the night, and lacking anywhere else to go, he travelled to the heart of the Roman empire to beg Caesar to help him.

Herod's presence in Rome was not an unusual one; many high-ranking foreigners travelled to the sprawling city to seek patronage and aid from the Roman senators who decided the fate of kingdoms. What was unusual was how unpopular Herod was within the city. The Jewish population saw him as a tyrannical traitor, the Romans saw him as an incompetent beggar. The decision by the senate to make Herod King of the Jews was only made through a lack of a better option. As far as Caesar and the senators were concerned, Judea needed a leader who was strong and loyal to the Roman cause. Herod wasn't strong, nor was he particularly loyal, but he understood power and the protection Rome could offer him if he became their puppet.

With thousands of Roman legionaries behind him and one of Rome's greatest war heroes, Mark Antony, by his side, Herod marched proudly back to his homeland as a conqueror in 37 BCE. He would not be satisfied with a mere governorship this time; he wanted ultimate power. He decided to ignore

HEROD I
Judea, 73/74 – 4 BCE

Brief Bio A client king for the Roman Republic (soon to become the Roman Empire), Herod wheedled his way to kingship. In biblical stories he is remembered as the tyrant who authorised the Massacre of the Innocents in Bethlehem. He was just as cruel in historical fact, suffering from paranoid and violent delusions of persecution.

"The Jewish population saw him as a tyrannical traitor, the Romans saw him as an incompetent beggar"

Life in the time of Herod

Roman rule

The Middle East, which consisted of the Jewish and pagan kingdoms located around the coastline of the Mediterranean, was influenced and controlled by the Roman rulers through vassals and puppet kings. The Romans needed the kingdoms for their resources, and to guard the eastern flank of the empire from the ever-present threat of the Persians.

Culture shock

Herod's kingdom was made up of a number of different tribes that settled in the area or who were cast out of Persia over the previous three centuries. Contrasting cultures were active in the region, some adopting Judaism while others followed Roman, Greek or pagan traditions, creating deep social divides.

Fractured

Due to the fractious nature of Judean society, many areas within the kingdom that Herod ruled did not recognise him as a legitimate king. Herod himself had very little in the way of military muscle to keep the different communities in line, and often had to rely on his Roman patrons to subdue the population.

Political games

Herod's position as a Roman vassal was not an easy one. Roman politics was going through a radical transformation during this period, which involved violent civil wars. Herod had to make sure he was backing the right man, or if he wasn't, change sides quickly to avoid being disposed of.

Rebel groups

Due to the brutal repression under Herod through the Roman legions stationed in Judea, a number of rebel groups sprung up, bent on ending his reign of terror for good. These groups were forced to fight a guerrilla war, as they could not raise a standing army that could beat Caesar's legions.

Herod at the Feast of Herod, where John the Baptist was beheaded

the outlying provinces and concentrate his forces around Jerusalem with the approval of Antony. The siege lasted for 40 days. The defenders were desperate to hold onto their new-found freedom from Roman oppression, but in the end Herod breached the walls and thousands of bloodthirsty Roman warriors stormed the city. The devastation was horrendous; the Romans slaughtered men, women and children, brutally slaying the people who dared defy Caesar's will. Herod was outraged; he wanted to subdue the population, not butcher them, and he knew all of Judea would never forget the Jewish blood spilled that day. His complaints to Antony fell on deaf ears - as far as he was concerned, it was all in a day's work.

Antony left Herod in the smouldering ruins of his new kingdom with enough Roman guards to keep an eye on him. From now on, Herod would be taking his orders directly from Rome. Immediately, Herod self-styled himself as high ruler of what remained of Jerusalem and the rest of Judea. His subjects were less than convinced; his claim to the throne was based on little more than the Roman bodyguards he had surrounding him. As a way of trying to gain some respect after putting his own people to the sword, he married his second wife - a Hasmonean princess called Mariamne - in 32 BCE. Mariamne was from an old Judean family that could trace its origins back to the conquest of

> Herod's patrons were the Romans; they gave him his political legitimacy and enough military muscle to keep Judea under his rule

Alexander the Great, and Herod hoped the marriage would give his rule an amount of legitimacy.

The marriage failed to gain the love of the people, and as he began to settle down to the task of ruling his unhappy kingdom, he felt more vulnerable. He feared assassination at every turn, particularly from his own family. He had his brother-in-law from his first marriage drowned in his own pleasure pool because he feared the Romans would prefer him as ruler of Judea. Then in 31 BCE, Herod received word that Rome had become engulfed in a power struggle between Octavian Caesar and Herod's old friend Antony. Like all vassals reliant on Rome's good will, Herod was forced to take sides, and in keeping with his preference for backing the strongest player, he chose Antony. The odds were very much stacked in Antony's favour, but he lost the struggle nonetheless, and Herod found himself in a very awkward position; the man in charge of Rome was the man he sided against. He sent a

Defining moment
Fall of Jerusalem
37 BCE

Herod, with the help of a number of Roman legions supplied by Mark Antony, invades Judea and lays siege to Jerusalem. The walls are surrounded and huge siege engines are built to devastate the city's populace hiding within the city. After 40 days of fighting, the townspeople begin to weaken through starvation, and Herod breaches the walls. When the Romans storm the city, they butcher the population. This angers Herod because his reputation would now be tarnished by the Romans' actions. Despite Herod's desire to appease the population after the siege, he still has the popular Antigonus executed because he represents a threat.

Timeline

74 BCE

Birth of Herod
Herod is born in Idumea as the second son of Antipater - a high-ranking official in the kingdom of Judea. Antipater quickly manoeuvres his son into a position of authority.
74 BCE

Appointed governor of Galilee
Through his father's influence, Herod is made governor of Galilee - a Judean satellite state. His father continues to gain influence throughout Judea because of his good relations with the Romans.
49 BCE

Flight to Rome
After the anti-Roman king Antigonus II takes power in Judea, Herod is forced to flee and persuade the Romans to help him regain his power in the region.
40 BCE

Elected King of the Jews
During his stay in Rome, Herod convinces the senate that he should be made King of the Jews. The Romans agree with the proviso that he acts as a vassal on his return to Judea.
40 BCE

Marriage to Mariamne
Herod marries a Hasmonean princess, Mariamne, who is also a member of the Judean ruling class, in an effort to give his new status as King of the Jews legitimacy.
32 BCE

number of grovelling letters to Octavian promising his undying loyalty in return for being allowed to keep his job as King of the Jews. Octavian reluctantly allowed him to remain king, again more through a lack of a better option than any reflection on Herod's skill as a leader.

Despite having survived one of the most destructive civil wars in Rome's history, Herod remained uneasy. He became estranged from his wife after he had her placed under guard to prevent her from claiming the throne for the Hasmoneans if he died during the fighting. He heard more rumours of threats against his life, he feared Mariamne would try to grab power by killing him in revenge for having her arrested, his behaviour became increasingly erratic and he fell into a strange psychotic state of paranoia. While he was suffering from this break from reality, he became convinced Mariamne was going to kill him, so he acted. He had her beheaded, but as soon as the axe fell, he came around from his delusion and realised he'd made a terrible mistake. He wept uncontrollably for weeks and began hallucinating visions of his dead wife screaming in agony in the corridors of his palace.

In an effort to try and turn his mind away from these terrifying visions, he began to construct a grand temple designed to be the envy of the ancient world. Construction started just after the death of Mariamne, and was only halted briefly after a great famine struck the city. When Caesar's aide Marcus Agrippa visited the city in 15 BCE, he was amazed at the temple's construction and how modern Jerusalem looked since its sacking by Antony. Agrippa held court with Herod, and Herod, knowing

that weakness in front of the Romans could be dangerous, managed to hide his precarious mental state. Underneath this façade, he was a man edging ever closer to madness.

After Agrippa left for the gates of Rome, Herod quickly returned to the depths of paranoia. He brutally slaughtered any who spoke out against his dictatorial regime, and the country lived in fear of his violent moodswings. He burned alive a group of rabbis and their students who had pulled down a Roman imperial eagle in a building in Jerusalem. He then executed two of his eldest sons because he thought they were plotting against him. By 4 BCE, he feared that he had become so unpopular that no one would mourn his passing after he died. In a fit of depraved madness, he ordered the families of the nobility throughout the kingdom to attend him on pain of death. He then had them rounded up and placed under guard in the city's hippodrome. The guards were ordered to murder them when he died so his death would be mourned.

As the families in the hippodrome huddled together, terrified at the prospect of being put to death as a sacrifice to the passing of their own king, Herod laid on his deathbed racked with pain. He was suffering from kidney failure and the paranoid delusions that had finally left him senseless. He saw visions of his beloved Mariamne and was tortured by her mutilated face. When he finally died screaming in agony in 4 BCE, the holy men of Jerusalem proclaimed that his horrific death was, 'the penalty that God was exacting of the king for his great impiety.' Herod's sister countermanded the order to kill the Judean families and the kingdom celebrated; Herod 'the mad and wicked' was dead.

> In a fit of psychotic rage, Herod killed his two eldest sons because he thought they were plotting against his kingship

A biblical connection

Herod has been reviled in the bible as the monstrous tyrant who threatened the life of the baby that Christians believe was the son of God. Jesus of Nazareth's birth came at the end of Herod's reign, when his psychotic episodes had become increasingly dangerous to the people he suspected were plotting treason against him. According to the Bible, it was during one of these paranoid episodes that he heard word of a child being born proclaimed as the 'King of the Jews'. This was highly threatening as far as Herod was concerned, as he had never been fully accepted by his Jewish subjects as their true king, and any kind of usurpation from another individual claiming to be their ruler had to be destroyed. He went into a fit of rage, ordering all the sons of Bethlehem, the birth place of Jesus, murdered in what became known as the 'Massacre of the Innocents.' While the Bible is not considered historically accurate by scholars, Herod's violent reaction was alluded to by Roman sources writing after the event, and archaeologists have speculated the massacre occurred at some point in 5 BCE, a year before Herod died. His actions have since been immortalised through the story of the Nativity, and his reputation for uncompromising brutality has never been forgotten in Christian traditions.

Herod orders the execution of all first-born males in Bethlehem

---

Defining moment
Trouble in Rome
31 BCE

A Roman civil war threatens to engulf Judea in factional fighting and Herod must decide which man to support - Octavian Caesar or his old friend Mark Antony. Antony's force, stationed in Egypt, appears to be the strongest, and initially Herod sides with him. After Antony's defeat, Herod endears himself to Octavian, pledging his loyalty to the new Roman leader. While Octavian is unconvinced of Herod's honesty, he recognises that he has served Rome well in the past, so allows Herod to stay on as King of Judea as long as he can control the population.

The Battle of Actium as depicted by Lorenzo A. Castro

Defining moment
Death of Herod
4 BCE

Herod dies in March or April 4 BCE after succumbing to 'Herod's evil', thought to be kidney disease and gangrene. He had already executed two of his eldest sons after another bout of paranoid madness, and he leaves Judea in open rebellion against Roman authority. The divided communities that make up the Judean state immediately demand independence, and only the presence of Roman legions under Octavian subdue the population adequately for Herod's three remaining sons to rule a third of the kingdom each under Roman patronage.

---

4 BCE

Mariamne arrested
In a fit of paranoia, Herod orders for Mariamne to be arrested after he fears that if he dies she will try and take the throne away from his son. This deeply offends Mariamne, and she becomes extremely hostile towards him.
31 BCE

Death of a princess
After further rumours about a plot to poison him, Herod condemns Mariamne to death to prevent her from trying to seize power. This action haunts him for the rest of his life.
29 BCE

Famine
A great famine strikes Judea and its surrounding provinces. Herod Is forced to halt some of his grand architectural projects in order to buy grain to feed the population.
25 BCE

The grand temple
As a way of appeasing the Jewish population, Herod builds a grand temple in Jerusalem. Little remains of the site today, but it was said to be one of the largest buildings in the entire city.
20 BCE

Visit of Markus Agrippa
Agrippa visits the city to make sure Herod's loyalty has not abandoned him, and is astonished by the new masonry projects commissioned by the King of the Jews.
15 BCE

Burning of the teachers
In one of Herod's most brutal acts, he orders the death of a group of rabbis who were found destroying a Roman eagle within Jerusalem. They are thrown in a pit and burnt alive.
4 BCE

circa 69 – 30 BCE
Cleopatra

In 30 BCE, a love affair between a powerful queen and a respected military leader caused scandal in Rome and ultimately brought about the end of a royal dynasty

Cleopatra VII remains an icon of both the ancient and modern world. Today, she continues to captivate and puzzle historians, remaining one of history's most enchanting and enigmatic figures.

The alliance of Mark Antony and Cleopatra changed the face of the world. A coalition which began as a political statement soon evolved into a tumultuous, and later tragic, love affair.

Despite her florid reputation, Cleopatra took only two lovers - both were rulers of Rome. Cleopatra recognised Rome as the leading power of the ancient world. Egypt, rich in gold and grain, provided the material resources to fuel that power. Both affairs had begun with a political agenda. They had enabled the queen to establish a secure and profitable union between Rome and Egypt. Despite this, however, events took an unexpected turn when she met the younger general. Cleopatra and Mark Antony fell in love, embarking on a passionate and unpredictable relationship that brought both riches and remorse. Their partnership, as lovers and politicians, both immortalised and destroyed a dynasty - it brought to a close 3,000 years of pharaonic rule.

Long before her meeting with Mark Antony, the queen had borne a child to her first Roman lover, Gaius Julius Caesar and she had named the child Caesarion - 'little Caesar'. In doing so, Cleopatra had secured for herself an enormous power base, for Caesar had no heir. Despite its material wealth, Egypt had suffered years of famine that had

CLEOPATRA VII
Egypt, circa 69-30 BCE

Brief Bio

Cleopatra was the daughter of Ptolemy XII Auletes and Cleopatra V. Born in Alexandria in 69 BCE her bloodline propagated a series of brother-sister marriages that were frequently corroded by family violence and murder. After a tumultuous reign, Octavian of Rome invaded Egypt and ended her rule. Rather than face the humiliation of defeat, Cleopatra committed suicide.

MARK ANTONY
Rome/Egypt, 83-30 BCE

Brief Bio

Marcus Antonius was born in 83 BC and, as a young man, was known as something of a playboy in Rome. But after fighting alongside Julius Caesar on the battlefield, he quickly established his military prowess. After Caesar's assassination, he formed a power trio with Marcus Lepidus and Octavian, but his growing love of the Egyptian queen Cleopatra would prove to be his downfall.

weakened the reserves of her granaries and her people. The country was in eclipse. Her allied states had also felt the grip of Rome tightening around their throats. Alexandria had long been important to Rome. As a gateway to the East, it was a major port with a large cosmopolitan community. It was renowned for its libraries, culture and trade. Egypt also had an abundant source of grain with which it fed its imperial army. On the other hand, the Romans regarded the Egyptian people and their religion with suspicion - its cults, along with its strange animal-headed gods, were an abomination to the refined Roman senses.

While her alliance with Rome continued, Cleopatra - and her throne - remained secure. For this reason, Cleopatra courted Rome and its leading figures. From the beginning, Cleopatra was an enigma to a man like Mark Antony. Having grown up in Rome, he was familiar with upper-class women who were cloistered in the home and whose only role in life was to be that of good wives and mothers. The women of Rome were largely regarded as vessels of chastity; Cleopatra was the antithesis of a Roman woman.

Growing up in a political, dangerous household where life was precarious, she was descended from a long line of rulers - all named Ptolemy - who could trace their line to the time of Alexander the Great. In order to keep their bloodline pure, female rulers often married their brothers. This practice brought outward strength but inner conflicts; during her early life Cleopatra witnessed brutal power struggles within her own family. Indeed, as her power grew, she had no choice but to execute her rival siblings.

Cleopatra had to live by her wits. She was a highly educated woman with a sharp mind and a keen instinct. She spoke several languages, including Egyptian - making her unique among her peers. She was a cultivated woman, a patron of the arts and devoted to books. Despite her later reputation as a femme fatale, she was not considered beautiful. It was said she had a charismatic presence, was a fine conversationalist and had a sweet, seductive voice - a trait she may have cultivated as a child. Most importantly, Cleopatra was a survivor; she knew that in order to sustain her throne, she needed to control the might

of Rome, and Mark Antony could offer this. Mark Antony and Cleopatra were as fire and water. Born in January 83 BCE, Antony was a true son of Rome. Like Cleopatra, he sought decadence and danger - he had quickly gained a reputation for drinking and gambling, and seems to have been attracted to exotic religious cults. Later, he earned fame and fortune among the militia; as the commander of a cavalry regiment he received great honours fighting with Caesar's armies in Gaul. Antony and Caesar formed a mutual friendship and a distant kinship had strengthened their alliance. As Caesar's star ascended, so too had Mark Antony's, and when the elder man became dictator, Antony was appointed Magister Equitum (Master of the Horse) and governed Rome in Caesar's absence. Better suited to the battlefield, Mark Antony made an impetuous politician - highly volatile, his excesses in wine and women became the topic of

much public gossip, for these often included affairs with other men's wives.

After the assassination of Caesar, Cleopatra and Mark Antony fled Rome and Cleopatra returned to Egypt. With Caesar dead, her position had become tenuous. The Romans regarded a female ruler with abhorrence and she desperately needed an ally in the Senate. When revolt failed to materialise, Mark Antony returned to the Forum to find a city outraged at the atrocities that had befallen Caesar.

The assassins were executed or fell into obscurity, and it was left to Octavian (Caesar's appointed heir), Lepidus (his trusted commander) and Mark Antony to calm the storm. The three men formed the Second Triumvirate granting themselves equal powers of government.

Antony was now in a strong position. As the three men began to carve out Roman territory each assigned themselves important provinces. Mark

"Octavian arranged a marriage between Mark Antony and his sister, Octavia – infuriating the Egyptian queen"

A 19th-Century depiction of Cleopatra on the River Nile

The men who ruled Rome 43 - 33 BCE

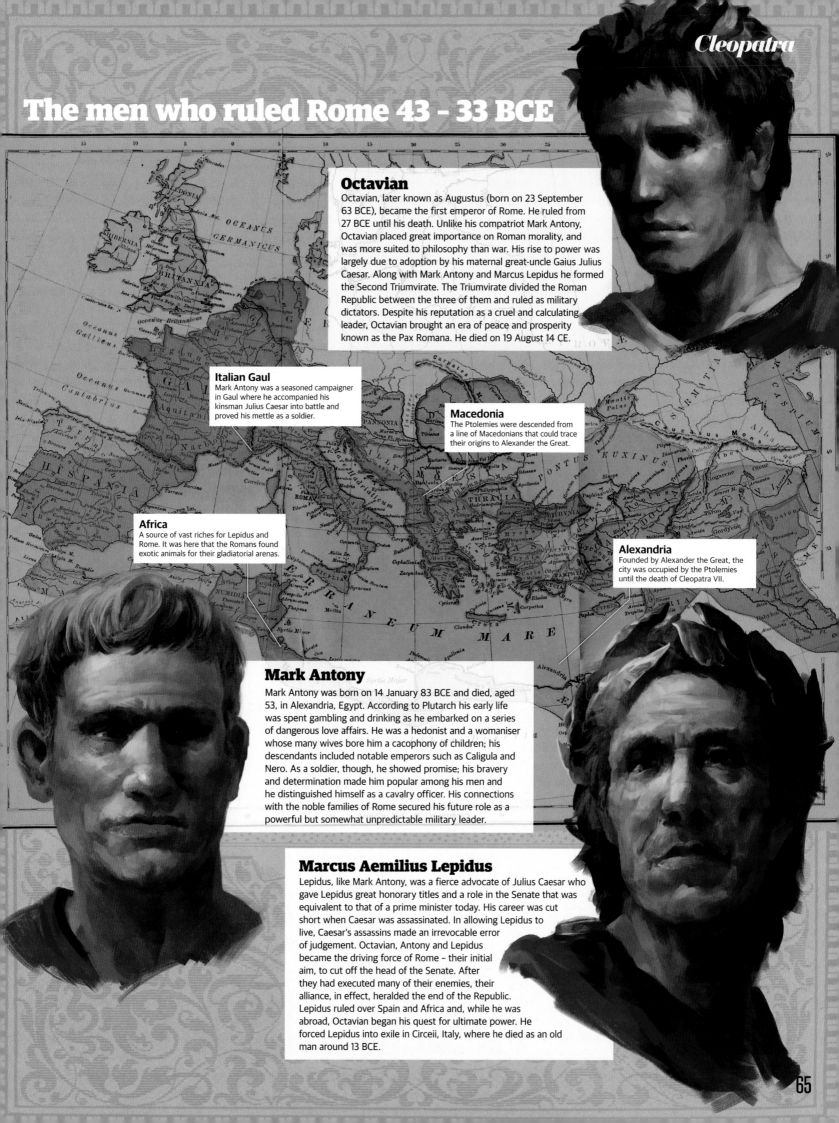

Octavian

Octavian, later known as Augustus (born on 23 September 63 BCE), became the first emperor of Rome. He ruled from 27 BCE until his death. Unlike his compatriot Mark Antony, Octavian placed great importance on Roman morality, and was more suited to philosophy than war. His rise to power was largely due to adoption by his maternal great-uncle Gaius Julius Caesar. Along with Mark Antony and Marcus Lepidus he formed the Second Triumvirate. The Triumvirate divided the Roman Republic between the three of them and ruled as military dictators. Despite his reputation as a cruel and calculating leader, Octavian brought an era of peace and prosperity known as the Pax Romana. He died on 19 August 14 CE.

Italian Gaul

Mark Antony was a seasoned campaigner in Gaul where he accompanied his kinsman Julius Caesar into battle and proved his mettle as a soldier.

Macedonia

The Ptolemies were descended from a line of Macedonians that could trace their origins to Alexander the Great.

Africa

A source of vast riches for Lepidus and Rome. It was here that the Romans found exotic animals for their gladiatorial arenas.

Alexandria

Founded by Alexander the Great, the city was occupied by the Ptolemies until the death of Cleopatra VII.

Mark Antony

Mark Antony was born on 14 January 83 BCE and died, aged 53, in Alexandria, Egypt. According to Plutarch his early life was spent gambling and drinking as he embarked on a series of dangerous love affairs. He was a hedonist and a womaniser whose many wives bore him a cacophony of children; his descendants included notable emperors such as Caligula and Nero. As a soldier, though, he showed promise; his bravery and determination made him popular among his men and he distinguished himself as a cavalry officer. His connections with the noble families of Rome secured his future role as a powerful but somewhat unpredictable military leader.

Marcus Aemilius Lepidus

Lepidus, like Mark Antony, was a fierce advocate of Julius Caesar who gave Lepidus great honorary titles and a role in the Senate that was equivalent to that of a prime minister today. His career was cut short when Caesar was assassinated. In allowing Lepidus to live, Caesar's assassins made an irrevocable error of judgement. Octavian, Antony and Lepidus became the driving force of Rome – their initial aim, to cut off the head of the Senate. After they had executed many of their enemies, their alliance, in effect, heralded the end of the Republic. Lepidus ruled over Spain and Africa and, while he was abroad, Octavian began his quest for ultimate power. He forced Lepidus into exile in Circeii, Italy, where he died as an old man around 13 BCE.

Actium

The ancient battle that changed the world

The battle took place on 2 September 31 BCE, on the Ionian Sea on the border of the city of Actium. It was thought that Antony's fleet had the advantage. It boasted 500 ships – each a war galley designed with turrets. Known as quinqueremes, Mark Antony's warships each weighed 300 tons; they were especially designed to ram enemy vessels. Commanded by his general, Marcus Agrippa, Octavian's fleet consisted of 250 ships. Agrippa launched his initial attack from the left wing of the fleet and attempted to outflank Mark Antony – the battle was brutal and prolonged.

Unfortunately, many of Antony's soldiers were dying of malaria and his ships were undermanned. Therefore, Octavian's fleet was greatly encouraged. These Liburnian vessels were manned by well-trained and rested soldiers, and the ships were fast and agile. As they outmanoeuvred their enemy, the deck soldiers used fire arrows and slingshots to diminish their capability. Realising the severity of his situation, Mark Antony decided to retreat and regroup. He took advantage of a break in the enemy formation and made a dash for it. In doing so, he abandoned many of his men to their fate.

Defeated by Octavian's fleet, Mark Antony fled the battle, leaving his soldiers to die

Antony had set his heart on Cleopatra and Egypt. He sent a message to his lover asking her to meet him at Tarsus in modern-day Turkey, determined to win her support for his military campaigns.

On this particular meeting she presented herself as the embodiment of the goddess Venus. The imperial queen of Egypt arrived on a golden barge; decked in fine linen and precious gems, she was attended by servants dressed as sea nymphs. While she drifted towards Mark Antony like a creature from myth, she refused to disembark. As queen of Egypt, she expected Antony to wait on her.

Mark Antony's temper was inflamed, but so were his passions. Plutarch said of their relationship: "observing Cleopatra's looks and her subtlety and tricky wit in conversation, he [Antony's agent] at once knew that Antony would never think of doing such a woman any harm, and that in fact she'd have the greatest influence over him."

Not surprisingly, Antony chose to spend the winter of 41-40 BCE with Cleopatra in Alexandria - the result of this visit was the birth of twin children, Alexander Helios and Cleopatra Selene II, whose names are linked with the dual powers of the Sun and the Moon.

Rome was greatly disturbed by this turn of events. In order to secure his loyalty, Octavian arranged a marriage between Mark Antony and his sister, Octavia - a move that infuriated the Egyptian queen. To avoid a public insult, Mark Antony stumbled into an acrimonious and dangerous union. Meanwhile, the queen of Egypt financed his army, allowing him to capture Jerusalem where he installed Herod as the puppet king of Judaea. Four years later, Antony visited Alexandria again en route to make war with the Parthians. His relationship with Cleopatra had gathered

"Roman law dictated Cleopatra should be treated as an enemy, taken back to Rome and paraded before the mob"

momentum and he had made Alexandria his home. Despite his union with Octavia, he married Cleopatra and they had another child.

Soon, Antony grew tired of luxurious living, exotic palaces and hunting in the Egyptian Delta; he longed for the glories of war. When Antony invaded Parthian territory with an army of about 100,000 Roman and allied troops, the campaign proved disastrous. He never recovered from the shock of defeat. Octavian took this opportunity; he demoted Lepidus, belittled Mark Antony and seized unilateral power. He reminded Rome of the menacing relationship between Antony and his abominable foreign queen. While feigning shock at the abandonment of his sister, he told the citizens of Rome that Mark Antony was now

living as an Egyptian; this was regarded as an act of treason. Antony and Cleopatra responded to the attack with theatrics. After a successful invasion of Armenia, Mark Antony infuriated his fellow Romans by holding a Triumph (formal celebration) in the city of Alexandria. Mark Antony then issued a series of proclamations known as the Donations of Alexandria, when he named Cleopatra and her children heirs to his conquered territories. It was, in effect, a declaration of war. Mark Antony named Caesarion the legitimate son and heir of Caesar - Octavian, of course, being the 'adopted' son of the former dictator. Octavian had no choice but to retaliate. He told the Senate that Antony had "gone native" and that he had been effeminated by the Egyptian queen. Mark Antony divorced Octavia and

End of an era

Cleopatra's surviving children were adopted by Octavia, became Roman citizens and faded quickly into obscurity. Egypt, now a Roman province, was ruled by a prefect. Greek remained the official language. While Alexandria continued to flourish, it became a site of many religious and military uprisings. In 269 CE Alexandria was claimed by yet another woman, when Zenobia, the ferocious warrior Queen of Palmyra, conquered Egypt. Zenobia – an admirer of Cleopatra – was quick to behead her detested Roman foes. She ruled Egypt until 274, before she herself was taken hostage by the Roman Emperor Aurelian; in an ironic twist of fate, Zenobia appeared in golden chains during Aurelian's Triumph in Rome.

The legacy of Greco-Roman Egypt still survives. It can be seen in a series of magnificent temples that were built along the River Nile. These include the Temple of Hathor at Dendera, where fabulous images of Cleopatra and Caesarion still dominate its walls.

The delicate amalgamation of the Egyptian and Roman cultures can be seen on many mummy portrait panels from the Greco-Roman period. Contrasts are visible in paintings and sculptures where traditional Egyptian iconography is paired with Roman symbolism. The result - a hybrid blend of the ancient and even more ancient - is now all that remains of the former bond between Rome and Egypt: Antony and Cleopatra.

accused Octavian of forging Caesar's will. Rome was drawn into a civil war - which culminated in the defeat of Antony at the Battle of Actium.

After his clear victory, Octavian returned to Rome. During the 12 months that followed, he left Antony and Cleopatra to contemplate their defeat and consider their demise. Egypt's neighbouring territories were largely annexed to Rome; for this reason, Antony and Cleopatra's attempts to regroup and raise an army proved futile.

It was in August 30 BCE that Octavian finally invaded Egypt. Antony made one last valiant attempt to usurp the Roman leader, but in the end, his fate had been cast. He did what was required of all honourable Roman soldiers and fell upon his sword. In an attempt to safeguard her children Cleopatra made a tentative effort to make terms with Octavian. In his final hour, Antony was brought to Cleopatra's mausoleum and he died in her arms. Octavian allowed Cleopatra to conduct burial rituals for Antony's body. While he presented an outward show of friendship, he naturally wanted her dead. He was, in fact, in a difficult position.

"Antony made one last valiant attempt to usurp the Roman leader"

Roman law dictated that Cleopatra should be treated as an enemy of the state. She should be taken back to Rome in shackles and paraded before the mob. However, a female ruler was a rare entity - the display could end up backfiring on Octavian and prove highly distasteful.

He was relieved then, when Cleopatra took the courageous decision to end her own life. Some historians believe that she was bitten by a snake hidden in a fig basket. Others suggest that she drank wine laced with hemlock. An account of her death can be found in Plutarch's *Lives*.

'The messengers [of Octavian] came at full speed, and found the guards apprehensive of nothing; but, on opening the doors, they saw her stone-dead, lying upon a bed of gold, set out in all her royal ornaments. Iras, one of her women, lay dying at her feet, and Charmion, just ready to fall, scarce able to hold up her head, was adjusting her mistress's

diadem. And when one that came in said angrily, "Was this well done of your lady, Charmion?" "Extremely well," she answered, "and as became the descendant of so many kings". As she said this she fell down dead by the bedside.

In Rome, the son of the orator Cicero announced the deaths of Antony and Cleopatra with relish. Mark Antony was stripped of his accolades, his image erased from coinage and his statues removed. Under threat from Octavian, Iullus Antonius - Mark Antony's eldest son - committed suicide. Concurring with Arius Didymus - "It is bad to have too many Caesars" - Octavian also had Caesarion murdered. The remaining children of Cleopatra and Antony were spared and taken to Rome where they were adopted by Antony's family.

With the death of Cleopatra, the Sun had finally set on the Hellenistic Dynasty - and indeed on the 3,000-year rule of the pharaohs.

Cleopatra attempts to make peace with Octavian for the sake of her children

The Historia Augusta boasts that Zenobia would often march for miles on foot ahead of the rest of her troops

ZENOBIA

Palmyra, 240 – 274 CE

Brief Bio Claiming descent from the iconic Cleopatra through the Seleucid bloodline, Zenobia was a capable rider and a noted scholar, unlike many of the women in the ancient Mediterranean world. Her capabilities extended to military tactics and economic strategy. She was determined to rule Egypt, but ultimately failed.

240 – 274 CE

Zenobia

Armed with the bravery and beauty of her ancestor Cleopatra, Zenobia defied the Romans to rule her own empire in the Middle East

Blame William Shakespeare – or Elizabeth Taylor – for the fact that Cleopatra has overshadowed all other strong, cunning and comely queens of antiquity. Three centuries after the legendary Cleopatra ruled from the Pharaoh's throne in Egypt, her blood heiress, as well as equal in courage and beauty, rose to power in the eastern oasis of Palmyra, in modern-day Syria. After the assassination of her war-hero husband, Zenobia assumed confident control of this wealthy city state on the fringes of the fading Roman Empire in the 3rd Century CE. Claiming independence from Rome, she would drive her loyal armies across Egypt and Palestine, briefly ruling a large and stable empire of her own. But her kingdom, and life, would ultimately be cut short by the sword of the conquering Roman Emperor Aurelian.

The true story of Zenobia is shrouded in centuries of legend. The earliest historical source is the wildly unreliable *Historia Augusta*, a colourful work of fiction posing as fact from the 4th Century CE. The 18th Century historian Edward Gibbon, in his monumental work *The Decline and Fall of the Roman Empire*, relied heavily on descriptions of Zenobia found in the *Historia Augusta* to paint his own romanticised portrait of the Palmyrene queen.

"Modern Europe has produced several illustrious women who have sustained with glory the weight of empire," wrote Gibbon. "But... Zenobia is perhaps the only female whose superior genius broke through the servile indolence imposed on her sex by the climate and manners of Asia. She claimed her descent from the Macedonian kings of Egypt, equalled in beauty her ancestor Cleopatra and far surpassed that princess in chastity and valour.

Zenobia was esteemed the most lovely as well as the most heroic of her sex."

Modern historians have pieced together a more reliable biography of Zenobia from early Christian sources, archaeological inscriptions and ancient coins, but much of her life story is still up for debate, starting with her lineage and ethnicity. Much is made of Zenobia's claimed relation to Cleopatra along the famed Seleucid bloodline on her mother's side. Her father also ruled Palmyra and was descended from a long line of Roman citizens, as well as royalty dating back to Julia Domna, the influential empress wife of Roman Emperor Lucius Septimius Severus.

Whether or not either of these genealogies are true, it's clear that Zenobia was born into a wealthy and powerful family in a city state at the height of its own wealth and power. Palmyra is located in the middle of the desert halfway between the Euphrates River valley and the Mediterranean Sea.

Underground springs transformed the land into a fertile oasis and a critical stop on the Silk Road trade route that brought spices and textiles from the exotic East to the bustling markets of Rome. Palmyra's security forces offered protection to passing caravans while the government exacted an import tax – 25 per cent of every camel load – to fill Palmyra's substantial coffers.

Zenobia, as described by Gibbon, was an olive-skinned beauty who spoke Aramaic, Greek, Latin, Arabic and Ancient Egyptian. Unlike the delicate noblewomen of Rome – who wouldn't leave the house without a protective veil and covered carriage – Zenobia was a capable camel and horse rider who enjoyed wild lion and panther hunts as much as her husband.

> **Tracing her ancestry, historians now believe that Zenobia may have had Aramaean or even Jewish origins**

Aurelian the unstoppable

After the Imperial Crisis of the 3rd Century, the Roman Empire owed its survival to the hard-nosed military mastermind Aurelian. Born into a family of humble peasant farmers in the Danubian provinces of the Roman Empire near the Balkans, he joined a long line of tough and disciplined military men. Aurelian rose to prominence as a strict and stalwart army officer during one of the messiest periods in Imperial history. In 268, the Emperor Gallienus was under fire from the so-called Thirty Tyrants, Roman military and political leaders who aimed to topple the throne. Aurelian, along with his compatriot Claudius, put down the rebellion, but may have played a role in Gallienus' assassination. Claudius succeeded as Emperor, but died after only 18 months, making room for no-nonsense Aurelian to assume the crown. He whipped the Roman legions into shape and marched them on the barbarian marauders — groups such as the Goths, Vandals, Alemanni and Juthungi — threatening Roman sovereignty in northern Italy. By this point, Zenobia had established herself as the Queen of the East and ruler of the independent Palmyrene Empire. If Aurelian had any hesitation about crushing a woman, he didn't show it, and brought the full force of his best legions against Zenobia, finally offering her a measure of mercy if she would surrender her empire at the gates of Palmyra. When she refused, Aurelian dragged her captive to Rome and had her entire inner circle executed. He returned two years later during a short-lived revolt.

Zenobia was the second wife of Odaenathus, the ruler of Palmyra and a critical ally of Rome in the East. During Odaenathus' rule, Palmyra was an important buffer state between the Romans and the Persian Sasanian Empire. Rome allowed Palmyra to remain independent in exchange for its strategic neutrality in the region. In 260 CE, the Persians captured the Roman Emperor Valerian and conquered the eastern Roman stronghold of Antioch. Fearing a Persian expansion towards Palmyra, Odaenathus struck first, decimating the Persian army as it returned victorious from Antioch. Later Palmyrene campaigns pushed the Persians all the way back to their capital. These victories won Odaenathus praise and titles from Rome and may have triggered visions of his own future rise to be Emperor himself.

Odaenathus would not live long enough to find out. He was murdered by a nephew along with his son Hairan, from his first wife, over a hunting argument. Odaenathus' death left Zenobia's young son Vaballathus as heir to the throne. Since the boy was too young to rule — between five and ten years old — Zenobia assumed the role of regent, a position that quickly evolved into the undisputed political and military leader of Palmyra. On coins recovered from the years after Odaenathus' murder, archaeologists first find them with Vaballathus'

> Zenobia's chief counsellor, Cassius Longinus, was a noted scholar, Platonic philosopher, as well as a literary critic

face on the front and Zenobia's on the back. Very quickly these positions are reversed.

As the de facto ruler of Palmyra, Zenobia picked up exactly where her husband left off, with her own dreams of a Palmyrene Empire. Historians argue about Zenobia's specific motivations and political calculations. During the 3rd Century, the Roman Empire suffered an extended period of great tribulation known as the Imperial Crisis. The Empire had gone through 19 emperors in 30 years, most of them killed by ambitious generals or their own Praetorian Guard. Britain and Gaul had split from the Empire, the Goths were invading from the north, there was a smallpox epidemic in the provinces and pirates were disrupting trade along the Libyan coast.

In Rome's moment of weakness, Zenobia saw an opportunity, but did she see herself as Rome's partner in empire, or its conqueror?

What happens next is undisputed. In the year 269 CE, with the support of her husband's battle-tested General Zabdas, Zenobia marched the Palmyrene army into Egypt, what she called her ancestral homeland. When the Roman prefect of Egypt objected to Zenobia's occupation, she swiftly had him beheaded. Zenobia bestowed upon herself the title of Queen of Egypt and commissioned a ten-volume history of Cleopatra to commemorate the victory. If the Roman Emperor Claudius had his

> ## "When the Roman prefect of Egypt objected to Zenobia's occupation, she swiftly had him beheaded"

Defining moment
Assassination of Odaenathus
266 CE
Zenobia's husband, Odaenathus, died far from the battlefield. One story sees him going on a hunting trip with a rude nephew, Maeonius, who Odaenathus punished by taking away his horse and locking him up for a few nights. Insulted, young Maeonius killed the Palmyrene king at a party. Other accounts implicate Rome in the murder. Another story puts Zenobia herself at the centre of the plot. Odaenathus was killed along with his eldest son, putting the throne in the hands of Zenobia's son Vaballathus and under her capable control.

Timeline

240 CE

A Queen is born
Cleopatra claimed to be descended from Isis and Zenobia hitched her own star to Cleopatra's. She was born into the ruling family of Palmyra and schooled in language, philosophy, horse riding and hunting.
240 CE

Her match in marriage
Zenobia became the second wife of Odaenathus, whose bravery and cunning on the battlefield were a perfect match for his ambitious young warrior bride.
258 CE

An heir in waiting
Zenobia bore Odaenathus a son, Vaballathus, but the direct heir to the Palmyrene throne was Hairan, a child by Odaenathus' first wife. In Zenobia's day, it was common for competing wives to jostle — or even kill — to get their son on the throne.
259 CE

Taking Egypt
Zenobia and her trusted general marched uncontested into Egypt while Rome's military was busy fighting off Goth invaders and Libyan pirates. The Egyptian people embraced Zenobia as the rightful heir to Cleopatra's greatness.
269 CE

own objections, he was too busy fighting off the Goths to worry about the upstart empress in Egypt.

Without Roman resistance, Zenobia the warrior queen was given free rein to extend her territory into Syria, Lebanon and Palestine. At its greatest extent, Zenobia's empire stretched from the Nile River in the south up through the Sinai Peninsula and Palestine, north to the Black Sea and west to modern-day Ankara, Turkey. Around this time, Zenobia changed her coins yet again to add the title Augustus, or empress, alongside her own portrait.

In 270, a new face appeared on the scene in the form of Aurelian, a lifelong military man who rose to the ranks to become Emperor of Rome and Restitutor Orbis, or restorer of the world. Aurelian brought order and discipline back to the Roman military. He pushed out invading Germanic tribes such as the Vandals from northern Italy and erected the fortress-like Aurelian Walls around Rome. Next he marched against the Goths in the Balkans and crushed them. By 272, Aurelian had dealt with Rome's most pressing problems and was ready to turn his attention east to the so-called Palmyrene Empire and its warrior empress. The *Historia Augusta* relates Zenobia writing a letter to Aurelian proposing that they rule the Mediterranean as co-emperors. If that letter ever actually existed, then Aurelian likely ignored it.

Aurelian and Zenobia first met in battle at Antioch. Zenobia's forces were anchored by heavily armoured cavalry called clibanarii, using a style of warfare borrowed from the Persians. Both horses and riders were covered with thick armoured plates to withstand a line of Roman archers known as sagittariorum. The clibanarii had a weakness, though, and Aurelian exploited it brilliantly. In Latin, clibanarii means the camp oven-bearers, because the armoured suits heat up like a furnace in the midday Sun. Aurelian feinted retreat and lead the cavalry on lengthy chases, timing his greatest offensive to coincide with the greatest heat of the day. Zenobia's overheated cavalry were no match for Aurelian's well-trained legions and Zenobia retreated to Emissa, modern-day Homs.

Aurelian attacked Zenobia again at Emissa, using Palestinian slingers — armed with rocks and slings, like young David who fought Goliath — to disrupt

and confuse the Palmyrene cavalry. At one point, the 70,000-strong cavalry turned in on itself, trampling its own horsemen in the chaos. Zenobia was right there alongside her troops. "In both [battles] the Queen of Palmyra animated the armies by her presence," Gibbon writes. Facing defeat at Emissa, however, Zenobia decided to flee to the stronghold of Palmyra on her speediest camel.

Back in Palmyra, Zenobia failed to gather enough forces to engage in conventional warfare. Aurelian laid siege to the city for months, which, according to Gibbon, drew criticism from Rome.

In *The Decline and Fall of the Roman Empire*, Gibbon quotes a letter from Aurelian: "The Roman people speak with contempt of the war that I am waging against a woman. They're ignorant both of the character and of the power of Zenobia. It's impossible to enumerate her warlike preparations, of stones, of arrows and every species of missile weapons. Every part of the wall is provided with two or three ballistae and artificial fires are thrown from her military engines. The fear of punishment has armed her with courage."

In the end, the gods favoured Rome, Palmyra swiftly fell and Zenobia, along with her son and heir, was captured. The *Historia Augusta* recalls Zenobia being paraded through the streets of Rome in golden chains. Other accounts say she died on the journey from Palmyra, while others still claim she committed suicide — like her tragic heroine Cleopatra — rather than suffer the indignity of submitting to the Emperor or facing the jeering Roman crowds.

> Zenobia's rule of Palmyra, including her rebellious campaign against the Roman Empire, lasted less than five years

Defining moment
Siege of Palmyra
274 CE

According to exaggerated accounts in the *Historia Augusta*, Aurelian's final offensive against Zenobia at the desert oasis of Palmyra was almost a failure. As the Roman legions marched from Emessa, they were hounded by Syrian robbers and target practise for Persian assassins. His troops exhausted from two massive battles, Aurelian attempted to strike a deal with Zenobia, promising her life and the freedom of her people in return for peaceful surrender. Zenobia said that she, like Cleopatra, preferred death to dishonour. She threatened Aurelian with talk of reinforcements from Persia. Aurelian surrounded and starved out the city, bringing Palmyra to its knees.

Life in the time of Zenobia

Stealing from Rome's own breadbasket
Rome supplied free rations of wheat to its citizens to win their political loyalty, but much of the wheat was imported from Egypt. When Zenobia conquered Egypt, she allegedly cut off the wheat supply, a tactic not unlike kicking a hornet's nest.

By name only
The wealthy city state of Palmyra held a unique position in the Roman Empire. It functioned as an independent colony, free to collect its own taxes, but privy to the protection of the emperor. Palmyra grew fat off the taxes levied on caravans travelling the Silk Road to the west.

Spice security
As a critical stop on the Silk Road, Palmyra was responsible for protecting the silk and spice caravans along the stretch of road within its boundaries. The task fell to private armies of swift horsemen that earned a reputation for their prowess at repelling bandits.

Lost in translation
Zenobia's full name in Greek was Septimia Zenobia, but was most likely a Latinisation of the Arabic al-Zabba, which was itself a translation of Zenobia's true Aramaic name, Bat-Zabbai, or 'daughter of Zabbai'. Zenobia's native language was Aramaic.

Roman triumph
Some sources claim that a captured and chained Zenobia was paraded through Rome as part of Aurelian's massive triumph in 274 CE, featuring 800 gladiators and conquered captives from every barbarian tribe. Some say she rode in a golden chariot he had built for her entrance into Rome.

274

Face fit for a coin
Zenobia ordered the Alexandria mint to produce new coins featuring her silhouette and the presumptuous inscription, 'S. Zenobia Aug', shorthand for Septimia Zenobia Augusta, Empress of the East.
270 CE

Bread baroness
Zenobia further provoked Rome by cutting off Egyptian wheat exports to the Imperial capital, where politicians assuaged the plebeians with free bread and circuses. If she was picking a fight, she would certainly get one.
271 CE

Eastern empire
At its peak, Zenobia's Palmyrene Empire absorbed the entire eastern shore of the Mediterranean, stretching from the Nile to the Black Sea. Most of her conquered territory submitted to their new empress without resistance.
272 CE

Aurelian strikes back
Emperor Aurelian follows his conquest of the Goths by turning his attention — and his armies — east to the Palmyrene Empire. In a rare move by the severe general, Aurelian spares the citizens of conquered Palmyrene cities, causing even more to surrender peacefully.
273 CE

768 – 814 CE

Charlemagne

The 'father of Europe' and ruler of much of France and Germany, Charlemagne made his name as a king, but left a legacy as the first Roman emperor since the 5th Century...

O ver 300 years, Europe had fallen into darkness. With the power of the pope and the once mighty Roman church beset by enemies, the legacy of the western Roman Empire toppled as steadily and as surely as the Caesars had themselves, stability withdrawing like overstretched legionnaires and knowledge fading away like the crumbling Roman roads that cross-hatched the continent.

Europe needed a strong leader to pull it back from the precipice, and it got a brace of them in the form of the Carolingian dynasty, a family of self-made kings who stabilised their lands by force, expanded their frontiers with terrifying aggression and ensured the primacy of the Christian church at the point of the sword. Yet, through this crucible of violence emerged a western Europe reforged to survive another 1,000 years.

By the 6th Century, most of what is now France, western Germany, Switzerland, the Netherlands and Belgium was inhabited by the Franks, a Germanic tribe split into several small kingdoms that had rushed into the power vacuum left by the fall of Rome. These petty principalities had been united not by their monarch - rulers in name only, the rois fainéants, the 'do-nothing kings' of the Merovingian dynasty, had been increasingly sidelined by their own ministers - but by the

CHARLEMAGNE
Western Europe, 742 - 814 CE

Brief Bio

Taking the throne of the Franks in 768, Charlemagne rose from relatively humble royalty to a position of greatness. Adding King of Italy to his portfolio in 774, he eventually ruled all of continental western Europe by the year 800. A pious man, his relationship with the church increased his political power.

Charles Martel, grandfather of Charlemagne, defeats the Moors at the Battle of Tours in 732 CE

Mayor of the Palace, the executive of the royal administration who was half-prime minister and half-Shogun-esque warlord.

Pepin of Herstal had warred his way to stability between 680 CE and his death in 714 CE, bringing the other Frankish lands to heel and taking Christianity to their furthest and most pagan reaches. His son, Charles Martel, was a stronger hand yet. Though Pepin had nominated his grandson as successor, Charles - born out of wedlock and excluded from the court - was having none of it, and took the not-quite-throne by force. Despite not being Pepin's choice of heir, he more than honoured his father's vision, expanding the centralised control of the Frank lands and expanding his rule further into modern Holland, Denmark and Germany with a standing army and revolutionary use of heavy cavalry, the foundation of Europe's knights. He defeated the pagan Saxons in the east and halted the advance of the Moors - the North African and Spanish Muslims of the powerful Umayyad Caliphate - who attempted to follow up their conquest of Spain by pushing across the Pyrenees mountains into France. 'Charles the Hammer' was even offered high office by the Pope, which he declined, but it was an omen of his grandson's own journey to come.

Succeeding his father Pepin the Short in 768 CE - who had given up the pretence of being anything other than supreme ruler by forcing the last Merovingian king into a monastery and taking the title of 'King of the Franks' for himself - Charlemagne, which means 'Charles the Great', shared the zeal of his predecessors. At war for most of his life, Charlemagne took Charles Martel's fight against the Moors into northern Spain, continued the conquest and conversion of the Saxons and launched new campaigns against the Lombards of northern Italy, the Slavs in Croatia and Avars in Hungary.

Leading his personal guard, the scara cavalry, into battle with his sword Joyeuse, Charlemagne's exploits have one armoured foot in myth and the other in fact, with separating the two being a difficult task, but his journey from king to the first Roman emperor since the fall of the Roman Empire has little to do with his legend as a warrior king and everything to do with the insecurity of the church.

Pope Leo III succeeded Adrian I on the day of the previous pontiff's burial, so fearful was he that the Frankish king to whom his predecessor owed his lands and safety would feel a right to interfere in the election of the new pope. Yet, despite his

wariness he was quick to bring Rome's most powerful ally on side, along with the letter that announced his succession, Leo included the keys to St Peter's Basilica and the Pope's banner. The not-so subtle message was that he viewed Charlemagne as the defender of the Holy See, and trusted him with Rome's protection. The Frank was equally magnanimous in return, congratulating the pontiff and sending vast riches, the spoils of his war against the Avars, but not without condition, suggesting that as he happened to be the stalwart defender of Christianity, the pope had a duty to pray for the Frankish armies as they continued their conquest.

Charlemagne would honour his side of this implied bargain, and in return Leo elevated him to an office left vacant since the 5th Century.

While Leo engaged in his letter-writing campaign with the monarch to the north west and used the Avar loot to become a patron of the arts, the family of the late Adrian I launched a conspiracy to remove him from his post and replace him with his nephew Paschal the Primicerius. On 25 April 799 CE, during the procession of The Greater Litanies through the Eternal City, Leo was attacked by armed thugs who stabbed him in the eyes and attempted to tear out his tongue at the root. After dragging him to the church of San Silvestro in Capite and trying to gouge out his eyes again, the bloodied pope was left unconscious as a prisoner at the monastery of St Erasmus. Accused of perjury and fornication by his rivals, the wounded - but amazingly not blinded or voiceless - Leo fled Rome to Spoleto, 126 kilometres (78 miles) north of the city, where under the protection of the Duke of Spoleto he

St Giles pardons the Emperor. Though a popular legend, there's no evidence that the two ever met

"Charlemagne's journey from king to emperor has everything to do with the insecurity of the church"

was able to make his way to Charlemagne at Paderborn in Saxony.

That such a loyal servant of the Frankish king could be found so close to Rome, deep within Italy's central Umbria region, neatly underlines the unbalanced relationship of power between the Franks and the Roman Catholic church that had initially caused Leo such anxiety. Though the territory had been given to Rome in 776 after the defeat of the Lombards, the king retained the power to choose the Duke, making papal control as meaningless as that of the last Merovingian kings under Charlemagne's ancestors.

Clearly, the threat of political interference from Charlemagne had been trumped by that of actual bodily harm, and Leo begged for the monarch's aid. He had no authority to do so - neither he nor the conspirators in Rome were subjects of the Franks, and no law yet existed that would make bishops subordinate to secular authority. With conflict left in Saxony to pursue, Charlemagne let the matter stew for a year and kept the recovering pontiff as his guest. Finally heading to Rome in November 800 CE with a sizeable (and no doubt fairly threatening) entourage, Charlemagne summoned a council of the city's religious authorities and patiently listened to the accusations put to Leo, before allowing the deposed pontiff to make an impassioned plea of innocence.

Unsurprisingly, Charlemange took Leo's side, and ordered the conspirators' executions, but Leo requested that they instead be exiled, with the unpopular pope perhaps seeing an opportunity to impress with capacity for forgiveness.

Crowned 'Emperor of the Romans' on Christmas Day that same year by the grateful pope, the official report insists that Charlemagne was ambushed like some sort of early-medieval surprise party. The king's biographer, the monk Einhard, claimed that his liege had such "aversion [to being crowned Emperor] that he declared he would not have set foot in the church... if he could have foreseen the designs of the pope."

Birth of the modern Europe

3 big ways in which Charlemagne changed the continent

01 Man of letters
Frustrated by his own difficulty in mastering the written word, Charlemagne rolled out a system of reforms to the very shape of writing, insisting on a double space to separate words, an indent at the start of a paragraph and punctuation marks to indicate where the reader should pause or stop. Question marks and lower case letters also appeared.

02 Silver age
Due to a shortage of gold, Charlemagne and the Anglo-Saxon King Offa standardised their currencies based on a pound of silver – in Latin, libra – which was broken down into 20 sous, each of 12 deniers. This is the origin of many global currencies past and present, from the British pound to the Italian lira.

03 Out of the dark
Charlemagne's interest in the arts led to the Carolingian Renaissance, a flowering of art, literature, poetry and learning. The Dark Ages traditionally cover the 6th to 13th centuries, but for the Franks it was over before it began, and 90 per cent of surviving Roman manuscripts do so because monks copied them.

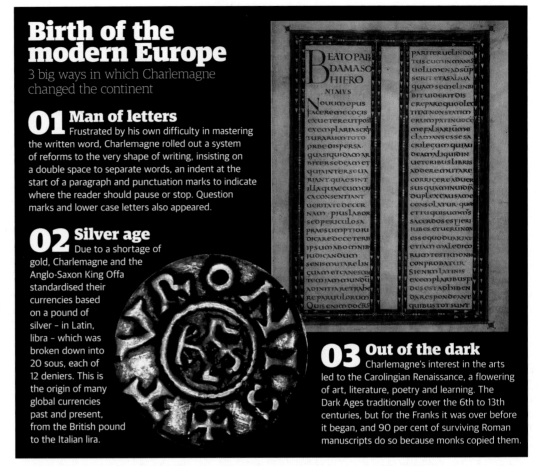

"The way Charlemagne signed his name changed nothing of the way he conducted his affairs"

It's entirely possible that Charlemange and Leo came to some agreement during their year together. After all, the idea of grinning priests hiding a bejewelled imperial crown as if it were a birthday cake is too ludicrous to contemplate. Documents from his reign reveal that Charlemagne preferred using the title 'Charles, the most serene Augustus crowned by God, the great, peaceful Emperor ruling the Roman Empire' rather than the simpler and more often used 'Emperor of the Romans'. These aren't entirely the actions of someone with an aversion to the role, and the king's humility may have been as expertly stage-managed as Leo's mercy.

Nonetheless, with his rule over the Frankish lands uncontested and his empire secured through sheer military prowess, Charlemagne no more needed to declare himself Roman emperor than the fearsome Charles Martel needed to be king, but the vulnerable pope required an emperor to protect him and a vast Empire with the church at its heart. Only Rome had nostalgia for its lost empire, the Franks held their 4th Century resistance to Roman rule, and their role in dismembering the Roman Empire as a point of fierce pride.

Ultimately though, the way Charlemagne signed his name changed nothing of the way he conducted his affairs, and the impact of his ascension - reluctant or willing - to Europe's highest office would take another 150 years to make itself fully known.

The first Holy Roman emperor, Otto I, took the title in 962 CE and reinvented himself in the Frankish king's image, creating a powerful multi-ethnic state and a crown that would endure for over 1,000 years.

Through the Holy Roman Empire, Charlemagne's rule defined not just the primacy of France as one of Europe's imperial, religious and cultural superpowers, but of numerous Austrian, German and Italian states too.

A career that began for Charlemagne as king of the Franks ended not just as emperor, but also as the father of the Europe that we can still recognise today.

Charlemagne orders the construction of a city to ford the River Main - Frankfurt, or Frank Ford

© Getty

849 – 899 CE
Alfred the Great

Warrior, scholar and king of the Anglo-Saxons, Alfred led a great crusade to unite his kingdom and rid it of Viking invaders

I n the dark and forboding landscape of 9th Century England, the Anglo-Saxon civilisation, which had called the British Isles home for 400 years, stood at the brink of collapse. Brutal warriors descended on English shores from dragon-headed long boats, looking for plunder and bloodshed. Children huddled close to their families inside their thatched long halls, fearing the panicked screams of terrified neighbours – the calling card of these merciless raiders. The Viking horde was not satisfied with just crops or gold, although for rural farmers like the Anglo-Saxons this was bad enough. They wanted to enslave and brutalise the people themselves, and destroy the original Anglo-Saxon society. With the other Anglo-Saxon kingdoms divided or conquered, Wessex stood alone against this unstoppable menace. It was in this bleak and embattled world that King Aethelwulf's wife Osburh gave birth to their fifth son at an unremarkable Berkshire village in 849 CE. They named him Alfred and he would change the fortunes of the Anglo-Saxon cause forever.

Alfred was forced to grow up quickly, learning the ways of an Anglo-Saxon warrior. He was taught to ride, hawk, hunt and most importantly how to defend himself with a shield and kill with a sword. The family he grew up in was a close-knit group and, in keeping with Anglo-Saxon families at the time, many generations of the same kin lived under one roof and passed down their knowledge to the young. While Alfred saw the practical lessons he was learning from his father's warriors as a duty, his real interests lied in the scholarly works his

father engrossed himself in. He particularly enjoyed poetry and one story involving this passion showed an unrelenting determination that would follow him into adulthood. His mother had promised one of her five sons an illuminated book of Anglo-Saxon poetry for the first one of them who could memorise the text off by heart. Alfred could not read, so he found a teacher and made him repeat every line in the book until he had it completely memorised. He won his prize and proved to his family that when he wanted something he was willing to do anything to get it.

Boyhood games and poetry recitals came to an abrupt end when a Viking army landed in the Anglo-Saxon kingdom of East Angles in 865. Stories of these iron-willed and bloodthirsty warriors had circulated in his father's court and it was widely feared that they were undefeatable. Alfred disagreed, if his years learning about his ancestors and hunting game had taught him anything it was that no enemy was undefeatable. The huge Viking war host led by the fearsome warriors Halfdan and Ivar the Boneless invaded Northumbria, looted York and then turned back to East Angles. The host captured the King of East Angles, Edward, and in a display of power killed him in a ritual sacrifice to their pagan gods. They renamed Edward's realm East Anglia then turned their attention to Wessex and quickly took the small town of Reading in 870.

There was little doubt in Alfred's mind that the terror and destruction the Vikings had wrought across the other Anglo-Saxon kingdoms would be brought to Wessex. He and his older brother Aethelred set out to meet them in open combat, mustering men to serve in their army. After days

> Alfred was the first King on the British Isles who established a universal set of written legal rights for the people of his lands

ALFRED THE GREAT
Wessex, 849 – 899 CE

Brief Bio Alfred was a highly trained warrior in a Britain that was comprised of smaller kingdoms and under constant threat of Viking raids. When he claimed the throne he brokered a deal with a Viking war leader who later reneged, killing Alfred's emissaries. Alfred revenged them with a crushing victory and consolidated power.

"Anglo-Saxons remembered him as 'England's shepherd, England's darling', history honoured him with a far grander title – Alfred the Great"

Alfred's success as King saw him become the de-facto ruler of Mercia and much of the other lands in mainland England

Alfred disguised himself as a minstrel to infiltrate the Danish camp

Alfred the warrior and tactician

Warfare during Alfred's reign was not for the faint of heart. Battles involved thousands of fierce warriors brutally killing each other with swords, axes, maces or any other sharp object that came to hand in uncontrolled melees. Battlefields would run with blood as the victor claimed their prize of crops, loot and slaves from the local populace. The Anglo-Saxon tactic of forming a shield wall to protect their warriors against incoming missiles was partially effective at keeping their soldiers alive so they could close in for hand-to-hand combat, but its effects were limited against a highly mobile foe like the Vikings who specialised in surrounding the enemy quickly. Alfred was aware of this problem and of the relative weakness of mustering a diffuse and at times reluctant community of settlements to stave off encroaching Viking raids. He ordered a fledgling Anglo-Saxon navy built with bigger ships than the Vikings and the construction of a system of forts throughout Wessex known as burhs to allow his warriors to effectively defend their homes from the pagan hordes. He also established a mobile standing army which could respond to foreign threats far more quickly than the hapless local fyrd or army. It also meant that the Vikings could no longer claim land and lordship over the people they conquered, allowing Alfred to consolidate his hold over his own kingdom.

of marching they met the Vikings on a ridge near Ashdown. The Vikings were surprised by the hot blooded aggression of Alfred; he attacked uphill like a 'wild boar' according to the chronicler Bishop Asser, tearing into the Viking lines and causing them to retreat while his brother was still at prayer. It was said afterwards that the field was 'covered in bodies'. After years of plundering the Vikings had finally met their match.

Alfred's triumph was celebrated throughout Wessex, but it was to be short lived. The battle of Ashdown was followed by defeat after defeat; large stretches of Wessex were now under Viking control. It was during these bleak days of 871 that Aethelred died and Alfred claimed the throne of his embattled kingdom. He knew he could no longer defeat the Vikings and attempted to pay them off, affording the realm some respite, but the raids soon continued and in 876 he locked swords with his greatest adversary, the Viking chieftain Guthrum at Wareham. In a siege that involved Alfred using long ships off the Dorset coast to block the Vikings' escape route to the sea, Guthrum was defeated and made to swear an oath of peace to Alfred on a ring of the Viking warrior god Thor. In an act which Alfred would never forget, Guthrum broke his promise, murdered Alfred's emissaries and inflicted a crushing defeat on Alfred's forces at Chippenham during a Christian feast day. It was an act designed to reaffirm Guthrum's commitment to his warrior gods.

Alfred barely escaped with his life, most of his men had been killed or captured by the Viking

> Alfred's commitment to Christianity was well known; the pope gave him a piece of what was thought to be the true cross

host and it seemed as if all was lost. He ran into the marshes and spent the next few months evading capture eventually holding up in a peasant's house. A story was told, written in later chronicles, that he was so consumed by the threat to his kingdom that when asked to watch over some cakes by a peasant woman, his mind wandered and they burned. The woman admonished him, saying, "Look here, man, you hesitate to turn the loaves which you see to be burning, yet you're quite happy to eat them when they come warm from the oven.' Rather than punish her, Alfred was said to have acted humbly. The tale not only showed how far the king had fallen but how his troubles had not affected his character.

Rather than accept his kingdom as lost, Alfred gathered his warriors around Southampton and used guerrilla tactics to turn the tables on the raiders until he could nail them down to one last engagement at Edington. It was the greatest battle of Alfred's career. The moment was captured by one of his scribes: 'then the band of bold men was quickly made ready, men brave in battle... warriors marched out, bore banners of victory... heroes beneath their helmets at the break of dawn; the shields rang resounded loudly.' Guthrum lead a huge charge into the Anglo-Saxon forces hoping to smash Alfred and his men with one bold gesture. Rather than retreat, Alfred was determined to stand his ground; there could be no more

Defining moment
Battle of Ashdown
8 January 871 CE

Alfred leads an attack on Viking positions at Ashdown after the Vikings begin to sweep through the area and into Wessex. Knowing that a muster of all available warriors would be the only way to secure victory, Alfred finds a Saraen stone and blows into it. The large boom that this creates musters all the men in the area to battle. The fighting lasts hours as the Vikings and Anglo-Saxons go head-to-head in close combat which leaves hundreds dead but eventually Alfred prevails and the Viking host retreats eastward. The battle of Ashdown becomes Alfred's first victory.

● **Viking invasion**
The Vikings launch an invasion of East Anglia and much of the English mainland is taken by the 'heathen army'. Alfred is made secundarius (advisor) to the king.
865 CE

Timeline

● **Birth of a warrior**
Alfred is born in Wantage, Berkshire. He is the youngest son of King Aethelwulf and his first wife Osburh. Aethelwulf insists his children succeed to the throne in turn making Alfred fifth in line.
849 CE

● **Pilgrimage to Rome**
Alfred goes on a pilgrimage to Rome where he is made a consul by the pope. He also spends time in the court of Charles the Bald of the Franks where he learns about his greatest enemy: the Vikings.
853 CE

● **Marriage to Ealhswith**
Alfred marries Ealhswith of Mercia as a way of showing solidarity against the invading Vikings. One account describes her as 'the true and dear lady of the English'.
868 CE

● **Battle against Ivar the Boneless**
Alfred and Aethelred fight the Viking host led by Ivar the Boneless in Mercia. Despite fierce fighting they cannot prevent the Vikings from crushing resistance wherever they find it.
868 CE

● **Alfred made heir apparent**
In order to prevent a succession crisis in the face of the Viking invasion the reigning king, Aethelred, agrees that Alfred should be next in line to the throne despite Aethelred having children.
Janurary 871 CE

defeat. He ordered his men to form an impregnable shield wall, as the Vikings crashed down onto them they were slaughtered on the shields and swords of the Anglo-Saxons. Alfred then led a charge into their camp at Chippenham and made 'great slaughter among them' until they retreated into their fortress and were 'brought to the extreme depths of despair.' Starving and trapped, Guthrum was forced to surrender.

Guthrum and the rest of his Viking army retreated from Wessex for good but this did not mean that they were out of England as a whole. In East Anglia and parts of Northumbria the Vikings had established settlements and were becoming neighbours rather than raiders. Alfred saw this and in an act which showed his keen intellect he forced Guthrum to convert to Christianity and became his godfather. By doing this he insured an oath of allegiance which would guarantee the stability of his kingdom. The Viking threat did not disappear after their defeat at Edington and as a warrior, Alfred knew that an attack on Wessex could happen at any time. He built up his defences and established a system of forts to help protect the countryside; he also instigated new laws based on the Bible which consolidated his grip on power.

His most decisive act during the years after his victories was the consolidation of the rest of the Anglo-Saxon kingdoms under his leadership. Reasoning that one kingdom united was stronger and more able to resist foreign invasion than a divided land with divided interests, Alfred targeted London, the most important trading town in the whole of England. London was controlled by a Mercian King Ceolwulf who had died at some point after 880 and it is

unclear if this was the result of Alfred laying siege to the city. Certainly this would have stained his reputation as England's 'darling' since London at the time was an Anglo-Saxon settlement. Whether London was captured or acquired, the city was brought under Alfred's control in 886. The symbolism of this act along with as his eldest daughter marrying Aethelred the lord of the Mercians united all of Anglo-Saxon England in a tenuous peace under Wessex.

By 890, old age had begun to creep up on Alfred. He suffered from crippling pain in his stomach and it was sapping his strength, along with the complexities of trying to rule a disparate group of settlements in his own kingdom and remain the most influential man in Mercia. Despite this he was determined to continue building his realm by enlightening his subjects. He translated a number of volumes from Latin to English including *The Ecclesiastical History Of The English People* and Gregory the Great's *Pastoral Care* which instructed bishops on their duties. Alfred's contribution to the development of the English church earned him such recognition that his most committed followers sought to get him canonised.

In 899, Alfred died aged 50, passing on a secure and powerful dynasty to his son Edward. The Anglo-Saxons would remain in a dominant position in England for the next 167 years until another great invasion in 1066 led to the investiture of a Norman King named William. Alfred had secured this legacy through his bravery, skill as a warrior and learned negotiating skills. Anglo-Saxons remembered him as 'England's shepherd, England's darling', history honoured him with a far grander title - Alfred the Great.

> It is widely thought that Alfred suffered from Crohn's disease which would explain his thin build and ongoing health problems

Kinship and Lord
Anglo-Saxon society was dominated by bonds of honour and loyalty to kin groups in individual settlements around the country and the tenuous fidelity these groups swore to the nobility and the king. This created a divided realm that only the strongest ruler could call upon in a national emergency.

Invaded land
The Anglo-Saxons themselves were invaders of the British Isles, the Angles and Saxon tribes originated from Germany and Denmark and established settlements across England subjugating the native Britons. In the time of Alfred, the Saxons had fully settled in Britain and were now under threat from the Vikings.

Language barrier
In many ways the British Isles were a cosmopolitan collection of different tribes, all of whom spoke a number of languages and dialects. The Angle, Saxon, Danish, Celtic and Latin languages combined together during this period to form the base of what we now know as the English language.

Divided religion
There was no dominant religion in Europe during this period, Christianity was becoming widespread but various forms of paganism still held sway in many lands including the British and Scandinavian kingdoms. The Anglo-Saxons had converted to Christianity in 601 and referred to the Viking invasion as the 'heathen invasion.'

Warrior society
Every Anglo-Saxon male who was 'free' could be called upon to fight for his home and family at any time by his lord in the fyrd or army. Often these groups would be poorly equipped as individual warriors had to arm themselves, and it took strong leadership to keep these unruly bands together.

Defining moment
Betrayed by Guthrum
876 CE
After a Viking incursion at Wareham in Dorset is defeated, the Viking chieftain Guthrum submits to Alfred and promises to withdraw his forces to Mercia. He seals his promise on a holy ring of the Viking god Thor. Instead of honouring his pledge to the warrior god, Guthrum betrays Alfred and escapes, reassembles his war host and destroys Alfred's army at Chippenham, forcing Alfred to flee into the countryside. The Anglo-Saxon chronicles speak of a dispirited, battle wary and lonely Alfred seeking shelter with peasants.

Defining moment
The Battle of Edington
878 CE
In the greatest battle of Alfred's career, Alfred confronts his old enemy Guthrum for the last time on the field of battle. The battle is a desperate struggle for the survival of Alfred's kingdom. Much of Wessex is now under threat from the Viking horde assembled in the northern part of the kingdom. Alfred orders his men to form a dense shield wall, a common tactic used by Anglo-Saxon armies and together they hold firm against the Viking tide which sweeps onto them. He wins a spectacular victory and pursues the Vikings to Chippenham where they surround and starve them out, forcing Guthrum to surrender.

- **London liberated**
Alfred takes control of London through a disputed action which may have involved him laying siege to the area. He gains de-facto dominance over all Anglo-Saxon territory by taking the most important trading city in the British Isles.
886 CE

- **The law codes**
After studying Latin, Alfred presents to his kingdom a collection of laws put together in a 'dooms book' which is based on Christian teachings from the Bible. He uses these laws to strengthen his influence in the other Anglo-Saxon kingdoms.
893 CE

899 CE

- **Crowned king**
After the death of Aethelred, Alfred is crowded King of Wessex. Word is then received that the Vikings have won more victories within the kingdom. Instead of fighting them, Alfred strives for peace.
23 April 871 CE

- **Treaty of Alfred and Guthrum**
Alfred signs a treaty with Guthrum which gives the Vikings control of East-Anglia on the condition that Anglo-Saxon rights are respected and the Vikings stop taking slaves from Wessex townships.
880 CE

- **A gift of the true cross**
In recognition of Alfred's true piety, Pope Marinus I presents a gift of what he believes to be a piece of the true cross as well as other priceless treasures to Alfred and his court.
883 CE

Death of a hero
Alfred dies in 899 aged 50, ensuring a secure land for his lineage, and Wessex as the dominant player of the three Anglo-Saxon kingdoms in England. He is remembered as Alfred the Great.
899 CE

HARALD HARDRADA
Norwegian, 1015-1066

Brief Bio

Born Harald Sigurdsson, Harald Hardrada was king of Norway from 1045 until his death at the Battle of Stamford Bridge in 1066. Son of Sigurd Syr, a chieftain from Norway's eastern territories, Hardrada garnered the nickname 'Harald the Ruthless' due to a series of brutal raids on his neighbouring territories.

1015 – 1066

Harald Hardrada

With the Viking Age setting in the West, one man set out to reclaim the lands, power and culture of his forefathers. His name was Harald Hardrada, and this is his story

Conqueror, exile, mercenary and warlord; Harald Hardrada was many things during his bloody, brutal and eventful life. However, he was one thing above all others: a Viking. Descended, according to Scandinavian saga, from the legendary first ever king of Norway, Harald Fairhair, Hardrada - named due to his style for 'hard rule' - came from a long line of war-loving Viking rulers who each, much to the terror of large swathes of Europe, had ravaged, pillaged and ransacked with a frequency that was previously unimaginable. The culture, landscape and language of Europe had irrevocably been altered by the Age of the Vikings, and Hardrada, born into one of its noble institutions, was brought up to be totally wrapped in its ideals and indoctrinated into a mindset, the likes of which had seen the nations of Scandinavia dominate their known world for almost 300 years.

It was this in-built, centuries-old lust for war and conquest that saw Hardrada engage in his first ever battle in 1030, a mere 15 years after his birth in Ringerike, Norway. Hardrada's brother Olaf Haraldsson had been forced into exile in 1028 after the Danish King Cnut the Great had taken the

Viking weapons

Battle axe

The axe was the primary weapon of all the Scandinavian cultures of the Viking Age, with a multitude of designs used between nations with differing shafts and heads. One of the most popular designs was the Dane Axe, a large two-handed weapon with long shaft and crescent-shaped wrought iron head. Often the axe head would be granted a steel cutting edge, a factor that helped it generate skull-splitting force.

Sword

If a Viking carried a sword then it would be his primary weapon. The problem was that swords were more expensive to produce than axes, and so were only carried by the rich and powerful. Viking swords were 90 centimetres in length and took a Roman spatha-like design, with a tight grip, long fuller and no pronounced cross-guard. Hilts and handles were often inlaid with embellishments like jewels or inscriptions.

Dagger

The standard secondary weapon for each Viking warrior, the dagger was an incredibly versatile weapon, granting an element of speed to the Viking's otherwise slow armament. In particular, the seax was a popular model that consisted of a symmetrical, straight blade of various lengths with a smooth, wooden hilt. Seax daggers such as this could also be used for everyday tasks like skinning animals and carving.

War of words

While it is true that Hardrada's reign was characterised by raiding, war and blood, he was also reportedly a sound diplomat and economist, and used his skills to bring a period of stability to Norway when much of Scandinavia was in turmoil. Two of the most notable examples of the king's ability to expand his empire by words rather than axe are, first, his arrangement of new international trade routes and deals – a decision that brought in much wealth to Norway, with deals struck with the Kievan Rus and the vast Byzantine Empire – and, second, his dissemination of Christianity throughout the lands of Norway. Indeed, Hardrada had been converted early to Christianity, and upon becoming king of Norway he implemented many policies geared towards promoting it – be that through direct communication or via the construction of churches and the reparation of existing ones.

Norwegian throne for himself. However, upon Olaf's return in 1030, Hardrada drummed up the support of 600 men from the Norwegian Uplands and joined with Olaf to take down Cnut. As such, on 29 July 1030, Hardrada took the fight to the Danish at the Battle of Stiklestad, fighting with his brother for control of his ancestors' country. Unfortunately, despite showing considerable military might on the battlefield, Hardrada was defeated by the far larger and stronger Danish army, with Olaf being killed in the fighting.

Hardrada barely escaped with his life, having been badly wounded in the melee. In fact, were it not for the covert help of his friend Rögnvald Brusason – the future Earl of Orkney – Hardrada would never have reached the remote farmstead

in eastern Norway that he did a few weeks after the battle, nor been able to recover from his serious wounds. A month went by, and with each passing day the reality of what had occurred became all the more apparent to Hardrada. He had let down his brother, father, nation and revered forefathers. He had been defeated at the first hurdle, part-crippled by a foreign invader that remained in control of his country. Unable to bear the guilt any longer, one month after his defeat Hardrada exiled himself to Sweden, journeying north over the mountains under the cover of darkness.

Over the following year, little is known of Hardrada's movements or activities, with not even the sagas of old recalling what transpired. All that is known today is that almost a year

Viking longships were light and manoeuvrable, and could reach a speed of up to 15 knots

Prince of plunder
The lands that felt Hardrada's wrath first-hand

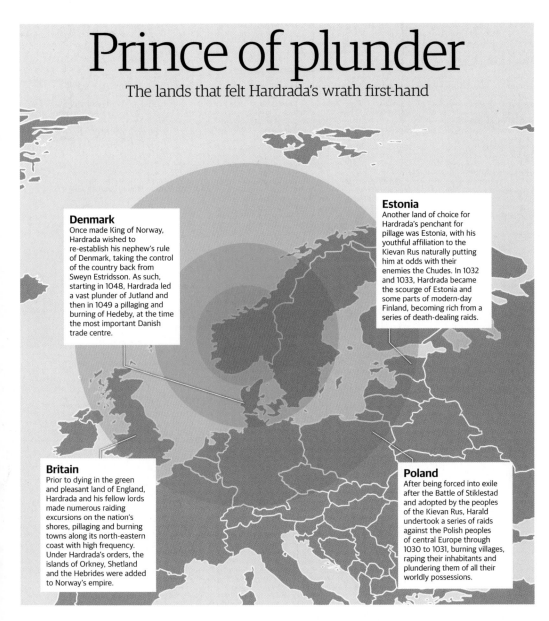

Denmark
Once made King of Norway, Hardrada wished to re-establish his nephew's rule of Denmark, taking the control of the country back from Sweyn Estridsson. As such, starting in 1048, Hardrada led a vast plunder of Jutland and then in 1049 a pillaging and burning of Hedeby, at the time the most important Danish trade centre.

Estonia
Another land of choice for Hardrada's penchant for pillage was Estonia, with his youthful affiliation to the Kievan Rus naturally putting him at odds with their enemies the Chudes. In 1032 and 1033, Hardrada became the scourge of Estonia and some parts of modern-day Finland, becoming rich from a series of death-dealing raids.

Britain
Prior to dying in the green and pleasant land of England, Hardrada and his fellow lords made numerous raiding excursions on the nation's shores, pillaging and burning towns along its north-eastern coast with high frequency. Under Hardrada's orders, the islands of Orkney, Shetland and the Hebrides were added to Norway's empire.

Poland
After being forced into exile after the Battle of Stiklestad and adopted by the peoples of the Kievan Rus, Harald undertook a series of raids against the Polish peoples of central Europe through 1030 to 1031, burning villages, raping their inhabitants and plundering them of all their worldly possessions.

Three ruthless victories

Asia Minor campaign
1035
Following his joining of the Byzantine Varangian Guard, Hardrada was dispatched to Asia Minor to put down a widespread piratical Arab uprising. A series of running battles continued in which Harald pushed the Arab forces back into mainland Asia. Following this initial success, Hardrada led a search-and-destroy operation deep into the Asia Minor, slaughtering thousands and taking over 80 Arab strongholds.

Battle of Ostrovo
1041
While the leader of the Varangian Guard, Hardrada led the Byzantine forces against a Bulgarian army in Greece. In 1040 Peter Delyan, a native Bulgarian, led an uprising against Byzantine rule and declared himself king. Hardrada killed his foe, crushed his forces in battle and re-suppressed Bulgaria to such an extent that it remained under Byzantine rule for another 145 years.

Battle of Fulford
20 September 1066
Hardrada's last great victory, the Battle of Fulford, saw him land in England and defeat northern Earls Edwin and Morcar of York in a battle involving over 15,000 soldiers. Harald's tactical masterstroke was positioning his troops so that he could absorb the heavy English infantry charge before countering down his right flank and breaking the enemy's lines. This victory won him the city of York.

to the day after his defeat at Stiklestad, Hardrada arrived in the town of Staraya Ladoga in the Kievan Rus region of north-eastern Europe. The Kievan people were a wild bunch of Slavic tribes renowned for their hardiness, combat prowess and expertise in trade, with their geographical position placing them very much at the gates between the largely Byzantine-controlled East and the Scandinavian-occupied West. So when Hardrada emerged from the wilderness in 1031, his ancestry and prowess in combat saw him warmly welcomed by the Rus' ruler Grand Prince Yaroslav the Wise, whose wife Ingegerd was a distant relative of his.

Badly in need of military commanders and recognising Harald's ability in combat, Yaroslav immediately made Hardrada leader of his forces

and dispatched him to the western border to fight the Polish peoples at war with the Rus. The faith Yaroslav placed in Harald's breeding was well founded, with the warrior completing a crushing campaign against Poland, slaughtering hundreds of thousands of Poles and driving them back into their country's distant heartlands. Following this victory, Yaroslav left Hardrada to engage the Chude peoples of Estonia and the Pechenegs nomads that had been fighting on and off with the Rus for decades, with similarly bold but horrific results. Hardrada was reportedly demonic on the battlefield, driven by some seemingly unnatural force in the pursuit of his enemy's blood, transcending into a berserker state that no man could oppose.

These victories for the Rus saw Hardrada gain a fearsome reputation, with a band of 500 men pledging their loyalty to him. Hardrada and his band of mercenary warriors were now the most feared fighting force in Europe and, after securing the Kievan territories in 1033, they set off on a quest for fame and riches. They began heading south to Constantinople, the capital city of the fabulously wealthy Byzantine Empire. Arriving there in 1034 and immediately introducing himself to the Byzantine Emperor Michael IV, Hardrada and his men were immediately employed in the Emperor's Varangian Guard, an elite fighting force controlled directly by the ruler. In theory, the Varangian Guard were supposed to simply protect the Emperor, but due to Hardrada's desire for battle, he was, soon after, fighting on almost every front of the empire.

From Arab pirates in the Mediterranean to rebel forces amassed in Sicily and onto Arab strongholds throughout Asia Minor, Hardrada became the scourge of any Byzantine enemy. He was deployed like a rampaging bull on the battlefield, one that

"Hardrada was demonic on the battlefield, driven by some seemingly unnatural force in the pursuit of his enemy's blood"

Hardrada's last hurrah

Follow the events of the last Viking king's final battle at Stamford Bridge on 25 September 1066

7. Hardrada falls
Outnumbered and out-flanked, Hardrada entered a berserker state and with a trance-like fury began rending English soldiers limb from limb until he was hit in the neck by a stray arrow then impaled by English soldiers.

4. Shield wall formed
Hardrada mobilised his army, which descended towards the bridge on the eastern bank and erected a shield wall that halted their advance. Godwinson ordered his men to lock their shields and charge.

5. Brutal melee
The two lines of men, thousands strong on each side, smashed together in an epic melee brawl. The vikings tried to hold the English assault, but they were ferocious and unstoppable.

6. Shield wall fragments
The Vikings were unable to repel the English, and holes began to form in the shield wall, with the defensive line splintering. Godwinson ordered extra troops through the gap to outflank the enemy.

3. Retreat across the bridge
The western Viking force fled across the bridge, with a few elite warriors holding back the English at the choke point. However, the English beat the Vikings and crossed over.

2. Norwegians surprised
Hardrada had not been made aware of the English advance, with the possibility that the English army had marched between London and Yorkshire in just four days unthinkable. That is exactly what happened though, and the battle began with a vast infantry charge on Hardrada's force early in the morning. Hardrada was unprepared and completely overrun.

1. Forces deployed
The Vikings were split into two groups, with the bulk of the army on the east side of the River Derwent and a smaller force on the west. The English force approached from the south west, so at first the English were west of Derwent.

could seemingly not be killed in combat no matter how far the odds were stacked in his opponents' favour. Returning back to Constantinople in 1041, Hardrada was now famed not just for his battle prowess, but also for his immense wealth, with almost seven years worth of plunder being amassed into a vast fortune that rivalled that of many kings. Indeed, Hardrada had raided so much that he had to send large portions of his loot back to Yaroslav for safe keeping - no boat was capable of carrying the sheer weight of the bountiful precious metals and jewels.

While Hardrada's position under the Byzantine Emperor Michael IV was unassailable, with the Varangian Viking chief being highly praised for

his deeds, upon the Emperor's death in December of 1041 he quickly fell out of favour, becoming caught up in the middle of a war of succession. Realising that his position was never going to be same again, Hardrada escaped a now turbulent Constantinople just months later, returning by boat through the Black Sea to the Kievan Rus. Upon returning to a rapturous welcome from Yaroslav, Hardrada promptly married the latter's daughter Ellisif and, for a short time, settled down in theKievan capital. There he engaged in little combat, and remained in the Rus for a further three years, living relatively peacefully.

However, as the days and years dripped by, Hardrada was still tormented by his defeat at

Sticklestad. He hadn't set foot in his native Norway for almost 15 years and, despite his vast riches and subsequent victories, was haunted by the legacy left to him by his ancestors. Norway, he decided, must be returned once more to Norwegian hands. Setting forth from Novgorod in early 1045, Hardrada journeyed back to the country of his birth, arriving in Sweden once more later on in the year. Here, Hardrada received excellent news: Norway was already back in Norwegian hands, with the illegitimate son of Olaf, Magnus the Good, sitting securely on the throne. Apparently, Cnut the Great's sons had abandoned Hardrada's much-loved Norway, and were currently fighting for the control of England.

Life after Harald

Despite a succession of other Norwegian and Scandinavian kings following Hardrada's death, none of them truly had Viking in the blood, and the Viking Age ended as abruptly as it begun 300 years previously. Far from the war-loving, plundering and raiding mentality that won the Vikings almost all of northern Europe, these successors had neither the will nor the military might to maintain the Viking Age and their way of life, with Scandinavian influence subsiding, and gradually becoming subsumed into wider European culture over the following decades.

For example, Hardrada's successor was Magnus Haraldsson, who was left King regent upon Harald's departure for England. However, after only reigning for three peaceful and uneventful years, he died of ringworm, leaving his brother Olaf III to take the crown, who proceeded to rule Norway until his death in 1093. However, while his rule was long, it was not Viking, with the king renouncing any offensive foreign policies and diverting funds to the defence of Norwegian borders. This pattern of defensive and peaceful ruler continued, with the only combat experienced being that of the civil wars of the 12th and 13th centuries.

The domination of Viking culture had come crashing down with Hardrada's defeat at Stamford Bridge, and Europe was now entering a more peaceful and civilised age. For Hardrada, in his last glorious stand, had being fighting on the razor's edge of a more savage time; one that saw the lands, language and laws of Europe changed forever. The last true Viking king was dead, and with him, the Viking Age.

Hardrada set off immediately to Norway and, after arriving in 1046 and negotiating with Magnus directly, struck a deal that he would joint-rule the country in exchange for half of his immense wealth. For the next two years, both Magnus and Harald ruled Norway, holding separate courts and rarely meeting. Hardrada now had everything he could want, owning much land, ruling his country and being fabulously wealthy too. However, after two years of supposedly living an ideal life, the Viking blood within Hardrada's veins called once more, leading him into a campaign of revenge against Denmark for the death of his brother and the pillaging of his ancestral lands. As such, in 1048 Hardrada plundered Jutland, pillaged and burned Hedeby - the most important Danish trade centre in the entire country - and launched a colossal naval assault on the Danish royal pretender Sweyn Estridsson. This battle was the infamous Battle of Nisa, and saw Hardrada lead 300 ships against Sweyn in a conflict that left many ships on both sides 'empty'.

Despite defeating Sweyn at Nisa and successfully launching multiple Viking raids on Denmark over the next six years, Hardrada never did take the Danish throne, and due to lack of finance was forced to begrudgingly declare peace with him in 1064. Now recognising that he would never reclaim the Danish throne as his own, Hardrada shifted his attentions towards another rich and historic land: England. England had been controlled by Cnut the Great's son Harthacnut until 1042, when he died childless. As such, Edward the Confessor had crowned himself king in his absence and proceeded to rule the island nation for over 20 years. When Hardrada heard in early 1066 that Edward had died on 5 January, he immediately decided to launch one more glorious Viking conquest. Now 50, Hardrada must have known that his time on Earth was coming to an end and, before he passed on to the afterlife to meet his hallowed ancestors, he needed to succumb once again to the call of his blood.

For the native English who witnessed the approach of 300 longships and 15,000 men on 8 September 1066 in north-east England, it must have felt like observing the coming of the

"Before he passed on to the afterlife to meet his hallowed ancestors, he needed to succumb again to the call of his blood"

apocalypse. The force was one of the greatest Viking armies ever to be assembled, and if unopposed would bring the nation to its knees. Stepping forth on English soil, Hardrada could taste the coming war, and after just 12 days he was not to be disappointed, with a 5,000-strong subsidiary English force crushed at the Battle of Fulford - see the 'Three ruthless victories' boxout for more information. Striding through the English dead, finally back in his element after years of inactivity and luxury, little did Hardrada know that this was to be his last victory. Just five days later, his army was surprised by the fierce force of the now English king Harold Godwinson, who marched over 180 miles in four days to meet with the Viking warlord at the Battle of Stamford Bridge. It was a battle that would end Hardrada - for a step-by-step account of the battle, please see the 'Hardrada's last hurrah' boxout - and, as history shows, have a profound effect on the course of England and Europe going forward.

Mere weeks after defeating Hardrada at Stamford Bridge, Godwinson himself would too be defeated by the Norman prince William, in large part due to troop exhaustion from the combat and enforced marching to and from York. As such, William became William the Conqueror, and instigated a centuries-long period of Norman rule over England, radically transforming its economy, language, architecture, law and education. Indeed, by the time the Norman presence in England had dissipated, the medieval age had long since transformed into the Renaissance, and its new, intoxicating culture, religion and science had swept away much of Europe's once-strong Viking presence.

When Harald Hardrada fell on the battlefield in England, it was more than just the flame of one great life being extinguished; it would prove to be the death of the last Viking warrior king.

Hardrada's lineage

Great great grandfather
Harald Fairhair
850 - 932 CE
Noted by many historians to be the first king of Norway, Fairhair became a legendary figure during the Viking Age, with his deeds relayed in numerous epic sagas. He supposedly won many battles against Norwegian opponents on his way to becoming the country's ruler, and famously had anywhere between 11 to 20 sons.

Great grandfather/ grandfather
Halfdan Sigurdsson of Hadafylke
935 - 995 CE
Little is known about Hardrada's grandfather, other than that he was supposedly Halfdan Sigurdsson, the alleged son of King Sigurd Hrise of Norway, Hardrada's great grandfather. Both Hrise's and Halfdan's lineage is unconfirmed, with only information as passed down from Icelandic sagas mentioning their link to Harald.

Father - Sigurd Syr
970 CE - 1018
According to Icelandic sagas, Syr was a prudent and modest man who was known for his hands-on approach to the management of his lands and properties. Records also indicate that he was a wealthy man, and that in 998 CE, chose to be baptised with his wife into the Christian faith.

Nephew - Magnus Olafsson
1024 - 1047
At times both king of Norway and king of Denmark, Hardrada's nephew Magnus garnered the nickname 'Magnus the Good'. He was crowned king of Norway at 11 and king of Denmark at 18, ruling both lands until his mysterious death aged 23. Upon his death the kingdoms were split, with Hardrada taking the Norwegian crown, and Sweyn Estridsson the Danish Crown.

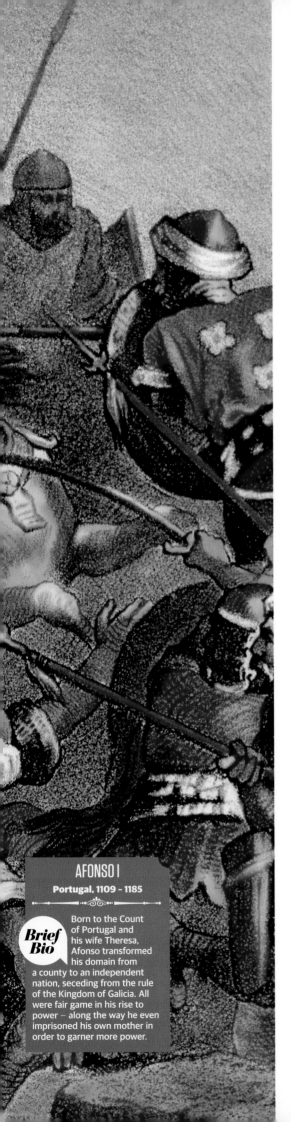

—1109 – 1185—
King Afonso I

The legendary first King of Portugal, Afonso I spent his tenure on Earth fighting a brutal series of wars to ensure his kingdom's independence

K ing Afonso I of Portugal was known by many different names during his lifetime, including Afonso Henriques, Prince Afonso of Portugal and Afonso the Conqueror, however it was as King Afonso I of Portugal that he cemented his place in history, with his bloody deeds in battle founding an entire nation. Today, Portugal is a thriving country, sharing a landmass with its neighbour Spain, however, in the 12th Century, this land was segregated along very different lines, with the Kingdom of León and Kingdom of Galicia, among others, each fighting among themselves and with the Moorish peoples of the Iberian Peninsula for control of the region.

It was into this hectic mix that Afonso Henriques was born, the son of Henry, Count of Portugal, and Theresa of León. Both his parents reigned jointly as Count and Countess of Portugal, with the pair paying allegiance to King Alfonso VI of León. However, upon Henry's death, Theresa reigned alone and soon remarried a powerful but disliked Galician count, who proceeded to exile his enemies from the kingdom. The Portuguese nobility, angered by the allegiance with Galicia and the banishment of their own, threw their support behind Afonso and as soon as he turned 14 he made himself a knight on his own account, elevating himself in the Cathedral of Zamora.

Now a knight and with the support of the majority of the Portuguese nobility, Afonso found no difficulty in raising an army, and moved against his mother and the Galician count's troops, defeating them near Guimarães in the Battle of São Mamede. With a decisive victory his, he then

AFONSO I
Portugal, 1109 – 1185

Brief Bio Born to the Count of Portugal and his wife Theresa, Afonso transformed his domain from a county to an independent nation, seceding from the rule of the Kingdom of Galicia. All were fair game in his rise to power – along the way he even imprisoned his own mother in order to garner more power.

46 years of Moor war

Why did Afonso I spend 46 years of his life in bloody battle with the Moorish peoples of the Iberian Peninsula?

While today Afonso I is mainly remembered for his foundation of Portugal as an independent country, separating itself through battle from the Kingdom of León in 1139 CE, he in fact spent far more of his life fighting against the Moors of the Iberian Peninsula than his enemies closer to home. This was largely due to Afonso inheriting the centuries-old Christian church-led 'Reconquista', a holy mission to reclaim territories that had once belonged to them from a series of now predominantly Muslim states. The importance of Afonso using his power as King of Portugal against the Moors was ensured by the support of the pope in Rome, who not only recognised his new country's independence, but claimed that he was free under the eyes of the Christian God to take as much Moorish territory as he liked, while also being free to pillage and loot to enhance his kingdom's wealth.

Afonso took this to heart during his reign, frequently ordering or encouraging his troops or allies – such as the Knights Templar, who Afonso welcomed to Portugal with open arms – to fight the Moors wherever possible. As a consequence, Afonso I oversaw more than ten wars between Portugal and the Moors during his reign, including one of the largest and most famous sieges in history, with the Siege of Lisbon seeing much of the Christian world's troops descending on the city to place it in Catholic hands. Interestingly, however, despite Afonso's many conquests, the Reconquista would not come to an end in his lifetime or even that of his son or grandsons, with the religious warfare continuing on and off right up until the close of the 15th Century, over 300 years later.

A statue of Afonso I that stands today in Guimarães, Portugal

proceeded to banish his mother for her crimes to a monastery in Galicia, where she lived out the remainder of her days in disgrace. Afonso, who was now Duke of Portugal and sole ruler, then proceeded to fight off his mother's nephew, Alfonso VII of León, thereby freeing the Kingdom of Portugal from dependence on the dominant Kingdom of León. On 6 April 1129, Afonso took the next step in his epic journey, declaring himself Prince of Portugal.

His mother and the rival Kingdom of León dealt with, Afonso then proceeded to turn his troops onto the Moorish peoples who inhabited

his kingdom's southern territories. The Islamic Moors had travelled across from Africa over the preceding centuries, sometimes taking terrain on the Iberian Peninsula by force, other times merely by expanding trade routes. Either way, with the rise and spread of Catholicism throughout Medieval Europe, the Moorish presence was considered heretical and something that needed to be eradicated. As such, as Afonso rose to power he found himself indoctrinated into the Reconquista, an established movement by Christian countries to conquer all Islamic peoples throughout Europe.

As such, over the next decade from 1129 to 1139, Afonso led a series of successful campaigns against the Moorish people of the region, culminating on 25 July 1139 with a crushing victory at the Battle of Ourique over the long-established Almoravid Moors of Ali ibn Yusuf. This victory was so complete that Afonso was immediately proclaimed King of the Portuguese, an act that elevated him to a rank equal to the rulers of the other realms of the Peninsula. Afonso's coronation was held the next day, officially making him King Afonso I of Portugal and the newly-established country's first monarch.

While Afonso's position and country were now established in terms of politics and arms, it was still largely unrecognised by the highest Christian authority in the world, the Catholic church and Pope in Rome. Afonso therefore immediately moved to rectify this, wedding Maud of Savoy – daughter of Amadeus III of the long-established and respected Christian House of Savoy – and sending an envoy of ambassadors to Rome to negotiate becoming a vassal of the papacy, as the kings of Sicily and Aragon had historically done before him.

> "With the rise and spread of Catholicism through Medieval Europe, the Moorish presence was considered heretical"

Timeline

1109

Born in Guimarães
Afonso Henriques is born to Henry, Count of Portugal and Theresa of León. His parents reign jointly as Count and Countess of Portugal until Henry's death, after which time Theresa reigns alone.
25 June 1109

Defeats his mother
After Theresa remarries a disliked Galician count, Afonso is backed by the rest of the Portuguese nobility and he defeats her forces at the Battle of Sao Mamede before exiling her permanently to a monastery in Galicia.
1128

Mother dies
Banished to Galicia, Afonso's mother's health deteriorates and she dies in 1130. In the same year, Afonso invades Galicia and the Knights Hospitaller install themselves in Portugal.
1130

Moors conquered
Now proclaimed Prince of Portugal, Afonso continues to conquer by taking Leiria and overthrowing its Moorish inhabitants. King Alfonso VII of Castile and León proclaims himself Emperor.
1135

Independence of Portugal
The Kingdom of Portugal is declared independent from the Kingdom of León after the Battle of Ourique. Prince Afonso Henriques finally becomes Afonso I, King of Portugal, the new country's first monarch.
25 July 1139

Afonso I accepting the surrender of the medieval Muslim peoples of Taifa of Badajoz

Impressed with his dedication to the faith, the Pope accepted Afonso as a new king and as a vassal to the Catholic church in Rome, rather than to his cousin, Alfonso VII of León.

Portugal was now completely independent from its rivals and one of the most dominant Catholic countries in Europe. With wealth and power flooding into the new country, Afonso proceeded with several construction projects, including many monasteries and churches, and granted religious institutions such as the Knights Templar - an incredibly powerful Christian military order that grew to great fame through its participation in the Crusades - unprecedented privileges and territory. In return, Afonso's troops were bolstered by the best Christian knights in the world, with the combined might allowing him to undertake even more military campaigns against the remaining Moorish peoples in the region.

Indeed, starting in 1147, Afonso first led the successful capture of the city of Santarém and then, with the aid of thousands of Christian Crusaders, Lisbon, with the Moorish overlords of the city's ruling Kingdom of Badajoz overthrown. This latter conquest was and is today seen as a pivotal battle in the Reconquista, with it signalling the beginning of the end of widespread Moorish occupation of the region and the dominance of Islam in the south of the Iberian Peninsula. Afonso I was now one of the most powerful kings in the western world, recognised by his people, the Pope and even many of the region's rival rulers.

However, one ruler who still did not recognise Afonso's legitimacy was his old nemesis, Alfonso VII of León, who still considered him merely a powerful illegitimate rebel. As such, throughout the 1150s and 1160s, the leaders of León and Portugal engaged in a series of bitter battles, with Afonso eventually struck down in a battle near Badajoz and captured by soldiers loyal to León. He was freed shortly after, however, though this was only after forfeiting many conquered territories in Galicia to his old rival. Despite this constant call of illegitimacy from the King of León, when Pope Alexander III acknowledged that Portugal was an independent crown in his 1179 CE papal bull Manifestis Probatum - papal bulls were the most official of Catholic charters - any lingering claims were quashed.

By the time the country of Portugal entered the 1180s however, Afonso was now an incredibly old man, with a life of near-constant warfare eventually taking its toll on the ruler's health. He did still make one last campaign in 1184 to help his son Dom Sancho fight off a remnant army of Moors who were besieging Santarém, however for the last five years of his life Afonso I enjoyed the fruit of his now-secured kingdom. Finally, on 6 December 1185 CE, Afonso I of Portugal died of old age, with the people of Portugal proceeding to celebrate his reign in song, word and deed - something that they still do today.

How one looks at the reign of Afonso largely depends on context. Today, Afonso's bloodlust and religious intolerance is hard to view objectively, considering that he essentially embarked on a series of genocidal campaigns against Islamic people. The banishment of his mother to die alone in a foreign kingdom is also ethically questionable. However by the standards of other Medieval rulers, Afonso's protection of his own kingdom at all costs and pursuit of religious warfare is very much of its time, with the aggressive us-versus-them mindset par for the course. In many respects, Afonso I was a king of extremes, with his decisions always determined and followed through with a zealous certainty that, whatever their outcome, could not be questioned.

Top five facts – Afonso I

Heavy sword
According to legend, it took ten men to carry Afonso I's sword due to his supposedly inhuman strength and military might. He also reportedly challenged rival monarchs to hand-to-hand duels.

Tomb forbidden
In 2006 researchers from the University of Coimbra in Portugal attempted to open the tomb of Afonso I. Unfortunately, many Portuguese people objected and the permission was rescinded.

Knights Templar
Afonso I was a key ally to the Knights Templar and Christian crusaders in general, granting them land, castles and plunder rights from any Moorish territory they conquered.

Reconquista obsessive
Afonso was reportedly obsessed with the Reconquista, a centuries-old mission to retake the Iberian Peninsula from the Moors. The Reconquista finally ended with the fall of Granada in 1492 CE.

Sancho succeeds
After living to the ripe old age of 76, Afonso is finally succeeded by his son Sancho, who becomes Sancho I of Portugal. Sancho proceeds to rule the country for 27 years.

Marries Maud
After spending the first five years or so of his reign fighting the Moors, King Afonso I decides it's time to strengthen his position and marries Maud of Savoy, daughter of Amadeus III, Count of Savoy and Maurienne.
1146

Lisbon taken
The army of King Afonso I is bolstered by a Crusader army from England, and combined they besiege the Moor-held city of Lisbon. Afonso takes Lisbon and the Moorish inhabitants flee, with the city's gates opening to the Christian army.
1147

Afonso captured
Decades later, Afonso I is captured after an engagement near Badajoz and made a prisoner of the King of León, his son-in-law. He is forced to forfeit many territories in Galicia to pay his ransom.
1169

Recognised by Pope
Pope Alexander III, in the papal bull Manifestis Probatum, recognises Afonso I as King of Portugal and the country as independent. He also recognises the country's right to conquer any lands held by the Moors.
1179

1185
One last stand
Despite being over 70 years old, Afonso I still comes to the aid of his son Dom Sancho, who was being besieged in Santarém by the Moors. One year later Afonso dies on 6 December
1185

© Corbis, Wagner

1122 – 1204
Eleanor of Aquitaine

How the Duchess of Aquitaine survived two husbands and her warmongering children to become the most powerful woman in Europe

In 1173, Henry II was confronted with unbelievable news: three of his sons had taken up arms in rebellion against him, backed by King Louis VII of France. To make matters worse, they were supported by their mother and his wife, Eleanor of Aquitaine.

This act of defiance may have come as a surprise to Henry, but he should have known what she was capable of it. He was aware when he married Eleanor that she was a woman of power, pride and ambition who would not let anything stand in the way of the greater good for her or her sons. This fiery temperament and willingness to confront her problems publicly had already caused trouble for her first husband.

Eleanor was born to one of the most powerful men in Europe: William X of Aquitaine. The Aquitaine territories were vast, encompassing roughly a quarter of all of medieval France, and the kingdom had a reputation for hosting cultural, religious and material riches. When William died, she inherited it all. William had decreed that King Louis VI of France would act as her guardian in the event of his death, prompting Louis, who knew an opportunity when he saw one, to arrange her engagement to his son, Prince Louis, with the wedding taking place on 25 July 1137. While William and Eleanor made their first trip around France as newlyweds, Louis VI passed away. Between them, Louis VII and Eleanor now had France and Aquitaine under their control.

The match of territories might have been harmonious, but the union between Louis and Eleanor was not a happy one. In her marriage agreement, Eleanor made sure that she retained control of Aquitaine, at least until a male heir came of age. Perhaps more importantly, their personalities were completely incompatible: Eleanor loved to travel and took great joy in the cultural and social opportunities her position allowed her; by contrast, Louis lived and ate simply, and it was obvious to everyone at court that he was intimidated by Eleanor.

The death blow to their marriage came when Eleanor insisted on accompanying her husband on the Second Crusade in 1147. His failures and their public arguments led to scandalous rumours about them both and, despite marriage counselling from Pope Eugene III, Louis and Eleanor grew further and further apart. A male heir might have been their saving grace, but when their efforts resulted in two daughters, they had their marriage annulled. Eleanor was now aged 28 and in need of a husband.

Although we might assume that she would relish her freedom, Eleanor's power and possessions put her in a very dangerous position. When she set out into the French countryside, there was a real danger that she might be kidnapped and forced to marry by men with designs on her kingdom. She had to make her way through the Loire Valley without being recognised or waylaid. If she was going to marry again, this time the decision would be hers.

She settled on Henry Plantagenet. At this time, he was the Duke of Normandy, but his plan to take the throne of England, then occupied by King Stephen, was about to come to fruition. He was younger than Eleanor, but his ambition and fiery temperament matched hers, and her power, standing and renowned beauty were attractive to him. In 1152, Eleanor wrote to Henry and asked him to marry her instead of mounting

> Eleanor of Aquitaine is often credited with creating a Court of Love at Poitiers, although there's no historical evidence to support this

When Eleanor fled to marry Henry, she had to avoid being kidnapped and forcibly married by his brother Geoffrey

ELEANOR OF AQUITAINE
France; England, 1122 - 1204

Brief Bio As Queen Consort of France from 1137 to 1152 and then Queen Consort of England from 1154 to 1189, Eleanor co-ruled some of the most powerful territories in medieval Europe. The beautiful and charismatic queen was a strong leader, but above all she protected the interests of herself and her children.

"Eleanor was a woman of power, pride and ambition who would not let anything stand in the way of the greater good for her or her sons"

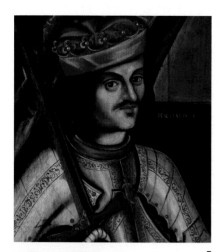

The Third Crusade

Once Richard I took the throne of England, his thoughts turned quickly to the glories of war, and the opportunity arose to prove himself in the Third Crusade. When Saladin, the sultan of Egypt, took Jerusalem in 1187, Richard, Frederick Barbarossa of Germany and King Philip of France joined forces to take back the Holy Land.

Their attack got off to a terrible start when Frederick drowned while crossing a river, prompting much of the German forces to turn back. However, Philip had lost none of his crusading zeal, and led the attack on Acre. A siege ensued, with Richard arriving nearly a year after it began. Brutal, criminal methods of violence were used, including the massacre of 2,600 Muslim prisoners, eventually forcing the city's surrender in 1191. Saladin paid off Richard and Philip not to sack the city, but by this point Philip had lost his enthusiasm and, tired and jealous of his companion, returned home. Richard stayed on until 1192, attacking Jerusalem but he eventually realised that the time had come to leave. He had become aware that John was plotting his downfall at home and, after a final stunning victory at Jaffa, he signed a three-year truce and sailed for England. He left behind a legacy of atrocity, but had created a legend for himself as Richard 'the Lionheart'.

his invasion of England. He hurried to meet her, and they were were wed on 18 May, uniting the kingdoms of Normandy and Aquitaine. She soon became pregnant, and Louis' humiliation would be compounded when Stephen died and Henry was crowned king on 19 December 1154.

The bustling metropolis of London provided Eleanor with culture and entertainment. She had long been renowned for her patronage of the arts, and it was a role she continued to play. Henry was determined to produce heirs, and although her first son, William, died at the tender age of three, she bore four living children by the end of 1158 (Henry, Matilda, William and Geoffrey), and by 1167 she would have a further three (Eleanor, Joan and John). They would be his downfall.

Henry manoeuvred his children like chess pieces, giving and taking away power when it suited him. His eldest, Henry, known as 'the Young King', was vain, proud and easily manipulated. When his father gave Henry's youngest brother John castles that he wanted, Henry left for the court of Louis VII, his father in law.

Richard's rebellion was almost certainly fuelled by his mother. There have been many reasons given as to why Eleanor, who had been at her husband's side for 20 years, would encourage rebellion; his incorrigible cheating, for example (leading to the well-known story of Queen Eleanor and the fair Rosamund). The most likely explanation is that she resented being sidelined, and the fact that Henry clearly wanted control of Aquitaine. The kingdom was owed to Richard, Eleanor's favourite child, and she would do anything to protect his interests.

> Eleanor was a tremendous patron of the arts, and Aquitaine was renowned for its music, art and culture

Eleanor rode out to join her three sons at the court of her first husband from Poitiers. She understood the danger that she was in, and disguised herself as a man in an attempt to avoid recognition. It did not work. She was captured and arrested, and the scandalous news about her open rebellion against her husband became public knowledge. She remained imprisoned at Chinon until the rebellion was over and some months after, and her husband crushed his sons' uprising. In July 1174 he had her moved to Salisbury Castle. Although she was kept comfortable and made the occasional public appearance, she was moved from castle to castle and was not allowed to leave England. Most distressingly, she was not permitted to visit her homeland of Aquitaine.

The years passed, and Henry the Young King continued to prefer the company of foreign monarchs. Henry II attempted to pacify him in 1182 by forcing Richard and Geoffrey to pay homage to him. Richard, now Duke of Aquitaine, refused, and the Young King rebelled. It was a poorly thought-out campaign, ending with his death on 11 June of dysentery. Henry II then requested that Richard give Aquitaine to John. Richard refused once more, and Henry released Eleanor and instructed his son to surrender Aquitaine back to his mother. When Geoffrey died in 1186, his close friend King Philip II of France began to plot war against Henry II. He began negotiating with Richard, and the Duke of Aquitaine did homage to the King of France in 1188. A year later, they attacked Henry's territory together. Stunned, the king acknowledged Richard before his death.

Defining moment
The Second Crusade
1147-49

Eleanor had agreed to provide troops from Aquitaine, but insisted on travelling with them to help treat the wounded. The king grew jealous of her close relationship with her uncle Prince Raymond of Toulouse, who was a far more capable military commander. Rumours sprang up that they were engaged in an incestuous relationship, and her rows with Louis led many to believe that Eleanor was sabotaging the Crusade. In fact, it was Louis who made the final fatal error by insisting that they press on to attack Jerusalem. The assault failed, and so had their marriage.

Timeline

1122

● **Eleanor of Aquitaine is born**
Eleanor is born to William X of Aquitaine and Aenor de Châtellerault, and proves to be intelligent and vivacious. Her mother and older brother both die when she is four, in the process leaving her as the sole inheritor of her father's will.
1122

● **Eleanor marries Louis**
The kingdoms of France and Aquitaine are matched when Eleanor agrees to marry Louis, the son of her guardian and the French King. Louis' father dies days after their marriage, creating a powerful union.
25 July 1137

● **Eleanor marries Henry**
In a move that humiliates Louis, Eleanor marries Henry, his rival and the Duke of Normandy. He is younger than she is, but they share a common ambition, and their united kingdoms are a threat to Louis.
18 May 1152

● **Henry is crowned King**
Eleanor and Henry's powers continue to grow when Henry invades England's territories and King Stephen dies, leading to his coronation as king of England. The kingdoms of Normandy, Aquitaine and England are now united.
25 October 1154

● **Eleanor is imprisoned**
Following her open support of her son's revolution, Henry II keeps Eleanor as his prisoner, rarely allowing her to make appearances at court and forbidding her to leave the country. She is moved from castle to castle.
1174

With Richard now on the throne of England, Eleanor returned to power once more. Richard understood that he was in an unstable situation, and needed someone he could trust to keep a hold of the reins while he was away. Eleanor was the perfect choice. Her years of imprisonment had not dampened her wits, and she remained fiercely protective of her son. Soon after he was crowned on 13 September 1189, Richard joined the Third Crusade with Philip while Eleanor kept a close eye on her ambitious son, John.

Not only did Eleanor watch over her son's kingdom while he was away; she travelled all over Europe to promote their diplomatic interests. She journeyed over the Alps in the depths of winter of 1191 to accompany Berengaria of Navarre from Pamplona to Sicily to marry Richard. Eleanor understood how powerful her reputation was, and took the opportunity to conduct diplomatic business on her travels, impressing foreign courts with her presence.

On her return to England, she had to deal with John. When William Longchamp, the man who

had been left in charge of the country's security, failed in his task, John leapt at the chance to condemn him and was appointed governor in his place. It was only Eleanor's control over her son that kept outright revolution at bay, but Richard was captured while attempting to return home from the Crusades in November 1192. She oversaw the attempts to free her son, including the raising of ransom money, and she delivered the payment in person to Germany. Perhaps more impressively, she convinced the proud Richard to submit to the Emperor as his vassal to secure his freedom.

Having returned, Richard forgave John and secured his allegiance, but tragedy struck when, in 1199, he was mortally wounded at the siege of Châlus-Chabrol castle. Eleanor rode across France to be at her son's deathbed. John was now king of England, and Eleanor did not let his past actions affect her behaviour.

She helped to secure his kingdom by recruiting mercenaries to crush the rebellion of his grandson Arthur, and securing the territories of her son and herself. She continued to travel in the interests of diplomacy, making a final trip to northern Spain, where she had chosen one of her grandchildren to be the bride of King Philip's son, Louis. Eleanor lived to the age of 82, continuing to act in the interests of her son and of Aquitaine. When she died, it was a heavy loss to both. Her fiery temperament and fierce protectiveness of her children had propelled Richard I into power and kept John in it. She had been a diplomat and an icon, a prisoner and a patron of the arts, not to mention the most powerful woman in Europe.

> When Eleanor died in 1204, she had reached the venerable age of 82 and had outlived all but two of her children

Defining moment
Richard is captured
1192
Richard was aware that his journey home from the Third Crusade was not going to be easy. He had caused offence to some of the most powerful men in Europe after denying them spoils and marriage alliances, and his brutal conduct was notorious. His route was cut off at several points, eventually forcing him to disembark in the Adriatic and journey across land. He was caught in Vienna, where Austrian Emperor Leopold sold him to German Emperor Henry VI. He was kept prisoner until 4 February 1194, when Eleanor ransomed him for 100,000 marks.

Life in the time of Eleanor of Aquitaine

Thomas Becket is assassinated
Henry VIII might have severed England's ties with Rome, but Henry II had similar, if less radical, ideas. He wanted England to have more independence from the pope, but Archbishop of Canterbury Thomas Becket refused to sign the legal documents, and their disagreements worsened. On 29 December 1170, Becket was brutally murdered in Canterbury Cathedral.

The first troubadours
The first historical use of the word 'troubadour' is to be found in the 12th century in the Occitan region of southern France. The troubadours were lyrical poets who performed their songs – often at court – about love and chivalry. They have long been associated with Eleanor of Aquitaine.

The Knights Hospitaller
This legendary fighting unit was formed in the final years of the 11th century, and were key to both the Second and Third Crusades. The Knights Hospitaller, or Knights of St John, were monks who would tend to the wounded and dying before becoming their own military and religious order. The three ranks were the brothers infirmarians, brothers chaplains and the military brothers.

First leper hospital
Disease and sickness were terrifying prospects in the Middle Ages, and one of the most terrifying contagions was leprosy. Anyone who became afflicted with the disease was shunned and cast out of the city, but there were exceptions. The first recorded leper hospital was St George's outside of Copenhagen, where it operated from 1109 until 1609.

The longbow is developed
Warfare and its technology underwent a revolution during the 12th century, from Japan, where the Samurai pledged to serve the Shogun, to Wales. It there that historians believe the first longbow was invented, which would in later years prove crucial in England's wars against the French.

Henry demands return of Aquitaine
When Richard refuses to give Aquitaine to his brother John, Henry knows he will only listen to one person: his mother. Eleanor is forced to request for the return of Aquitaine, to which her son reluctantly agrees.
1183

Richard is crowned
Eleanor makes a triumphant return to the political arena when Henry II dies, allowing the ferocious Richard to claim the crown for himself. She looks on proudly as her favourite son takes control of the realm.
6 July 1189

Eleanor transports Berengia of Navarre
Eleanor proves invaluable to Richard, her diplomacy and reputation counter-balancing his warmongering. She agrees to transport Berengaria of Navarre across the Alps to marry her son.
1191

Richard dies
After all of her efforts to keep his kingdom out of John's hands and free him from his German prison, Richard is killed while laying siege to a castle. Eleanor hurries to his deathbed, and is with him when he dies.
6 April 1199

Eleanor is captured outside Poitiers
Despite her age, Eleanor is vital to John's reign as King, touring Europe on diplomatic missions. She is captured outside Poitiers by his enemies, but her son hurries to her aid and frees her.
1199

1204
Eleanor dies
At the age of 82, Eleanor dies at Fontevraud Abbey, where she had become a nun. She is buried there alongside her second husband and her favourite son, leaving behind her legacy as the most powerful woman in Europe.
1204

1157 – 1199
King Richard the Lionheart

Richard the Lionheart was the most famous Christian king of the Medieval period, waging a religious war against the Muslim East, attempting to conquer the Holy Land and Kingdom of Jerusalem

One of the most bloodthirsty, tactically astute and arguably wise kings that England ever saw, King Richard I - famously known as Richard the Lionheart - took the military might of the Medieval Christian West into the heart of the Islamic East in order to re-conquer the Holy Land (Palestine) from the Sultan of Syria, Saladin. Indeed, with his Third Crusade - often referred to as 'Richard's Crusade' - the English King led literally thousands of knights thousands of miles into a territory that had long been fraught with religious tension and then, through a series of military victories, heightened those further, cutting a hole not just through the rival troops of Saladin but also through Islam itself.

For Richard though, the quest to the Holy Land was but part of a life that was characterised by conflict and combat, with him born into one of the most infamous dynasties in Europe, the House of Plantagenet. Son of King Henry II of England and Eleanor of Aquitaine, Richard was born into a family famous for feuding, with his father's legacy of fighting with all and sundry, including his own

wife who he ended up imprisoning in a house-arrest situation due to her strong influence over not just his sons but also many of the barons and nobility in England and specifically France. As such, it is no surprise that during his early years not only did he fight against his father but also, following the pair briefly reconciling, against his father's kingdom's own barons he put down a series of revolts.

Indeed, by the time Richard successfully took down the supposedly impregnable fortress of Taillebourg in the spring of 1179 while fighting rebels, he had won a reputation as a highly skilled military commander and fierce combatant, with an infamous reputation of cruelty and brutality against anyone who stood against him. His hunger for conquest however did not stop in defeating rebels; soon after the revolts had been quelled Richard challenging his father for the throne. This led Richard to end up not just fighting his father but also his brothers, with only the passing of his older brothers Henry and Geoffrey as well as eventually his father allowing him to ascend as King.

"He led thousands of knights thousands of miles into a territory that had long been fraught with religious tension"

RICHARD I
England, 1157 - 1199

Brief Bio
Nicknamed 'the Lionheart' for his ferocity and faith, the son of Henry II and Eleanor of Aquitaine was obsessed with the Crusades, prosecuting a holy war in the Middle East to achieve Christian control of the Holy Land, particularly Jerusalem. He figures in many myths, notably *Robin Hood*.

Having been born in England, Richard was officially invested as Duke of Normandy and then crowned King of England on 3 September 1189 at Westminster Abbey. Now finally free from the constraints of fighting his family and the rebels in his territories in England and France, Richard was free to undertake what had, since 1187 when he had taken the Christian cross as Count of Poitou (something he had done to renounce his past wickedness) and Saladin had taken Jerusalem, been his primary aim, retake the Holy Land from the Muslamic infidels. The problem was, while Richard's will and desire for combat was unabated by years of conflict, his inherited kingdom was not, with the royal coffers largely empty.

Richard therefore immediately set about raising the necessary funds to launch his own crusader army. Firstly, he agreed with King Philip II of France to undertake the crusade jointly – with both leaders scared that if one left Europe then the other would invade his territories – and then proceeded to raise taxes in England, free King William I of Scotland from his oath of subservience in exchange for 10,000 marks, and sell much land and property, with the proceeds being funnelled into assembling an army of 4,000 knights, 4,000 foot-soldiers and a huge fleet of ships. At one point Richard reportedly said that 'I would have sold London if I could find a buyer', so determined was he to proceed on the Third Crusade. This large army was to travel with Phillip's to Palestine and retake Jerusalem at any cost. Boarding his flagship, Richard I left England in the summer of 1190.

As can be seen in greater detail in the column on the right, his passage to the Holy Land was eventful, with him first stopping in Sicily – where he famously freed his sister from the usurper King Tancred I – but then also conquered the entirety of the island nation of Cyprus, overthrowing the despot ruler Isaac Komnenos and installing Richard de Camville and Robert of Thornham as its governors (interestingly he later sold the island to the Knights Templar, where it was then sold to Guy of Lusignan, one of Richard's fellow crusaders). Indeed, while as we shall see, Richard made many conquests in the Holy Land, his capturing of Cyprus not only greatly added to his reputation but was also strategically incredibly important, allowing the waters on the approach to Palestine to be controlled by Christian forces.

"His capturing of Cyprus not only greatly added to his reputation but was also incredibly strategically important"

Despite multiple conquests and himself even getting married on his journey into the East, Richard eventually arrived in the Holy Land at the city of Acre on 8 June 1191. He immediately joined forces with Guy of Lusignan and Conrad of Montferrat and took the city in the now-famous 1191 Siege of Acre. As his and his allies' flags were raised above the city, Richard's Crusade had well and truly begun, with what was to be the first of several victorious conquests now firmly under his belt. Buoyed by his victory, Richard soon left Acre and marched south with his Crusader army, fearing that if Jerusalem was to be taken then this military momentum needed to be maintained.

Momentum was indeed maintained thanks to Richard's leadership, with victory both in the Battle of Arsuf and at Beit Nuba, leaving the Crusader army a mere 12 miles from their ultimate destination of Jerusalem. By this point, Richard's multiple victories had left morale in Saladin's forces low and it has since been postulated that if the army had directly besieged the city it would have fallen to them quickly. However, news of a possible Muslim relief army and poor weather led to Richard ordering the army to retreat back toward the coast, with him fearing that if they tried to take the city right now they might become trapped and wiped out. Returning to the captured city of Ascalon, Richard fortified his position. It was here where he would make the first of multiple negotiations with Saladin, however at this stage they were unsuccessful, with the invasion still fresh.

The lion roars: Richard's top five victories

Messina (4 October 1190)

Arriving in Sicily to see his sister, Queen Joan, freed from prison, he proceeded to attack and capture the historic city of Messina. After looting it of every penny and burning it to the ground, Richard set up his base there, eventually forcing Joan's captor Tancred to sign a treaty ensuring Joan's release, an inheritance of 20,000 ounces of gold, and his nephew Arthur of Brittany enshrined as Tancred's heir. Richard proceeded to spend much of the year in Sicily.

Cyprus (1 May 1191)

Heading for Acre, a storm disrupted it and many ships landed on the south coast of Cyprus. Cyprus' despot ruler Isaac Komnenos proceeded to take Richard's sister prisoner. Richard, having finally discovered the stricken ships, arrived at the port of Lemesos and demanded his troops and sister to be released. Komnenos refused and so Richard landed his army, took the port and then the entire island nation, capturing Isaac and placing him in silver chains (the chains were silver as he promised not to place him in irons).

Acre (July 1191)

After landing in the Holy Land on 8 June, two weeks after his travelling companion Philip of Alsace, Richard proceeded to join him in the now famous siege of Acre. Richard finally secured the city's surrender on 12 July after weeks of combat, with the Christian troops entering the city and imprisoning the Muslim garrison. Richard, along with fellow Crusader Conrad of Montferrat, raised the banners of the Kingdom of Jerusalem, France, England and the Duchy of Austria.

Arsuf (7 September 1191)

Having left Acre, Richard proceeded south and was engaged by Saladin's forces at Arsuf in Palestine. Following a series of attacks by Saladin's forces, Richard charged the main body of Saladin's troops in a bold counter attack that broke their ranks. Importantly, while this victory gained Richard no resources, it did result in the coastal area of southern Palestine falling to him, making an assault on Jerusalem possible.

Jaffa (8 August 1192)

Richard lead a daring assault on the besieged city of Jaffa, which had been taken a month earlier by Saladin. Leading just 54 knights, a few hundred infantry and about 2,000 crossbowmen into battle, Richard caused the city's Muslim garrison to panic and then flee from the city, with Saladin himself unable to regroup them until they were five miles away. Saladin attempted a counter-attack, but it was in vain, his forces exhausted from years of warfare. After this battle that a peace treaty was agreed on by Richard and Saladin.

In June of 1192, Richard's Crusader army once more advanced towards Jerusalem, an action catalysed by the assassination of Conrad of Montferrat by the Hashshashin, an elite group of Islamic assassins. This time the Crusader army came in sight of the great city, however, due to disagreements between its component leaders on how best to proceed - Richard and the bulk of the crusading leaders wanted to force Saladin to hand over Jerusalem by attacking his base of power in Egypt, while the French Duke of Burgundy wished to make a direct attack on the city - they were once more forced to make a tactical retreat. Saladin attempted to punish the crusader's indecision by attacking them in a series of harassing running engagements, however the army stood strong and following another decisive victory at the Battle of Jaffa on 8 August 1192, both Saladin's and Richard's armies were heavily depleted.

A stalemate of inactivity ensued, with both Richard and Saladin realising their positions within Palestine were fragile and that continued fighting was unattainable. Another bout of negotiations between the two leaders proceeded and - as can be seen in greater detail in 'Richard VS Saladin: An Eternal War' to the right - finally a peace treaty was agreed upon on 2 September 1192. The treaty decreed that Richard would not take Jerusalem, however Christian pilgrims and merchants would be now free to enter the Muslim-held city as they wished completely lawfully. This would be how the Third Christian Crusade would come to an end, with Richard soon after departing the Holy Land for his homeland.

The story of Richard's Crusade, however, was not quite over with his departure from Palestine. His ship wrecked near Aquileia, Italy, and forced him to return over land through central Europe. It was during this land voyage that, as he passed by Vienna shortly before Christmas 1192, he was captured by the forces of Leopold V, Duke of Austria, who accused Richard of arranging the murder of his cousin Conrad of Montferrat by assassins back in the Holy Land. Richard proclaimed his innocence, but it was ignored by the Duke and Richard was imprisoned in Dürnstein Castle by the Duke, an action that saw him excommunicated by the pope. Regardless of the excommunication, Leopold V handed Richard over to Henry VI, the Holy Roman Emperor, who then

Richard vs Saladin: An Eternal War

Richard's crusade was one of the most personal of all, with what began as a duel of religions evolving into one between two of history's greatest leaders

While the Third Crusade was in fact one of the most complicated in terms of participants, with everyone from Philip II of France through to the Italian Conrad of Monteferrat and Guy of Luisgnan taking up arms to take the Holy Land, it was largely determined and eventually ended by just two men, King Richard I of England and Sultan of Syria Saladin. Indeed, some with the pair directing troops from afar, Richard and Saladin clashed more than ten times during the Third Crusade, with both taking or retaking territory in a continuous tug of war throughout the Palestine region. In the Battles of Arsuf and Jaffa both men were active participants in the field, with both winning much renown for their personal combat prowess.

Interestingly, however, while both Richard and Saladin spent much of the Third Crusade directing combat against each other, they were reportedly also great admirers of each other's abilities and met multiple times during the hostilities in attempts to negotiate

over matters. In fact, it was through one of these negotiations after the Battle of Jaffa that the Third Crusade finally came to an end, with Richard agreeing to demilitarise Christian-controlled regions and Saladin ensuring that Christian pilgrims and merchants could have access to Jerusalem. Military historians often point to Richard and Saladin's relationship as a key factor in more bloodshed not being spilt, arguably without their work the Third Crusade would have been prolonged.

As a footnote, little more than six months after Richard the Lionheart left the Holy Land after the two great men had agreed on a peace treaty, Saladin died of fever on 4 March 1193 in Damascus. As with Richard, who would return slowly to his homeland without wealth or ceremony, Saladin himself died with only one piece of gold and 40 pieces of silver to his name, the rest given away to his subjects or spent on the proceeding years of war. Clearly, for peace – no matter how temporary – it was a price worth paying.

Timeline

1157

Richard born
Richard is born at Beaumont Palace, Oxford, England as the son of King Henry II and Eleanor of Aquitaine. He is one of four brothers including Henry, Geoffrey and John.
8 September 1157

Aquitaine gained
Following him turning ten, Richard is invested with the duchy of Aquitaine and then, four years later, the duchy of Poitiers.
1168

Richard argues
After arguing with his brothers, Richard joins his forces with those of his father to subdue Henry, Geoffrey and their rebelling barons.
1179

Henry dies
Henry II's rightful heir to the throne - Henry the Young King - dies of dysentery, leaving Richard to become the rightful heir. Three years later Richard's other brother, Geoffrey, dies in a tournament.
1183

Richard crowned
Following the death of Henry II at Chateau Chinon, Richard is crowned King in Westminster Abbey, England.
3 September 1189

Fire sale
Having heard of Saladin's capture of Jerusalem, Richard begins raising funds for his crusade by selling off castles and territory in his control.
11 December 1189

"Returning to England, Richard found that his brother had tried to take the throne with the help of the French King Philip"

held him to ransom, demanding 150,000 marks for Richard's release.

His mother, Eleanor of Aquitaine proceeded to raise the large sum, though it took almost two years, with Richard only finally being freed on 4 February 1194. Upon returning to England and France, Richard found that his brother John had tried to take the throne with the help of French King Philip and that much of his territory in Normandy had been taken. He immediately began a campaign of reconquest, forming an alliance against King Philip and then beating him in multiple battles throughout the 1190s, the most famous being the Battle of Gisors, a conflict in which Richard coined the now famous motto of the British monarchy 'Dieu et mon Droit', which

translates as 'God and my Right', an indication that the monarch only answers to God.

As is related in 'Death in his mother's arms' to the right, this new campaign of conquest would end with Richard's own death, which came from a very unlikely source. Regardless though, upon his death his was eventually succeeded by his brother John, who would proceed to lose almost all of Richard's territory in mainland Europe and then go on to lose much more power by losing the First Baron's War in 1217, the latter leading to the creation of the Magna Carta. Indeed, following Richard's death on 6 April 1199, no king of England ever held as much power or territory than he did during his reign.

So what of Richard's legacy? One of the most powerful Kings of England in the country's long history, Richard was born into a firmly established - albeit warring - empire where the monarch's position as ruler was unquestionable. He was, as he said himself, answerable to no one but the Christian God and held the military might and privilege to do as he wished on Earth. Despite the romance surrounding his famous Crusade, as well as the scandalous family politics that coloured his life and his favourable rule when compared to his brother John, it can be easily argued that the legacy left by Richard is not a positive one, with him spending vast sums of his subjects' money on a series of wars either for his own personal gain or in the pursuit of religious zealotry and intolerance.

But perhaps that is to look upon Richard's actions with a modern perspective, one that is wholly unsuitable to decode the motives and mindset of the Medieval world. There is no doubt about it, life and death were very much part of the same blade during Richard's rule, with those who did not adequately defend themselves put to the sword for no fault of their own aside from that they stood in someone else's way. Regardless of his legacy though, one thing is clear, Richard's actions had a marked effect not just on Europe but on the western Middle East too, one that can still be seen today if you look in the right places.

Crusaders under Richard I gain sight of Jerusalem, though they were unable to seize it from the Saracens

Crusade begins
King Richard finally embarks on his crusade, setting sail for the Holy Land. His first port of call is Sicily, arriving at Messina two months later.
4 July 1190

Queen maker
King Richard marries Queen Berengaria of Navarre, the first-born daughter of King Sancho VI of Navarre at Lemesos, Cyprus.
12 May 1191

Richard captured
After travelling back from his crusade, Richard is captured by the Duke of Austria, who he had supposedly offended during the Siege of Acre. He pays a ransom and is freed.
1192

Richard dies
At the age of just 42, Richard the Lionheart dies at Chalus. His body is buried at Fontevraud Abbey in Anjou, while his heart is buried in Rouen in Normandy.
6 April 1199

Rebel sigil
Much of Hotspur's forces - most noticeably the archers - were recruited from Cheshire, an area hostile to King Henry due to its loyalty to the former king Richard II.

Royal forces
The victory at Shrewsbury was a decisive one for King Henry, marking the end of the biggest challenge to his reign and giving his rule a welcome degree of credibility.

Ruthless fighting
The fighting between the two sides was brutal and fierce, with former allies being forced into battle with each other. Amid a near constant hail of arrows, the death toll was heavy on both sides.

Hotspur

Hotspur was killed after being brought down in a last-ditch charge aimed at killing the king. In the melee that followed, no one knows who struck the decisive blow.

1367 – 1413

Henry IV
and the
Battle of
Shrewsbury

How did this close-fought battle legitimise the rule of Henry IV?

HENRY IV
England, 1367-1413

Brief Bio

The tenth king of England from the House of Plantagenet, Henry seized control from Richard II but found his own reign plagued by other upstarts, eager to do for him what he had done for the previous king: depose him, preferably violently. In the Battle of Shrewsbury he saw off a challenge from the fiery young Henry Hotspur, son of Henry Percy, the First Earl of Northumberland.

Perhaps ironically considering that his reign began with the seizure of the crown from the sovereign monarch, Henry IV of England's kingship was an insecure one. He was beset by rebellions from those who were either dissatisfied with his rule, believed themselves to be more credible claimants to the throne, or who saw the precedent that he started as part of a new status quo; one that allowed for the strongest to seize power, with birthright having been reduced – by virtue of Henry's original rebellious act – to a mere technicality.

The event that came the closest to putting a premature end to Henry's rule was the Battle of Shrewsbury, the culmination of a rebellion by the Percy family: chiefly Thomas Percy, the Earl of Worcester; his elder brother Henry Percy, the Earl of Northumberland; and his nephew, Henry 'Hotspur' Percy. Having assisted Henry with his successful overthrow of Richard II in 1399, the Percys found themselves increasingly dissatisfied with Henry's rule, in large part to his refusal to lend them sufficient funds to defend their lands against the Scots in the north (due to the parlous state of the royal treasury) or to grant them additional titles or lands, with one noteworthy sticking point being when the king gave the justiciarship of Wales – previously in the possession of Northumberland and Hotspur – to his son, Prince Henry, the future Henry V.

Allying themselves with Owen Glendower, the Welsh leader who was in open rebellion against English rule at the time, Hotspur gathered his forces from nearby Cheshire – including a large force of archers – and marched south towards Shrewsbury, where he planned to meet forces led by Northumberland and Glendower. However, Henry heard about the attack, and immediately mobilised his forces, sending a small force ahead to hold the town, along with a group led by Prince Henry, while the rest of his army marched towards Shrewsbury from the east. When Hotspur arrived, not only did he find the town held against him, but with the king coming from the east, he was caught between the town, the nearby river and an army, effectively cutting him off from Glendower's reinforcements and leaving him with little choice but to choose a place of attack.

With the primary aim of the rebels being to kill Henry himself, he disguised two knights in his own attire as diversions. Even with this clever precaution, however, the battle was closely fought, with the rebels getting the better of the early stages thanks to the devastating attacks from their archers, which decimated and scattered the royal vanguard. Despite this, a two-pronged attack from father and son turned the battle in their favour, forcing Hotspur into a desperate last-ditch charge at the King that resulted in his own death.

With the rebel leader dead and his surviving forces fled, the most serious challenge to Henry's rule was at an end. His rule had been legitimised, and his son's military prowess, later to achieve legendary status at the Battle of Agincourt, became clear for everyone to see. The Earl of Northumberland would later make another attempt at rebellion in the Battle of Bramham Moor in 1408, which also resulted in his defeat and death.

Royalists

TROOPS 14,000

INFANTRY 12,000

ARCHERS 2,000

HENRY IV OF ENGLAND

LEADER

Having usurped Richard II as king of England, Shrewsbury would prove to be the biggest challenge to his rule.

Strengths Strong and capable.

Weakness Unable to mobilise as many men as he'd have liked.

DISGUISED KNIGHT

KEY UNIT

One of Henry's strategies was an attempt to focus enemy attention elsewhere, prompting him to disguise two knights as him.

Strengths An effective decoy for the king.

Weakness Only effective as long as they're alive; potential for enemy to see through the ruse quickly.

SWORD

KEY WEAPON

The standard weapon for the royal infantry, it was interchangeable with other pole-type weapons, like bills or daggers.

Strengths Highly versatile.

Weakness Required high amounts of skill to wield effectively.

01 Spies observe Hotspur at Berwick Field

Hotspur based his army on a low hill in a predominantly open area sown with peas. The pea stems were wound together in order to trip up advancing horses and men.

02 The king marches

Henry and his army marched in formation, divided into two battalions: the vanguard (including the archers) were led by the Earl of Stafford, with the king in charge of the main army, and his son Prince Henry joining with another force from the south.

03 Final attempts at negotiations

Henry offered the rebels a chance at safe conduct if they could work things out, but the Earl of Worcester, sent in Hotspur's stead, refused to negotiate.

04 Initial assault

The Stafford-led Royal vanguard led the assault. Despite incurring heavy casualties from the rebel archers, the vanguard managed to engage them in contact after the archers ran out of arrows, thus sapping their strength. Regardless, the king's men were beaten back and retreated, with Stafford being killed in the process.

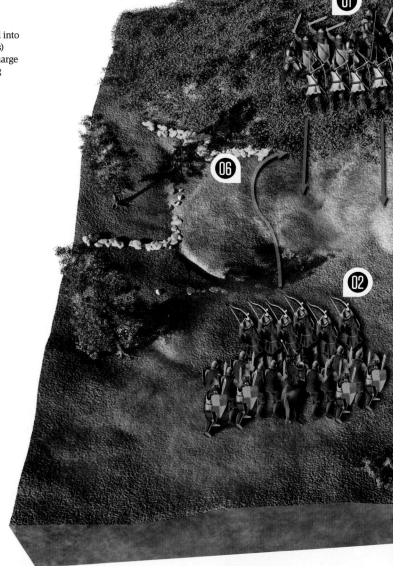

05 Henry attacks

With much of the vanguard either killed or deserted and the rebel forces pressing the attack, it fell to Henry to lead the assault. On his mark, his trumpeters gave the signal for the main bulk of his army to charge, with Henry leading the assault, meeting the rebel forces at the bottom of the slope. The fighting here was especially fierce, with the king being the main target of the rebels' attacks.

06 Prince attacks on flank

At the same time as the main assault, the king ordered Prince Henry to attack Hotspur's army on the flanks in order to divert the destructive archers from the main force. The attack went well, weakening Henry's forces and decimating the archers. However, the prince was grievously injured when an enemy arrow struck him in the face and penetrated his skull just below his visor, although he would ultimately recover from this wound.

Rebels

10 Rebels retreat

Leaderless and conscious of the lack of mercy they would receive in a land in which they were now defeated traitors, the rebel forces fled, with the wounded left behind being dispatched by the royalist forces.

09 Hotspur killed

Although they mowed down many men, Hotspur's charge was gradually slowed among the masses, and he was cut down from his horse and killed. The rebels initially thought they'd killed the king after slaying his standard bearer, but Henry revealed himself to proclaim that "Harry Percy is dead."

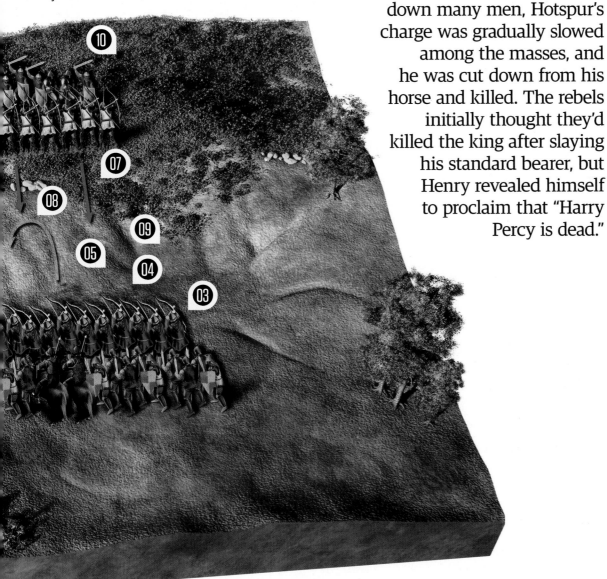

08 Dunbar orders king to fall back

In the nick of time, Henry's close ally, the Earl of Dunbar, realised what was about to happen. Subsequently, he shouted at the king to fall back, which he did, in the process narrowly avoiding being caught up and killed in the inexorable charge of Hotspur and his men.

07 Hotspur charges towards the king

With his forces rapidly diminishing and archers faltering under the two-pronged assault from the royalist forces, Hotspur decided that desperate times called for desperate measures. After gathering 30 of his most trusted men, including the Earl of Douglas and his uncle, the Earl of Worcester, they mounted their horses and charged directly at Henry's men, with the aim of cutting the king himself down.

TROOPS 14,000

INFANTRY 13,000

ARCHERS 1,000

HENRY 'HOTSPUR' PERCY

LEADER

The primary leader of the rebel forces, Hotspur led his forces into battle against the king.
Strengths Well-trained archers.
Weakness Lacking expected support from Glendower and Northumberland.

ARCHERS

KEY UNIT

Large quantities of archers comprised both forces, but it was arguably Hotspur who used his to the most effect.
Strengths Devastating in large numbers.
Weakness Vulnerable once arrows have been used up.

BOW AND ARROW

KEY WEAPON

A weapon that has lived on in folklore, at short range arrows could penetrate armour, and had a killing range of about half a mile.
Strengths Long range and difficult to defend against.
Weakness Requires large supply of arrows.

1386 – 1422
Henry V
and the
Battle of
Agincourt

Discover how Agincourt proved to be Henry V's defining moment

While his father, Henry IV, had been preoccupied with consolidating - and in the process effectively legitimising - his rule, his son, King Henry V of England, saw the opportunity to expand England's empire by taking back lands which he believed belonged to him, starting with France.

In 1415, he proposed to marry Catherine, the daughter of the French king Charles VI, in addition to audaciously demanding the handover of the Plantagenet lands of Normandy and Anjou as his dowry. Unsurprisingly, Charles refused this offer from the upstart young king, with one account claiming that he sent the young Henry a case of tennis balls - the upshot being that his time would be better spent playing games than attempting to invade France.

Unperturbed, Henry set sail for France, determined to capture the throne for himself. As well as the prospect of regaining the lost lands of his ancestors, success abroad would have the effect of galvanising support back home, and in the process focus attention away from his cousins' royal ambitions.

His success was almost instant. Upon landing, he captured the port of Harfleur, although while on the way to the port of Calais, he found his path blocked by an army that substantially outnumbered his own. Faced with this much-larger French army, he nonetheless put his tactical acumen to good use, decimating the French forces via the use of vast quantities of longbow archers to devastating effect. Between 7,500 and 10,000 French soldiers are estimated to have been killed according to various accounts, with about 1,500 noblemen taken prisoner, while the English forces' casualties are numbered at around 112, with high-ranking noblemen like the Duke of York and the Earl of Suffolk being counted among the dead. Even more French prisoners were originally taken, but in a show of calculated - but arguably justifiable - ruthlessness, Henry had ordered many of them to be put to death in order to avoid the possibility of them linking up with the remnants of the French forces.

Proving that this was no fluke, Henry followed up this stunning victory with the conquest of Normandy - a campaign that lasted for three years. By June 1419, Henry controlled most of Normandy. Agincourt had not only been a military triumph; it had been a moral victory too, galvanising the English both abroad and at home.

Facing defeat, Charles agreed to the Treaty of Troyes, which formally recognised Henry as the heir to the French throne - at the expense of his own son - and finally allowed Henry to marry Catherine. Flushed with success, in February 1421 he returned to England for the first time in three and a half years as a hero. His successful conquest of much of the his country's hated enemy had made him a hero back home, and the Battle of Agincourt in particular would forever serve as a poignant example of his strength and ingenuity in battle - yet another example of the plucky underdog spirit and ability to triumph against the odds that future British forces would demonstrate again and again.

Front line
The English front line consisted mainly of dismounted knights and men-at-arms. Out of shot, archers were posited either side, hiding in the woods that bordered the battlefield.

King Henry
Unlike the French king, Henry personally led his troops into battle. He was a king first and foremost but never stopped being a warrior - even on his deathbed he insisted on being carried to the next siege.

Crown
Unlike his father, who used decoys at the Battle of Shrewsbury years earlier, Henry's affixing of a crown on top of his helmet made sure he stood out. The crown was damaged in the battle after he took an axe blow to the head.

Prayer
While lined up for battle, Henry led his troops in prayer, asking for God to grant them victory against the French forces.

HENRY V
England, 1386 – 1422

Brief Bio
The hero of the Battle of Agincourt, Henry V believed that France was legitimately his and set out to get it, despite being heavily outnumbered. He achieved a decisive victory, winning lands and the hand of the King's daughter in marriage, but his early death curtailed his vision of an entirely English France.

English

TROOPS 6-9,000
LONGBOWMEN 5,000
KNIGHTS/MEN-AT-
ARMS 1,000

KING HENRY V
LEADER

The King was a skilled battle commander, leading his troops into battle and fighting alongside them.
Strengths Brave and experienced military leader.
Weakness His forces were numerically inferior to those of the French aggressors.

LONGBOWMAN
KEY UNIT

The effectiveness of the English longbowmen played a massive part in the success of the battle.
Strengths Long range and difficult to attack.
Weakness Relatively poorly armoured and vulnerable if attacked.

LONGBOW
KEY WEAPON

The longbow's six arrows per minute could wound at 400 yards, kill at 200 and even penetrate armour at 100 yards.
Strengths Accurate and destructive in large numbers.
Weakness Finite number of arrows available to them.

01 Camping for the night

On 24 October, about 30 miles from Calais in the town of Frévent, English scouts reported that an immense French army was blocking the road ahead. Seeing that they could not pass without meeting them in battle, Henry ordered his forces to camp there for the night.

02 Taking their positions

The English positioned themselves across the road to Calais in three groups of knights and men-at-arms: the right side led by Lord Camoys, the left by Sir Thomas Erpingham and the Duke of York in the centre. The French had the Constable of France leading the first line, the Dukes of Bar and d'Alencon the second and the Counts of Merle and Falconberg in charge of the third.

03 Forward banners

Bored of waiting for the French to begin the attack, Henry ordered his troops to advance. Once within range of the French archers, the English troops halted, the divisions closed, and the archers set a series of pointed stakes in the ground, forming a fence. Within the woods surrounding the two armies, Henry directed groups of archers and men-at-arms to move through the trees to get closer to the French.

04 Arrows away

Shortly after, Henry gave the order for his archers to shoot the French, who were massed together in a big, unwieldy group. Taken by surprise, the French forces incurred very heavy casualties.

05 French attempt to move forward

After the shock of this assault, the French forces tried to advance in order to take the battle to the English. However, having already suffered massive casualties, they were impeded by the dead and dying horses and men already shot down in front of them. Reduced to walking pace, they were easily picked off by the English archers concealed in the woodlands on the flanks.

10 French camp ransacked

With the battle over and any local resistance crushed, the English troops ransacked the largely abandoned French camp, having secured a victory that would live on in legend.

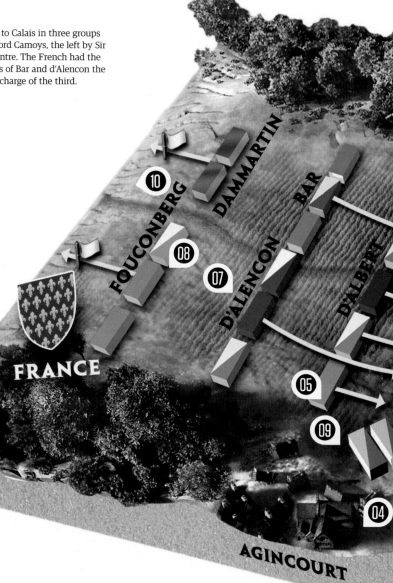

06 Archers join the fray and flanks

With the battle continuing along the fence of stakes, the English archers abandoned their positions and joined the knights in fighting against the French cavalry forces – most of which had been forced to dismount – which were reinforced by soldiers attacking on the flanks.

09 Local French force attacks baggage

Although the main battle was over, it threatened to reignite when a local French force circumvented the forest and attacked the English baggage. Fearing the substantial amount of prisoners would rebel and join this assault, Henry ordered them executed - which many were, until the attack was repelled.

07 French second line moves forward

The French second line, led by D'Alencon, moved forward in earnest to assist the beleaguered first line, but was overwhelmed in a similar fashion. Seeing the futility in continuing, he attempted to surrender to Henry, but was killed before he could reach the King.

08 Third line retreats

Seeing the fate that had met the first and second waves, the third line of the French forces waited on the edge of the field, pondering whether to join. After being greeted by a messenger sent by Henry, who informed them that if they joined the battle, none of them would be spared, they made their decision. Unsurprisingly, considering their options, they left the battlefield.

France

TROOPS 12-36,000
CAVALRY 1,200
KNIGHTS 8,800

CHARLES D'ALBRET
LEADER

The former Constable of France co-commanded the French army alongside Jean le Maingre.
Strengths Experienced soldier.
Weakness Low social rank, so orders were ignored by noblemen.

KNIGHTS
KEY UNIT

Much of the French forces consisted of heavy infantry, making them tough adversaries in open combat.
Strengths Heavily armoured and effective at hand-to-hand fighting.
Weakness Slow, cumbersome and easy to pick off by enemy archers.

HORSES
KEY WEAPON

Large numbers of knights on horseback often presented a fearful sight for their opponents.
Strengths Fast and powerful opponents in battle.
Weakness Cramped and boggy location made them useless.

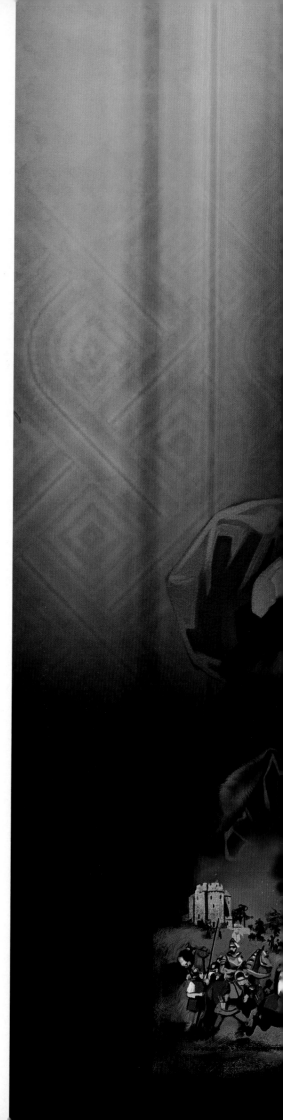

1491 – 1547
Henry VIII the Warlord

In pursuing dreams of victory in France, Henry threw England into decades of war and the chaos of a Europe in conflict

Henry VIII was born dreaming of war. When he took the throne in April 1509, with his bride Catherine of Aragon at his side, Henry knew exactly what kind of king he wanted to be. His would be a glorious reign that would restore England to the magnificence it deserved. His father, Henry VII, had become unpopular by levying punishing taxes to restore the country's finances, but the new king had no intention of focusing on matters as petty as the treasury. He would be a conqueror.

By the end of his life, Henry was a bloated and frustrated mockery of the athletic youth that he had once been. He had grown up jousting, riding and hunting, and would often participate in chivalry tournaments in disguise. He had grown up hearing the stories of the great Henry V - the hero of Agincourt - and had dreamed of the battles that years of peace had deprived him of. He was determined that he would repeat his ancestor's triumphs in France and expand England's territory beyond Calais - perhaps even as far as Paris. He wholly believed that France belonged to him and

"By the end of his life, Henry was a bloated and frustrated mockery of the athletic youth that he had once been"

HENRY VIII
English, 1491-1547

Brief Bio

As king, Henry spent lavishly, courted conflict and pursued his own leisurely interests. His most enduring legacy is that, to annul his marriage to Catherine of Aragon, Henry separated England from the Catholic church. However, he is still better known for his six wives and how he rid himself of five.

- fortunately for the English monarch - he did not have to wait long to stake his claim.

Henry had grown up in years of stultifying peace thanks to his father's treaties with France and Aragon in Spain. Meanwhile, just across the Channel, the continent was in the throes of war. The powers of Europe clashed over the possession of Naples, essentially turning Italy into one big battleground. A quarrel over the region of Romagna had set Venice against the Vatican, and so Pope Julius II rallied France, the Holy Roman Empire and Spain (under Ferdinand II) in the final weeks of 1508, planning to split the Venetian territories among them.

Venice fell, but Julius feared French occupation of Italy. He mounted an impulsive attack on his allies which backfired as French forces stormed south in retaliation. A terrified Julius formed the Holy League, and Spain and the Holy Roman Empire sided with the papacy in 1511.

Henry VIII had now been on the throne for two years with his queen Catherine of Aragon (Ferdinand's daughter) at his side. A strong royal family was vital to his dream of a glorious England and he announced that he would marry her shortly after his father died. Catherine was fiercely loyal and determined to meet her king's expectations. She became pregnant almost immediately but their child was stillborn. It was a matter of weeks until Catherine was with child again, and she gave birth to a son, Henry, on New Year's Day, 1511. Sadly, Henry would survive for just seven weeks.

At this point, Henry was a young king just beginning his reign. He was the head of a proud royal family and he had shown his subjects that he

"Wolsey was the perfect right-hand man, able to counterbalance the king's violent rages with his own skilled diplomacy"

was not the penny-pinching tyrant that his father was. The Holy League would enable him to serve his God and show France the power of England's might. The full force of that might would be delivered by Henry's expanding Royal Navy, which would boast the world's largest and most advanced warships. It is important not to underestimate the importance of the pope's blessing. He was still a devout Catholic and would go on to condemn the Protestant Martin Luther so harshly that the pope would give him the title 'Defender of the Faith'. His religion also included the concept of Divine Right; France was his God-given property. The Holy League should have been undefeatable.

However, the first attack ended in disaster. An English force sailed to Gascony in June 1512, due to meet up with Ferdinand's army and claim the region of Aquitaine for Henry. Unfortunately, Ferdinand decided that he was more interested in claiming Navarre for

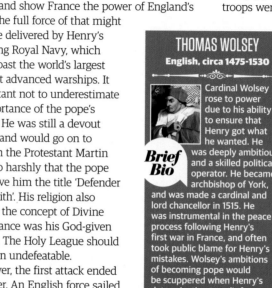

THOMAS WOLSEY
English, circa 1475-1530

Brief Bio

Cardinal Wolsey rose to power due to his ability to ensure that Henry got what he wanted. He was deeply ambitious and a skilled political operator. He became archbishop of York, and was made a cardinal and lord chancellor in 1515. He was instrumental in the peace process following Henry's first war in France, and often took public blame for Henry's mistakes. Wolsey's ambitions of becoming pope would be scuppered when Henry's determination to split from Catherine of Aragon destroyed England's relationship with Rome. Scrabbling to reconcile his position in Rome with his duty to his king, Wolsey's failure to deliver papal approval would prove to be his downfall.

himself and directed his troops in that direction. Ill-equipped and ravaged by dysentery, the English troops were forced to retreat. Henry was furious but resolute.

Less than a year later, a second invasion plan was underway, with much of the organisation left in the hands of the invaluable Cardinal Thomas Wolsey. Wolsey was the perfect right-hand man for a king like Henry, able to counterbalance the king's violent rages with his own skilled diplomacy while sharing a similarly rabid ambition. Wolsey was a fixer; he made sure that whatever Henry wanted, Henry got. What Henry wanted was France, and so, in April 1513, an army was raised and an attack was made on Brest.

This incursion proved even more disastrous than the attempt on Aquitaine, but Henry would not be dissuaded and personally accompanied the English landing at Calais in June. With his feet on French soil and standing at the

Debacle at Gascony
June 1512

Henry's only concern prior to the expedition to Gascony was that he couldn't be there. It was the first attack on France during his reign and it should have been the first step in a glorious campaign. Henry was all too eager to ally himself with his father-in-law, Ferdinand II, who had similar ambitions to claim French territory. Both kings had joined the Holy League, which had been created in response to France's military activity in Italy. The League had decided that Ferdinand and Henry should attack together and it should have been an impressive display of force.

The Marquis of Dorset was given control of the English forces and the invaders were due to march with Ferdinand on Aquitaine. However, once the Marquis set foot on dry land, he discovered that the Spanish king had not kept his word. Instead, Ferdinand was occupied with his own attack on Navarre, which better served

the Spanish king's own interests. The Marquis's troops quarrelled with the few Spanish forces that they had been given and many of his men succumbed to dysentery. As a result of all this, he had no choice but to retreat.

Although Henry can't be blamed for the failure of this attack, it shows the Holy League for what it really was. The kings were fighting with the pope's blessing and the glory of God, but they were all out for themselves. Once the fighting started, each monarch was really only interested in what land they could claim – their allies only functioned as a bank and backup.

Verdict

The forced retreat enraged Henry, pushing him towards leading his own attack, and also sowed the seeds of distrust that would come more prominently to the fore throughout his further campaigns

Ferdinand II of Aragon, depicted here surviving an assassination attempt in 1492, was a no-show when it came to marching on Aquitaine with England.

Victory at Flodden Field

9 September 1513

With the king's attention focused on France, the timing was ripe for an attack from the north. King Louis XII reached out to his ally in Scotland and James IV was very agreeable. He wrote to Henry instructing him to abandon his war on the French – an instruction that Henry roundly ignored. The Scottish troops rallied and marched south to the border, sending word that they intended to invade. Having appeased their sense of honour, they waited for the English troops at Flodden.

Catherine of Aragon was acting as regent while her husband was at war in France. Catherine was a woman who believed fiercely in duty, honour and loyalty, and the prospect of losing a battle in her husband's absence was too awful to even consider.

Together with the Earl of Surrey, Catherine raised an army from the Midlands to meet the Scottish invaders. Surrey met the Scottish army at Flodden Field and subjected them to a crushing defeat. The number of Scottish dead numbered in the thousands, and King James IV himself was among the fatalities.

While Henry's refusal to leave France may have been the final straw that prompted the attack, he had very little to do with the result of the battle – it was the Earl of Surrey who won the day. The Scottish king fell on the battlefield, and his cloak was sent to France as a trophy for Henry. A decisive victory, but not one which can be attributed to any military excellence on Henry's part.

Verdict

While the victory would assure Henry of England's military might, it was the start of a long and costly struggle with the Scots that would distract him from his goals in France.

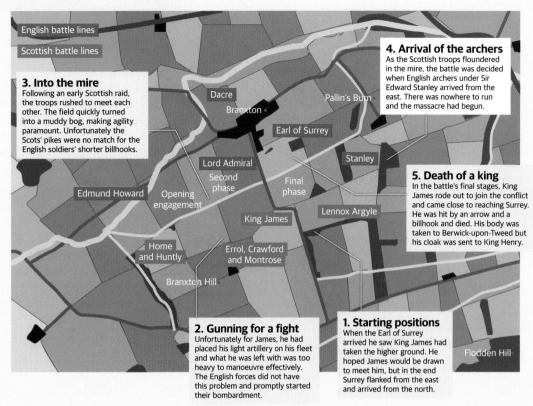

English battle lines

Scottish battle lines

3. Into the mire
Following an early Scottish raid, the troops rushed to meet each other. The field quickly turned into a muddy bog, making agility paramount. Unfortunately the Scots' pikes were no match for the English soldiers' shorter billhooks.

Dacre

Branxton

Pallin's Burn

Earl of Surrey

4. Arrival of the archers
As the Scottish troops floundered in the mire, the battle was decided when English archers under Sir Edward Stanley arrived from the east. There was nowhere to run and the massacre had begun.

Lord Admiral

Stanley

Second phase

Final phase

5. Death of a king
In the battle's final stages, King James rode out to join the conflict and came close to reaching Surrey. He was hit by an arrow and a billhook and died. His body was taken to Berwick-upon-Tweed but his cloak was sent to King Henry.

Edmund Howard

Opening engagement

King James

Lennox Argyle

Home and Huntly

Errol, Crawford and Montrose

Branxton Hill

2. Gunning for a fight
Unfortunately for James, he had placed his light artillery on his fleet and what he was left with was too heavy to manoeuvre effectively. The English forces did not have this problem and promptly started their bombardment.

1. Starting positions
When the Earl of Surrey arrived he saw King James had taken the higher ground. He hoped James would be drawn to meet him, but in the end Surrey flanked from the east and arrived from the north.

Flodden Hill

> "The Scottish king fell on the battlefield, and his cloak was sent to France as a trophy for Henry"

The Scottish army outnumbered the English by about 15,000 at Flodden, but some clever tactics won out.

Father of the Royal Navy

Henry might be known as the founder of the Royal Navy but its creation had begun during the reign of Henry VII. Five royal warships had been built by the time Henry VIII took the throne, but the young king wanted more from his military might.

Henry knew that Scotland had invested in their own navy and that he was potentially facing a two-pronged attack by sea. Henry ordered the construction of two great warships: the infamous Mary Rose (which embarrassingly and mysteriously sank while leading the defence against the French at the Solent) and the Peter Pomegranate. Henry's ambition knew no limits and the English Navy would be the biggest, the most advanced and the most fearsome. He equipped his ships with the latest guns and the heaviest cannons, while employing new innovations like hinged gun ports. By the end of Henry's reign, his fleet numbered 58.

Enormous gunships aside, perhaps the most important innovations Henry made to the navy were on land. He created the first naval dock in Portsmouth, he gave the Grant of the Royal Charter to Trinity House (which developed beacons, buoys and lighthouses), and he created the Navy Board and the Office of Admiralty. Henry is known as the father of the Royal Navy because he didn't just bulk up its muscle, he created its backbone.

Inside the Mary Rose

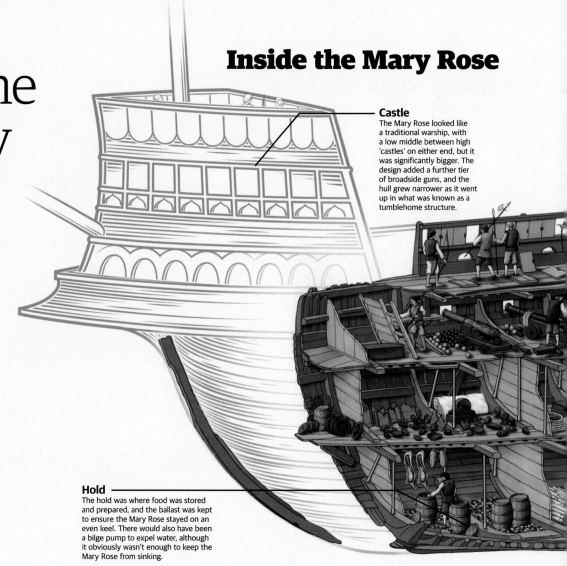

Castle
The Mary Rose looked like a traditional warship, with a low middle between high 'castles' on either end, but it was significantly bigger. The design added a further tier of broadside guns, and the hull grew narrower as it went up in what was known as a tumblehome structure.

Hold
The hold was where food was stored and prepared, and the ballast was kept to ensure the Mary Rose stayed on an even keel. There would also have been a bilge pump to expel water, although it obviously wasn't enough to keep the Mary Rose from sinking.

---

head of an English army, Henry was exhilarated. He made straight for the town of Thérouanne and promptly laid siege to it. The Holy Roman Emperor and fellow Holy League leader, Maximilian, joined him soon afterwards, helping to assure Henry that he was on the side of the angels. Finally, Henry tasted glory on 16 August 1513 when the French attacked in the Battle of the Spurs. The light French cavalry were unable to withstand the combined forces of the invaders and fled. Henry claimed the day as a great victory, which was consolidated when Thérouanne surrendered on 22 August. The subsequent capture of Tournai was just as important to Henry, and he kept that town as an English stronghold while giving Thérouanne to Maximilian as a gesture of their allegiance.

What had Henry actually achieved? He'd taken two towns from the French, but Paris was a long way away. Nothing he'd done would tip the scales in either direction, but this was just the beginning. Henry was in his element. He was re-enacting the glories of Henry V and who knew how far he could go? Even as Henry celebrated his victories in France, trouble at home soon threatened to bring everything to a halt. All too aware of the English forces currently on their soil, the French reached out to King James IV of Scotland and suggested

that this might be the perfect opportunity to mount an attack of their own. James marched south to Flodden Ridge with his armies to await the English.

While England may have seemed weak, Queen Catherine, acting as regent, had no intention of allowing such a challenge to go unanswered. An army was raised and met the Scots on 9 September. The English victory was brutally decisive and King James was killed. The gleeful queen sent the fallen monarch's bloody cloak to her husband in France, with the message: "In this your Grace shall see how I keep my promise, sending you for your banners a king's coat." Henry was conquering his enemies abroad, while his queen was seeing off attackers at home.

Sadly for the warrior king, peace was just around the corner, whether Henry wanted it or not. He had been acting as a war chest to his allies and England's

coffers were so depleted that there was simply no way that he could carry on alone. He would have to make peace. The next few years presented Henry with a new potential ally, and a new enemy.

The ambitious Francis I took the French crown, while the Austrian King Charles V was elected Holy Roman Emperor (adding Spain and a huge portion of Italy to his kingdom). Wolsey, aware of the financial sinkhole that the wars had been, worked hard to keep the peace. He managed to put quills to paper with the Treaty of London in 1518, while friendship would be forged at the Field of the Cloth of Gold on 7 June 1520. The plan was that Henry and Francis would spend a week enjoying the festivities and settling their differences, while Wolsey met with Charles V. It did not go according to plan.

For all Wolsey's good intentions, this attempt at friendship was doomed from the start. Henry had never wanted peace to start with,

THOMAS MORE
English, 1478-1535

Brief Bio
Thomas More trained as a lawyer and nearly became a monk before entering Henry's employ in 1517, taking on a variety of roles from interpreter to writer and chief diplomat. The two quickly became close confidants and More was knighted four years later, before becoming the speaker of the House of Commons in 1523. It was his strong Catholic faith that would prove his downfall. Although he was made lord chancellor in 1529, he rejected the formation of the Church of England with Henry at its head, so resigned soon after. His refusal to accept the new denomination would lead to his arrest and eventual execution on 6 July 1535.

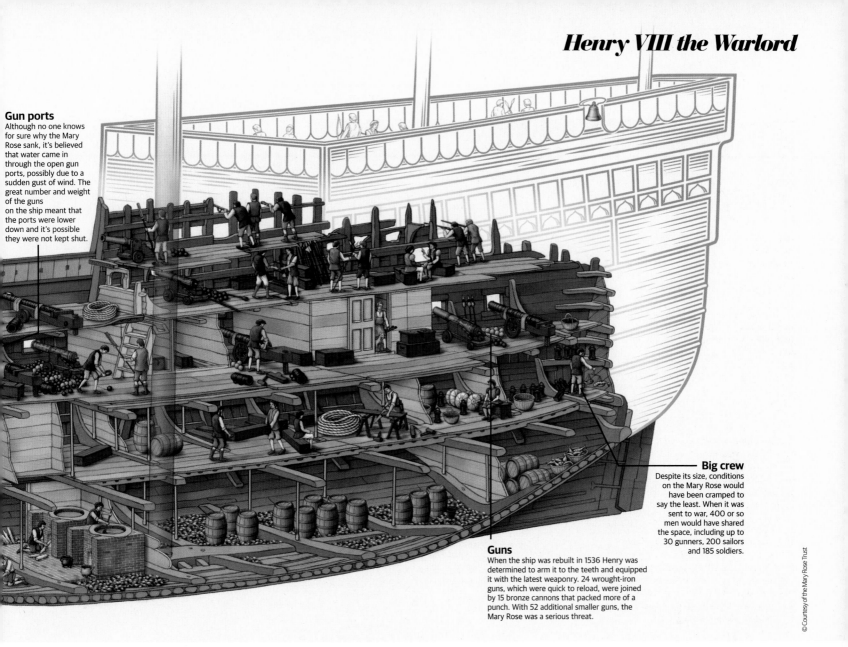

Gun ports
Although no one knows for sure why the Mary Rose sank, it's believed that water came in through the open gun ports, possibly due to a sudden gust of wind. The great number and weight of the guns on the ship meant that the ports were lower down and it's possible they were not kept shut.

Big crew
Despite its size, conditions on the Mary Rose would have been cramped to say the least. When it was sent to war, 400 or so men would have shared the space, including up to 30 gunners, 200 sailors and 185 soldiers.

Guns
When the ship was rebuilt in 1536 Henry was determined to arm it to the teeth and equipped it with the latest weaponry. 24 wrought-iron guns, which were quick to reload, were joined by 15 bronze cannons that packed more of a punch. With 52 additional smaller guns, the Mary Rose was a serious threat.

"Henry's ambition to conquer France was hamstrung by the fact that he couldn't afford it"

and Francis had no intention of bowing down to his English counterpart. Ambitious, stubborn and proud, the two men were too similar for any attempts at friendship to work. After the first meeting was concluded, the two kings engaged in a week of oneupmanship and competition. It was a week dedicated to flaunting power and status; the 'cloth of gold' referred to the ludicrously lavish tents. Henry was determined to prove his athleticism and joined the competitions, but Francis had a similar idea. Henry had to suffer the humiliation of losing to the French king in a wrestling match, and it is hardly surprising that the only result of the meeting was a greater sense of hatred. Instead, Henry turned his diplomatic attentions to Charles V.

Henry's alliance with the Habsburgs had continued throughout the years of peace, despite one or two hiccups involving marriage arrangements. Crucially, Charles and Henry shared a mutual loathing of Martin Luther and King Francis. His hatred of the French king meant that war was inevitable and Henry eagerly awaited the perfect opportunity to mount another attack. When hostilities resumed in 1521, Henry declared that England was now allied with the Holy Roman Emperor and signed the Treaty of Windsor in 1522 to make 'The Great Enterprise' official. At

this point in his plans, Henry could not afford a full-scale invasion and an attack on Picardy failed due to a lack of communication and, perhaps more importantly, trust.

Henry's ambition to conquer France and claim the throne for himself was hamstrung by the fact that he couldn't afford it. He had previously helped to bankroll Ferdinand and Maximilian and he had seen them make peace without him. Henry was scared that Charles might repeat his father's trick and, for his part, Charles had no particular interest in seeing Henry on the French throne. Their mutual distrust would only grow.

Trust wasn't the only problem. In an echo of 1513, Henry was distracted by the constant threat from the north. Whenever he began a campaign in France, the Scottish forces would threaten attack, forcing him to wage a war on two fronts. Henry was enraged and infuriated but he would not give up. He mounted another attack in 1523 to support

the rebelling Duke of Bourbon, but Charles sent no help and the English troops were forced to retreat.

The line was finally crossed when Charles captured Francis at the Battle of Pavia in 1525 and showed no interest in sharing his spoils with the English king. Henry decided that the time had come for a full-scale invasion. With nowhere near enough money, Henry and Cardinal Wolsey tried to create the 'Amicable Grant' tax to pay for the attack, but opposition proved so fierce that Henry was forced to scrap his plans and publicly blame Wolsey. The humiliation of backpedalling helped Henry to realise that he was not going to get what he wanted. He signed the Treaty of the More with Francis's mother, Louise of Savoy, and turned his attention towards his family.

Not surprisingly, Charles's rejection ranked Henry. The Holy Roman Emperor's increased presence in Italy once again caused the panicking Pope Clement VII to create the League of Cognac,

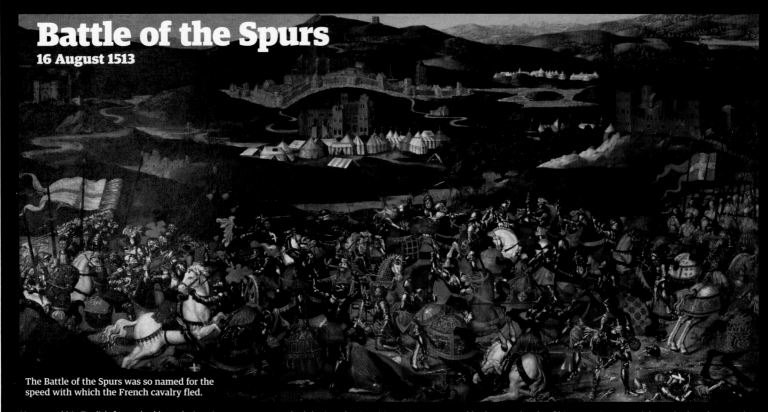

Battle of the Spurs
16 August 1513

The Battle of the Spurs was so named for the speed with which the French cavalry fled.

Henry and his English forces had been laying siege to the town of Thérouanne since July 1513. Following the embarrassment at Gascony, he had finally arrived in France to lead his army to great conquest. He camped close, but not too close to the city, and laid siege. A stalemate ensued until French action on 16 August tipped the scales.

The French forces had seen Maximilian's Holy Roman Army join Henry's and decided that the time had come to attempt a counterattack. On the morning of 16 August, French light cavalry, a few thousand strong,

attacked the invaders' positions. However, word had reached the Holy League's camp of the planned attack and a trap had been prepared, leading to a brutal skirmish. It was an attack that was ultimately doomed to fail, with Henry and Maximilian's combined forces coming to roughly 30,000 men. The speed with which the surviving French rode away led to the name of the battle.

It was not a significant military victory in any other term than morale. Henry had been looking for a victory to claim in France, and this encounter was the first real

battle of his campaign. He celebrated it but the actual gains from the Battle of the Spurs and the subsequent fall of Thérouanne would impress nothing but his ego. At great financial expense, Henry's dreams of Agincourt came a little closer.

Verdict
The victory at the Battle of the Spurs did more for Henry's ego than it did for the outcome of his campaign, essentially proving to be an incredibly expensive display.

---

which united Venice, Florence and France against Charles. Henry was not a member, but offered to help bankroll the group. His treaty with Francis in the Treaty of Westminster on 30 April 1527 was a sign that his mind was elsewhere.

Henry was desperate to be separated from Catherine and marry Anne Boleyn. He had no interest in a divorce and instead wanted to prove that it had been illegal to marry his brother's widow. This would soothe the good Catholic in him, but it set him against Charles V, who was appalled by what the accusation said about his aunt, Catherine. However, circumstances were not in Henry's favour; Charles had attacked Rome in retaliation for the League's advances. Pope Clement VII was now his prisoner and Catherine's nephew made his influence felt. Clement gained his freedom in December, but the emperor had no interest in peace talks with the League. Once again, Charles had frustrated Henry's plans and he declared war with the Holy Roman Emperor in January. However, England lacked the finances to do any more than declare itself at war; it's unlikely that this worried Charles too much. The situation

"Overjoyed at having the queen he lusted after, Henry realised that a Europe united against him was dangerous"

in Europe finally resolved itself in 1529 with the Treaty of Cambrai. However, Henry's determination to end his marriage had made enemies out of his old allies. Francis offered to plead his case to the new Pope Clement, but he was more concerned with cementing his own alliance with the Holy See. Anne Boleyn's pregnancy pushed Henry into taking decisive action and his marriage to Catherine was annulled by Thomas Cranmer in 1533. In the eyes of the English court, his secret marriage to Anne was now completely legal. Finally, Henry was recognised as Head of the Church and abolished the right of Appeal to Rome. England was no longer Catholic and the pope had no more influence over the king.

Although he was overjoyed at finally having the queen he lusted after, Henry realised that a Europe

united against him was a dangerous prospect indeed. He tried to take advantage of the frequent arguments between Charles and Francis, but in 1538 the excommunication order for Henry was finally delivered and the pope declared that the Vatican would support anyone who deposed the English king; his death was something God would turn a blind eye to. Luckily for Henry, Charles was busy with the Ottoman Empire and, if Francis planned to attack England, he had no intention of doing so alone. Henry knew that the differences between Francis and Charles would prevent them from ever remaining allies for long. He just had to be patient. Finally, in 1542, they declared war and Henry could return to the battlefield.

By this point Henry was obese, sickly and prone to violent rages. The war gave him a sense of

The Siege of Boulogne
19 July - 18 September 1544

The Siege of Boulogne would be the closest thing to an unqualified victory that Henry would get in all his years of war with France. However, the conquest of a single city at tremendous expense tells us that unqualified is not really the most accurate adjective to use. Henry had been waiting for an excuse to resume hostilities with France and he eagerly joined his old ally (and old enemy) Charles V when war broke out in 1544. He raised a huge invasion force to set sail across the Channel.

The English force was split into two;=, attacking Montreuil and Boulogne, with Henry himself joining the latter. While the attack on Montreuil failed, the Siege of Boulogne, though lengthy, would result in success. The siege began on 19 July and the English forces quickly took the lower part of the city. However, they were unable to breach the castle walls and the siege stretched from weeks into months. Henry wrote to his wife (number six, Catherine Parr) praising the strength of his opponents, but it was only a matter of time before the French were forced to surrender, which they did after Henry's forces tunnelled beneath the walls.

However, Henry's triumph would be short-lived. He learned that Charles, fearful of the Ottoman threat and caring little about Henry's personal ambition, had made his own peace treaty with France without England. Henry returned home to attend to Scotland, leaving Boulogne occupied, and Francis began preparations for a counterattack.

Verdict

Henry may have taken the city, but the financial cost was enormous. Although Charles's treaty led to threats of a French invasion, Francis's attempts ultimately failed.

Charles Brandon, First Duke of Suffolk, was left to defend Boulogne after Henry returned to England.

purpose and Charles was finally back on his side. For all their past differences, now there were no personal reasons why Henry and Charles could not resume their alliance. Catherine of Aragon had passed away and, by executing Anne Boleyn, Henry had removed the insult to Charles' honour. Across the Channel, Francis wasn't sitting idly by and he knew how to keep Henry distracted.

Scotland had proved to be a continual thorn in Henry's paw during his attempts to invade France, attacking every time his attention was focused across the Channel. Having hoped that James V would be a more amenable ally than his predecessor, Henry was livid when Scotland refused to follow him in separating from Rome. When James did not appear at the diplomatic talks at York in 1541, outright conflict followed. Following a minor Scottish victory at the Battle of Haddon Rig in 1542, the two armies met at Solway Moss. In a brutal echo of Flodden Field, the Scottish army suffered a humiliating defeat. James V died of fever about two weeks later and Henry, once again buoyed by such a decisive victory, turned his attention to France.

Henry was taking no half measures and invaded France on two fronts. Stretching his finances as far as they would go, he sent troops to Montreuil under the Duke of Norfolk, while another force attacked Boulogne under the Duke of Suffolk. While Norfolk failed, Suffolk succeeded. Henry himself arrived to take charge of the siege which lasted from July until September when the city fell. He basked in the glory of a French city claimed, but his elation was short-lived. Henry was forced to turn his attention back to Scotland, where a rebellion had sprung up. His retaliation was so brutal that it became known as the 'Rough Wooing'.

The Rough Wooing
December 1543 - March 1550

The Rough Wooing was the result of Henry's failed attempt to subdue Scotland while he turned his attention to France. Although he might have won a huge victory at the Battle of Solway Moss, Henry's hopes that the Scottish would be amenable to peace proved to be ill-founded. He had given them his terms, but Henry may as well have given them a blank piece of paper, as Scotland declared its renewed allegiance to France.

At the time, Henry was planning his invasion with Charles V and could not afford to be distracted by yet another full-blown conflict with his neighbours in the north. Deciding against open battle, Henry commanded that a force should sail north and show the Scots how furious he was. It was led by Edward Seymour, Earl of Hertford, who was told to "Burn Edinburgh town, so razed and defaced when you have sacked and gotten what you can of it, as there may remain forever a perpetual memory of the vengeance of God."

Towns and villages were to be burned down and destroyed, and the king's strict instructions as to what to do with anyone who opposed Hertford were clear; he was commanded to continue "putting man, woman and child to fire and sword, without exception, where any resistance shall be made against you." Hertford obeyed his liege's orders with relish, sending frequent reports of his conquests back to his king, and capturing Edinburgh and the nearby port at Leith. However, France did not sit idly by, but instead sent forces to help Scottish counterattacks. This dual campaign of aggression between England and Scotland would only be (temporarily) halted by the Treaty of Camp in 1546.

Verdict

Although it had the immediate effect that Henry wanted, which was to give a show of force and wrath, the Rough Wooing only served to deeper entrench hatred and distrust of the English.

The invasion of France fell apart when Charles signed another continental peace treaty that excluded England. Francis had no intention of making peace with Henry and mounted an invasion in the summer of 1545. It was a very real threat but, fortunately for Henry, the attack was a dismal failure and Francis was forced to retreat. The Treaty of Camp brought an end to the years of war in Henry's reign, as England, France, Scotland and the Holy Roman Empire agreed to peace in 1546.

He died a year later, sickly, angry and defeated. So what does Henry VIII's history as a military commander show us? It shows him to be a man unable or unwilling to grow out of the romantic, heroic dreams of his youth. He was constantly fighting for the glory that he saw for himself and for England. In his mind, France was English property that no one before him had been able to claim. He saw himself as the king who would bring it under English rule, and it was a childhood dream that became an adult delusion. By joining with allies who had no interest in his dream, and reacting rashly to insults, real and imagined, Henry spent many years at war with little to show for it.

1500 – 1558

King Charles I of Spain

The heir of three of Europe's leading dynasties and future Holy Roman Emperor, Charles I of Spain was arguably the most powerful man in the world, with a reign typified by military success and territorial expansion

The closest thing to an Emperor of Europe that ever existed during the 16th Century, Charles I of Spain - who was also more importantly Holy Roman Emperor (see 'Charles I or Charles V?' boxout for more information) - was not only heir to three of Europe's leading dynasties but also ruler of extensive territories that stretched throughout Europe and the Americas. Indeed, as well as controlling the Netherlands, Germany, Spain, parts of Italy and France, Charles also benefitted much territorially by the conquests of the Spanish conquistadores, with men like Hernan Cortes granting him control of large parts of modern day South America.

Charles was, however, born as the eldest son of Philip I of Castile in the Flemish city of Ghent in 1500, where he both received his education and cultural mindset. At the age of six Charles inherited his father's Burgundian Low Countries' territories and by the time he was 15, he could famously speak multiple languages including German, French and Flemish. At 15

> Charles, especially in his later life, became famous for his deformed lower jaw, the product of centuries of royal inbreeding

> During his reign Charles oversaw much of Spain's colonisation of the Americas

the first test for Charles as a ruler occurred, with a rebellion of Frisian peasants scoring a series of military victories over Charles' forces. Charles didn't panic, however, and after consulting with his advisers, managed to push the rebels back and, eventually, capture their leaders and decapitate them. It was Charles' first taste of war.

While Charles was being blooded in the Netherlands, his mother Joanna Queen of Castile was ensuring his succession in Spain. This came to a head in 1516 when Charles' grandfather King Ferdinand II of Aragon died, with Joanna then also inheriting the Crown of Aragon, a rule that included the lands of Aragon, Catalonia, Valencia, Naples, Sicily and Sardinia. Joanna used this opportunity to finalise Charles' succession, with it being arranged that he was named King of Castile and Aragon, and that he would rule jointly with his mother till her death. One year later Charles arrived in Spain to survey and control his new territories.

Due to Queen Joanna still being alive and the perception of Charles as

Charles spent much of his reign fighting the forces of Suleiman the Magnificent's Ottoman Empire

CHARLES I OF SPAIN
Spain, 1500-1558

Brief Bio A member of the woefully inbred Habsburg family line, Charles suffered from genetic defects including an incredibly painful jaw disorder; a family trait that unfortunately makes a Habsburg stand out a mile in any portrait. Ruling a large European territory as Holy Roman Emperor, he brought Spain into the mix of Dutch, German, Italian and French domains that he ruled.

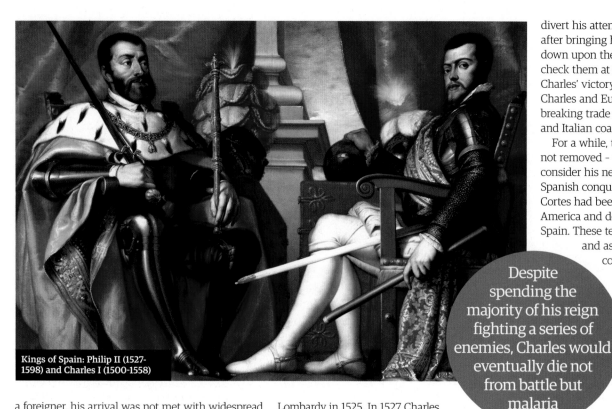

Kings of Spain: Philip II (1527-1598) and Charles I (1500-1558)

divert his attentions to repelling Suleiman and, after bringing his considerable military might down upon the Ottomans, finally managed to check them at the Siege of Vienna in 1529. Despite Charles' victory, Sulieman continued to haunt Charles and Europe in general, continuously breaking trade routes and devastating the Spanish and Italian coasts.

For a while, the threat of Suleiman - while not removed - was muted enough for Charles to consider his newfound lands in the Americas. Spanish conquistadores like the famous Hernan Cortes had been claiming much land in South America and dedicating it to Charles as King of Spain. These territories were rich in precious metals and as such Charles realised that they could prove invaluable in funding his empire. However, Charles was also seemingly concerned about the methods in which the resources and territories were being attained, with Cortes and company frequently slaughtering local populaces to ensure domination. This concern would eventually come to a head when Charles personally convened the famous Valladolid Conference to specifically decide how the lands and people of the New World should be treated.

Charles' American diversion could not last long though, as in 1536 and then 1542, Charles' french enemy King Francis I allied himself with Suleiman against the Holy Roman Emperor in order to check his power and control over, not just the lands of Europe, but also its religion. This agreement led to the Franco-Ottoman alliance and caused Charles no end of trouble, with a series of wars between the three powers ensuing

> **Despite spending the majority of his reign fighting a series of enemies, Charles would eventually die not from battle but malaria**

a foreigner, his arrival was not met with widespread acclaim by the local population and the Spanish officials treated him with great suspicion. Indeed, Charles was only finally confirmed as monarch after signing an agreement that mandated that he learn to speak Castilian, not to promote foreigners to court, respect the rights of his mother and not to take Spain's precious metals out of the region. Charles agreed to this and was begrudgingly accepted as ruler and for the following two years everything was going to plan, with Charles laying down his own style of rule and policies.

However, in 1520, due to Charles placing a high taxation rate on all his Spanish territories, a revolt sprung up. Challenged for the first time in Spain, Charles brought the full military might of his forces down upon the rebellion and, after learning how to deal with such uprisings in the Netherlands, brutally put it down quickly. With his Spanish territories now pacified, the young and powerful king then looked to expand his already impressive lands. He had much success too, capturing Milan in 1522 off a Franco-Swiss army at Bicocca and then

Lombardy in 1525. In 1527 Charles even managed to sack the grand city of Rome, virtually imprisoning the pope - his power was seemingly uncheckable.

However, Charles was soon to be tested like never before in battle, with the mighty forces of the Ottoman Empire's Suleiman the Magnificent invading Europe and making a beeline for Charles' central territories. A wave of terror spread throughout Europe, with Suleiman not only scoring numerous naval victories in the Mediterranean but also sacking and ravaging all European lands his men touched. Charles was forced to immediately

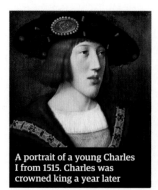

A portrait of a young Charles I from 1515. Charles was crowned king a year later

Charles depicted enthroned above his defeated rivals - note Suleiman the Magnificent on the far left

Timeline

1500

● **Charles born**
Charles was born as the eldest son of King Philip I of Castile and Joanna the Mad – a name most likely granted due to probable schizophrenia – in the Flemish city of Ghent. He would go on to be tutored by William de Croy.
24 February 1500

● **Comuneros revolt**
Following Charles taking the kingship of Castile and then proceeding to tax the region heavily to fight his many wars, the citizens revolted and Charles suppressed them brutally. Castile was then absorbed into the larger Habsburg empire officially.
1520

● **Isabella of Portugal**
Charles marries his cousin Isabella of Portugal on March 10th in Seville. Isabella would proceed to take over administrative duties of Spain, with Charles frequently away in his foreign territories. Their son Philip would eventually succeed Charles as King of Spain.
1526

● **Suleiman stopped**
Suleiman the Magnificent's Ottoman Empire invades central Europe, with the forces taking much territory. However, Charles checks them at Vienna and the advance is fatally halted. Suleiman however wins control of the Eastern Mediterranean.
1529

● **Crowned by pope**
Despite being elected as Holy Roman Emperor in June 1519, Charles is only eventually crowned thus 11 years later, with Pope Clement VII conducting the ceremony in Bologna. Charles would be the last Holy Roman Emperor to receive a papal coronation.
1530

"In many respects Charles reigned very well, inheriting and then controlling a simply massive empire"

throughout the 1530s and 1540s. In fact, the on-off fighting was only finally brought to a partial close with Charles' acceptance of the Truce of Adrianople in 1547. Charles did not want to sign the treaty, however the cost of continuous warfare was bankrupting his lands.

Indeed, with Charles frequently away fighting wars and leaving his lands in the administrative control of others, soon he found his power curtailed, specifically in Germany, the heartland of his Holy Roman Empire. As the year of 1550 rolled around, this unrest and usurpation of power spread into the Netherlands and Charles, realising that a full-blown rebellion was likely on the cards, introduced the death penalty there for any cases of heresy and political dissent.

At this point, whether it was obvious to Charles or not, he was now attempting to put out fires that had been kindled by decades of hard rule, high taxation and a nomadic lifestyle. Charles was now 50 and he increasingly found he had neither the will nor the energy to prop up his massive empire. Further, as he entered his 50s a deformity that he had lived with all his life, an enlarged lower jaw, got significantly worse, leaving him with chronic jaw pain and an inability to chew foods properly. Thanks to a life of consuming little but red meat,

> During his later life Charles also became famous for his chronic gout, which caused him much pain

he also began suffering seriously from gout, which became incredibly painful. Realising his time was almost up, Charles then decided to end his king- and emperorship on his own terms, abdicating his rule of the Netherlands in 1555, then his rule of the Spanish and Holy Roman Empires in 1556, with his son Philip appointed to succeed him. Following the abdications, Charles self-confined himself to the monastery of St. Yuste in Extremadura, where he was cared for in the last years of his life. Two years later, in 1558, Charles died after contracting malaria, with his body then buried at the monastery.

So what of Charles' reign? In many respects Charles reigned very well, inheriting and then controlling a simply massive empire where he, not only protected it, but expanded it considerably. Further, he frequently succeeded on the battlefield and was politically savvy enough to hold the other rulers in and around Europe from himself and his interests at arm's length. In addition, unlike many other kings of the age, despite his constant warring, Charles was not reported to be bloodthirsty, with him reportedly having strong distaste for combat. On the other hand however, Charles left the Habsburg Empire financially destitute, with Spain near-bankrupt, and this lands of Germany and the Netherlands bitterly divided over religion.

Charles in the armour of the Holy Roman Emperor

Charles I or Charles V?

As well as being Charles I of Spain, Charles was also Holy Roman Emperor Charles V. Here we explain how exactly that happened...

Today, Charles I of Spain is not remembered thus but instead as the Holy Roman Emperor Charles V. The Holy Roman Emperor was the leader of the Holy Roman Empire, which was formed out of the remnants of the collapse of the Western Roman Empire in 408 and then the Carolingian Empire in the late 880s. The Empire consisted of a series of multi-ethnic territories in central Europe – with Germany being the largest – that over period of 600 years dominated the politics and religion of the region, with its leader – the titular Emperor – crowned by the Catholic pope in Rome.

Charles I's grandfather was Maximilian I, who was King of Germany not Spain, as well as being Holy Roman Emperor. However, upon Maximilian's death, the complex laws of hereditary meant that he was the frontrunner as the new Emperor, with a council of electors eventually choosing him to succeed to the crown of the Holy Roman Empire – note, not the Spanish crown (King of Castile), which he had already accepted in 1516, or the rulership of the Netherlands and Burgundy, which he had inherited in 1506 – in 1519. Charles, however, was not officially the Holy Roman Emperor until he was crowned thus by Pope Clement VII in Rome 11 years later in 1530.

Further, despite officially abdicating as Holy Roman Emperor in 1556 in favour of his brother Ferdinand, the Holy Roman Empire's Imperial Diet did not accept the succession technically, so while Ferdinand was in fact the Emperor of the Holy Roman Empire from 1556 onwards, it was not until the year of Charles' death two years later that he was officially recognised thus.

Due to the size and importance of the Holy Roman Empire in its day, its titular leader trumps that of Spain's monarch, leading to the history books favouring Charles V over Charles I.

A famous portrait of Charles from 1548 painted by the old master, Titian

1558

Revolt of Ghent
Along with help from the Duke of Alba, Charles personally suppresses a revolt in Ghent, where political dissent had been firmly controlled for decades. The revolt was instigated by high taxation. After the revolt, Charles stripped the city of all its legal and political freedoms.
1539

Valladolid debate
Charles convenes a conference at Valladolid in order to consider the morality of using force against the indigenous populations of the New World, which Spain was taking a lead in colonising and exploiting. Unfortunately, little consequence comes of the debate.
1550

Protestant rebellion
Protestant princes, in alliance with King Henry II of France, rebel against Charles' Roman Catholic rule in central Europe, forcing him to retreat into the Netherlands. Charles abdicated his rule of the Netherlands three years later.
1552

Abdication nation
After previously abdicating his rule of the Netherlands and the county of Charolais the previous year, Charles finally abdicated his Spanish Empire in January. It is passed on to his son Philip, who already controlled Naples and Sicily.
1556

Charles dies
After living in self-imposed exile at the monastery of Yuste in Extremadura for two years, Charles eventually dies from an attack of malaria. His remains were buried at the monastery, however, 26 years later they were transferred to the Monastery of San Lorenzo de El Escorial.
21 September 1558

© Alamy

ELIZABETH I
British, 1533 – 1603

Brief Bio Elizabeth assumed the throne after the death of her Catholic sister Mary, upon which she faced an unstable nation torn apart by religious conflict. Over the course of her reign she fought enemies at home and abroad, uniting England under one church and oversaw the exploration of new lands.

1533 – 1603
The turbulent reign of
Elizabeth I

She fought off foreign invasions and domestic rebellions
but did she really preside over a golden age?

I n 1588, against the advice of her most trusted aides, Elizabeth I rode out on her grey gelding to address her troops gathered at Tilbury in Essex in preparation of repelling the expected invasion force of the Spanish Armada. Looking out at the assembled faces before her, she delivered a speech that would go down in history and for many would forever define her: "I know I have the body of a weak, feeble woman; but I have the heart and stomach of a king - and of a king of England too."

The speech would have to be transcribed and redistributed for the soldiers who were unable to hear the queen but they had all seen their monarch, armoured and on her steed, ready to stand by them to repel the Catholic invasion. This image of Elizabeth has been the key to our popular perception of her for centuries, but there's much more to her. Elizabeth was cunning and capricious, but she could be blinded by affection, if only temporarily. She was tremendously clever, with an almost unfailing sense of what her people wanted

or needed from her, but had to see off foreign invasion attempts and homegrown rebellions. While she was sitting on the throne of England the country became acquainted with some of its greatest triumphs and darkest hours.

When Elizabeth came to the throne in November 1558, the whole of Europe was on tenterhooks. How would the new Protestant queen follow the reign of her Catholic sister Mary? With an unstable nation and conspiracies at home and abroad, the situation required diplomacy, intelligence and bravery; three qualities which Elizabeth had always had in ample supply. In fact, the unstable situation was nothing new to her; Elizabeth's position had been precarious from the moment she was born. The daughter of Henry VIII's second wife, Anne Boleyn, she was immediately deemed as illegitimate by any Catholic nations, who regarded the king's divorce of Catherine of Aragon as illegal. In their eyes, Catherine's daughter Mary was the only rightful heir to the throne.

Although both parents had been desperate for a boy, Anne would be a doting mother to her infant child, but she was sent to the executioner's block in 1536 after failing to produce a male heir for her king. Although Henry's third wife Jane Seymour was kind to Elizabeth and Mary, she had her own child to attend to with the birth of her son and Henry's heir, Edward. Henry himself would not see much of Elizabeth until 1542, when he decided the time had come to reacquaint himself with his young daughter. He found her to be intelligent and charming, and decided that he would reinstate both Mary and Elizabeth back into his lineage.

In 1543, Henry married Catherine Parr, his last wife, and relations within the royal family warmed, as Mary took a maternal interest in young Edward, while Elizabeth enjoyed a sisterly relationship with both. However, when Edward took the throne upon their father's death, cracks started to form. First, Elizabeth had to contend with the amorous attentions of Catherine's new husband Thomas Seymour, which caused a scandal at court in 1548. Seymour's intentions were seen as treasonous, and Elizabeth was reported to be pregnant. The young princess denied these rumours, confounding her interrogator. "She hath a very good wit and nothing is gotten of her but by great policy," he wrote. This

"She was tremendously clever, with an almost unfailing sense of what her people wanted, or needed from her"

How good was Elizabeth at balancing the books?

While the popular image is that Mary left England in a sorry state, Leanda de Lisle explains that Elizabeth's fiscal behaviour was far from immaculate. Mary left England £227,000 in debt, while her sister produced debts of £350,000. "Mary's reign was not a 'disaster'. The popular image of Mary – always 'Bloody Mary', rarely Mary I – has been greatly influenced by a combination of sexual and religious prejudice," explains De Lisle. "Mary I had named Elizabeth as her heir, despite her personal feelings towards her sister, and so allowed the crown to be inherited peacefully. Elizabeth continued to refuse to name anyone. In 1562, believing she was dying, she asked for Robert Dudley to be made Lord Protector with an income of £20,000." Elizabeth was notoriously reluctant to engage in warfare because of its costs and risk, but the Spanish conflict dragged on for years, while she awarded monopolies to her favourites at court and crops failed. "While we remember Elizabeth's success in repelling the Armada in 1588," says De Lisle, "We forget that the war continued and impoverished the country and the crown, a situation made worse by the corruption of court officials including notorious high-ranking figures such as Robert Cecil. People starved in the 1590s and the elite even began to fear possible revolution."

Verdict

Elizabeth was forced to deal with circumstances beyond her control, such as poor harvests and an ongoing conflict with Spain, but the fact is that she was not the financial marvel many believe her to be.

Borrowing money in the 16th century

Before the English merchant Thomas Gresham came to prominence, the Tudors had borrowed money from the great European banks such as the Antwerp Exchange. However, these banks charged a high interest rate and it was generally acknowledged that going around Europe borrowing money did nothing to improve England's image as a serious power. Money could also be borrowed from independent merchants, such as Horatio Palavicino, from whom Elizabeth was forced to borrow money late in her reign. Gresham had previously helped Edward VI rid himself of most of his debts and founded the Royal Exchange in 1571 to challenge the power of Antwerp.

Now that Elizabeth could seek loans from within her realm, she was able to exert greater pressure to get what she wanted, while Parliament could grant her more funds if they chose. Royal revenues were supposed to cover the basic expenses of governance, while Parliament could add to the war chest. Later in her reign, she began to use increasingly severe taxation, which contributed to her decreasing popularity.

Queen Elizabeth I opening the Royal Exchange

Picture depicting the coronation of Elizabeth I in 1558

Portrait of Mary, Queen of Scots, who was executed after being found guilty of plotting against Elizabeth I

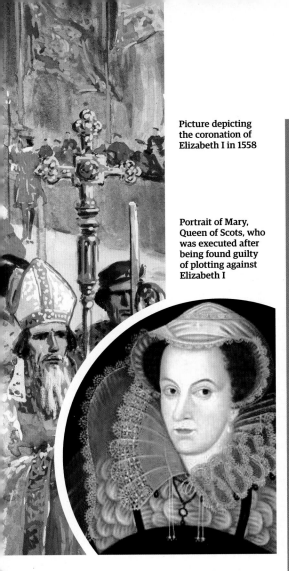

Was a religious compromise met?

The Church of England was one of compromise and middle ground. While Elizabeth was a Protestant, she didn't hold the puritanical beliefs of some of her council members. She introduced the Act of Supremacy in 1558, which reaffirmed England's separation from Rome and established her as the head of the Church. Elizabeth understood the dangers of trying to impose religion and allowed Catholicism to continue, provided it took place in secret.

However, Leanda de Lisle reminds us that we should not forget Elizabeth's willingness to crack down when necessary. "Elizabeth's conservatism and pragmatism has seen her described as a religious moderate, in contrast to the 'fanatical' Mary," she explains. "But as the new Protestant Queen of a largely Catholic country Elizabeth was necessarily moderate, and as her reign grew longer, she proved that, like Mary, she could be utterly ruthless when faced by a threat. The hundreds of executions of villagers following the Northern Rebellion far exceeded anything her predecessors had done in similar circumstances; her later persecution of Catholics was also relentless and cruel. It is a little-known fact that she also burned heretics – namely Anabaptists – these were far fewer in number than Mary's victims, but then there weren't that many Anabaptists!" She executed both Protestants and Catholics for publicly disobeying the laws of the Church of England. However, events in Europe show the English Queen in a much more favourable light. Comparatively, Elizabeth was extremely tolerant. The St. Bartholomew's Day Massacre in Paris showed the fervour with which Catholic Europeans detested Protestants. She was also much more tolerant than many of her advisors.

Verdict

Elizabeth successfully found a moderate middle ground in a very turbulent time during her reign, but would crack down mercilessly if the rules she had laid down were broken.

VS

Catholic

1 The services were held in Latin, countermanding the reformation's ideal that everyone should be able to understand. The English prayer book was banned.

2 Church furnishings were restored to their former lavish state and the buildings were now decorated completely with Catholic artwork.

3 Catholic Mass was reintroduced, and Holy Communion was now banned by law.

4 The clergy were not allowed to marry. Priests who had married before the new law came into effect were given a choice of two options: leave their families or lose their job.

C of E

1 The image of the minister became much simpler. They were not allowed to wear Roman Catholic vestments, such as the surplice.

2 All rood lofts, a screen portraying the crucifixion, a common feature in Catholic churches, were removed. The Pope was not the head of the church.

3 The Bishop's Bible, which was in English rather than Latin, was restored, opening it up to a wider readership.

4 There was a general removal of 'superstition', such as making the sign of the cross during communion. Simplicity was what the Puritans strived for.

---

practice would serve her well once Mary took the throne but not all players were as skilled in the game of thrones; Seymour was executed the following year.

When the staunchly Catholic Mary refused to convert, Edward began proceedings to remove both his sisters from the line to the throne, fixing his hopes on his cousin, Lady Jane Grey, instead. However, the prince was seldom in good health during his short life, so it was no surprise that he died before the contract could be finalised and Mary became the new Queen of England. Just as Edward had asked Mary to change her faith, the new queen was determined that her sister should convert. She acquiesced without enthusiasm, but it was clear to both Protestants and Catholics that her true allegiance still lay with her father's Church of England rather than the Pope's Catholic Church. Over the course of Mary's reign, many conspiracy plots were designed to get Elizabeth onto the throne. None of them succeeded, but they did almost manage to get her killed.

In 1554, Thomas Wyatt attempted a rebellion following the announcement that Mary would marry the Spanish king Philip. The queen's reprisal was brutal and swift, executing not only the ringleaders, but Jane Grey as well. Elizabeth claimed ignorance, a trick she managed to successfully repeat a year later after another attempted rebellion in 1555, but her sister's patience was wearing thin and Elizabeth was placed in the Tower of London, with some Catholic supporters clamouring for her execution.

"The queen's reprisal was brutal and swift, executing not only the ringleaders, but also Jane Grey"

Elizabeth's future prospects were looking anything but golden, and the next few months saw her walking a political tightrope. Mary, desperate to provide her husband and her country with a Catholic heir to end the uncertainty surrounding the throne, announced that she was pregnant, but by 1558, it became clear that Mary's condition was not pregnancy, but a devastating illness. Her health broke quickly, and she died on 17 November of that year after begging Elizabeth to keep England Catholic once she took the throne. Her wishes would not be fulfilled.

Elizabeth's coronation was a stunning balancing act. With countless eyes waiting for any hint of an overtly Protestant or Catholic gestures, Elizabeth managed to confound them all. Instead, the emphasis was elsewhere: Elizabeth's intention to restore England to a state of

prosperity. The new queen knew that if she was to have any chance of surviving her early years she would need trusted and astute advisors, and chose William Cecil and Robert Dudley. Cecil had worked for Edward, survived the reign of Mary and was fiercely loyal to Elizabeth. In contrast, Dudley's appointment and favour with the queen had nothing to do with his abilities as a politician. He had known Elizabeth since childhood and her affection for him had only grown stronger, and rumours abounded that she spent the nights as well as the days with him.

Cecil disapproved of Dudley and agreed with the majority of Parliament that Elizabeth should marry as soon as possible. The eyes of France and Spain were fixed on England and it made sense for the queen to create a marriage alliance with one of these major powers for her and the country's

Did Elizabeth have a genuine thirst for new worlds?

Although the expansion of trade into India occurred during Elizabeth's reign, in terms of exploration she is best remembered for England's attempt to colonise North America. The Spanish and Portuguese had already laid claim to much of South America, establishing lucrative trade routes, but North America was relatively unexplored. Elizabeth was reluctant to fund exploratory voyages for much the same reasons that she was reluctant to fund wars: they were expensive and risky. However, she could be won around with the promise of riches from one of her favourites and, when sailor Davy Ingram returned to England with alluring tales of riches and simple inhabitants, geographer Richard Hakluyt began plotting a serious expedition to be led by Walter Raleigh.

With the promise of fortune and the flattery of Raleigh, she agreed to a trip to form a colony named after her: Virginia. The first party launched, and Raleigh would follow. When the nobleman arrived, he saw the settlement had failed. The English were desperate to leave. Raleigh's second attempt was intended for Chesapeake Bay, but the first group, led by John White, returned to Roanoke. Raleigh arrived with his second group and found no trace of survivors. Elizabeth was disappointed that these costly ventures yielded no results. There was one purpose to these expeditions, as de Lisle explains very simply: "Making money."

Verdict

The Elizabethan era's reputation for exploration is largely due to the fact that there was money to be made from it. Piratical ventures were profitable; colonisation was not.

2. 1585
Following a positive report, Raleigh dispatches colonists to settle at Roanoke in Virginia. By the time he arrives on a later ship, the crops have failed and the English are desperate to leave.

3. 1587
Raleigh tries again to establish a colony at Chesapeake Bay, but instead the settlers travel to Roanoke. When Raleigh arrives, all 150 colonists have disappeared, with only a single skeleton remaining.

1. 1584
Walter Raleigh and Richard Hakluyt convince Elizabeth to fund an expedition to explore the possibility that a colony could be founded on America's east coast.

safety. King Philip II made no secret of his desire to marry Elizabeth, but she had no interest in marrying Mary's former husband. Henry of Anjou was suggested as a match, but he was still a child. Elizabeth spoke instead of being married to her nation, but scandal struck when Dudley's wife Amy died suddenly after apparently falling down the stairs in 1560. It was rumoured that Dudley had committed the deed for his queen, and Elizabeth was forced to expel him from her court.

In 1561, Elizabeth's cousin, Mary, Queen of Scots, returned to Scotland from France. For many Catholics, Mary was the true successor and she did little to downplay those clamouring for a Catholic monarch. Her arrival was perfectly timed, as Elizabeth was on the verge of death due to smallpox. However, she recovered and, with the scandal over Dudley dissipating, Elizabeth chose him to be Lord Protector, bringing him back into her court, before shocking everyone by suggesting a marriage between him and Mary. This was Elizabeth showing her political astuteness; she knew well that Scotland with a Catholic heir would

> "The Queen rallied troops by declaring that she would fight by their side to repel anyone who dare set foot on their land"

have too much power, but an heir produced by her favourite and Mary, Queen of Scots could potentially unite the two countries. However, Dudley refused and Mary had no interest in marrying her cousin's paramour.

Instead, Mary married for love, choosing Lord Henry Darnley. Seeing this may have prompted Elizabeth to renew her interest in Dudley, which greatly upset the council, in particular the ambitious Lord Norfolk. When the tension between Norfolk and Dudley grew too great, Elizabeth understood that she needed to assert her authority. "I will have here but one mistress and no master," she told Dudley. It was both a political statement and a personal one. The lack of a husband and heir was only made worse in 1566 when Mary gave birth to a son, James, but she was desperately unhappy. Darnley was a violent, drunken husband: many believed he brutally murdered her secret lover, David Rizzio. Darnley would meet his own nasty end a year later, when he was found strangled in the garden of a house. Mary quickly married the Earl of Bothwell, the man who had allegedly murdered Darnley, and Scottish forces rose against her. Imprisoned and forced to abdicate, she eventually fled to England. Elizabeth agreed to give Mary shelter, but her arrival in the north had given Catholics a figurehead and rebellion brewed.

The northern Earls suggested that Norfolk should marry Mary: soon, the Northern Rebellion had begun. As the rebel forces marched south, Elizabeth moved Mary to Coventry and mustered troops of her own. The southern Earls rallied to her cause, which stunned the rebel forces, who

began to retreat. Elizabeth's victory was quick and decisive, with 700 men being executed in a brutal display of power. Norfolk was placed under arrest, but a lack of concrete evidence postponed his execution, until he was implicated in the Ridolfi plot, which aimed to make Spain's Philip II king. Elizabeth ordered and rescinded Norfolk's execution three times – a prime example of how indecisive she could be at times – before finally deciding that he simply had to die.

If Elizabeth's position at home appeared shaky it was positively stable compared to how she was viewed abroad. The Pope decreed that anyone who murdered the heretical English queen would

be forgiven, a statement King Philip took to heart. Not wanting to risk open war, Elizabeth found other ways to aggravate her enemies. She quietly patronised the piratical exploits of John Hawkins and later his cousin Francis Drake. In 1577, when he planned to travel to South America to raid Spanish gold, Elizabeth met Drake with Francis Walsingham, one of her ambassadors to France.

The cautious Cecil had to be kept in the dark, but she told Drake explicitly that she supported him: "I would gladly be revenged on the King of Spain for diverse injuries I have received." Having sailed through the Straits of Magellan and captured a Spanish ship carrying up to £200,000 in gold,

The return of Mary, Queen of Scots to Edinburgh

Queen Elizabeth I knighting Francis Drake in 1581

Drake decided to sail across the Pacific, becoming the first Englishman to circumnavigate the globe. Elizabeth gloried in his achievement, and when she met the Spanish ambassador in 1581, she pointedly wore a crucifix Drake had given to her from the loot. She dined with Drake on the Golden Hind and knighted him. He had done her proud.

These piratical exploits stood in sharp contrast to the events of 1572. The St. Bartholomew's Day Massacre in Paris - the assassination of a number of French Calvinist Protestants - shocked England and the ambassador Sir Francis Walsingham was forced to take refuge. Elizabeth brought him back to London to become her spymaster, where he advised that Mary, Queen of Scots was a real danger. The uprising was not only a shocking scene for English Protestants; it was also a sign that the Protestant Netherlands and their booming wool trade would soon be in danger.

When William the Silent asked Elizabeth for military assistance, she did not want to be seen to intervene and give Philip of Spain an excuse to attack. Walsingham counselled war, while Cecil continued to preach marriage. So Elizabeth entertained the idea of marrying the Duke of Anjou, roughly ten years after it had first been suggested. Then, he had been an ugly youth and she had been a beautiful queen. Now, she was visibly older and the flattery of the French ambassador and Anjou's letters began to win her over. When they finally met, it appeared that Elizabeth really was in love, but there were genuine concerns over how the English people would react.

"The anxieties Elizabeth expressed to the emissary of Mary, Queen of Scots in 1561, that she too could not marry anyone without triggering unrest in one group or another, only deepened following Mary, Queen of Scots's disastrous marriages to Darnley and then Bothwell - which ended in her overthrow," explains Leanda de Lisle, author of Tudor: The Family Story. "Elizabeth continued to look publicly for a husband to fulfil national expectations that she would provide them with an undisputed heir, and surely she hoped it was not impossible. She was married to her kingdom - a phrase she had learned from Mary Tudor. But while Mary had married, Elizabeth did not because she feared revolt by those who disapproved of her choice."

Although she clearly wanted to marry the man that she had nicknamed her "frog," the English people found the idea of their Virgin Queen marrying a French Catholic absolutely repulsive. When a pamphlet appeared that condemned the union, Elizabeth decreed that both the author and his printer should have their right hands cut off. Her Privy Council was split in half, with the jealous Robert Dudley vehemently opposed. Elizabeth was heartbroken, but she agreed to abstain. She gave Anjou £10,000 to continue his war against Philip in the Netherlands, but did not see him again. He tried to take power for himself but failed and died a year later. When William the Silent was assassinated in his own house in 1584

Main players of

Council and Government

William Cecil

1520-98

A canny political operator who understood the difficulties that were ahead, Cecil was Elizabeth's first appointment and was fiercely loyal, dedicating his life to helping her. Although he believed she should marry, Elizabeth knew Cecil was invaluable and pressured him into staying on, even when he was sickly and deaf.

Robert Dudley

1532-88

Dudley had known Elizabeth since childhood, and was her first love. His appointment to court had more to do with her affection for him than any outstanding abilities as a politician, however, and his presence at court proved to be a continual source of rumour and scandal. Their relationship was rocky and driven by passion.

Francis Walsingham

1532-90

The Protestant Walsingham was allowed to return to England after Mary's death, and quickly became one of Elizabeth's most invaluable assets. A brilliant spymaster and politician, he understood the threat that Mary, Queen of Scots posed, and engineered her downfall. He also supported Drake and Raleigh's explorations.

Family

Henry VIII

1491-1547

Henry was desperate for a boy to carry on his family name, and was disappointed when Anne Boleyn gave him Elizabeth. He was absent for much of her childhood, but was kept informed of her progress nonetheless. When he finally met his daughter he was very impressed, so much so that he reinstated her and Mary into his legacy.

Mary Tudor

1516-58

Despite their differences, Mary, Elizabeth and their brother Edward had a relatively close relationship as children. When she became Queen, Mary was desperate for Elizabeth to convert and unable to understand why she wouldn't. She came close to executing her sister, but abstained, finally requesting that she keep England Catholic.

Catherine Parr

1512-48

Catherine and Elizabeth became close during her marriage to Henry, and Elizabeth lived with Catherine for some time after his death. However, Catherine's husband Thomas Seymour was more interested in their young charge than his wife, and she assisted in his attempts at seduction, dying soon after they failed.

the golden age

Explorers

John Hawkins

1532-95

Hawkins may have possessed a coat of arms, but he first managed to find favour with the Queen as a pirate. With Elizabeth's implicit permission, he planned and executed a series of daring raids on Spanish ports in the West Indies, but after a disastrous third voyage he returned to England, where he began working for the Queen in a more direct capacity.

Francis Drake

1540-96

Having sailed on his cousin John Hawkins' expeditions, Francis Drake had no love for the Spanish. He was willing to circumnavigate the globe in order to rob them of their riches and deliver them to Elizabeth, who was delighted with his exploits, and continued to commission him to undertake raids on Spanish ports.

Walter Raleigh

1554-1618

Raleigh gained Elizabeth's favour at court and quickly set his sights on expanding her empire. He decided he would establish Britain's first colony in North America, and told the Queen it would be named after her: Virginia. To his great dismay, the colony at Roanoke failed. He is often falsely credited with bringing potatoes and tobacco to England.

Enemies

King Philip II

1527-1598

The main religious threat to Elizabeth for the majority of her realm came from the King of Spain. The Pope might have given the bull that deposed Elizabeth but the fiercely Catholic Philip was the man with the army that could enforce it. He had attempted to woo the princess while still married to her sister but, once rebuffed, relentlessly opposed her.

John Whitgift

1530-1604

As the issue of religious tolerance became increasingly difficult to manage, Elizabeth hand-picked her old chaplain for the role of Archbishop of Canterbury. He was a stubborn man, as evidenced by his refusal to leave England during Queen Mary's reign. Like Elizabeth, he was a Conformist and ruthlessly punished those who publicly strayed from the 'right' path.

Pope Pius V

1504-72

As the head of the Roman Catholic Church, Pope Pius V saw Elizabeth's status of Queen of England and head of its church not only as an affront to his religion, but as an act of heresy. He went as far as to issue a Papal Bull on 27 April 1570, which declared that her subjects no longer owed her any kind of allegiance.

"She bitterly resented the circumstances of Mary's execution"

by a Catholic fanatic, it was clear that military intervention could not be put off any longer and so in 1585, to the relief of her impatient councillors, she agreed to send a small force of men. Dudley took command in the Netherlands but proved to be incompetent, losing territory to Philip's general, the Duke of Parma. Mary was now more dangerous than ever. Elizabeth ordered her imprisonment at the urging of Francis Walsingham, who had no intention of allowing her to live much longer. He arranged for a servant, one of his own spies, to suggest that Mary smuggle letters in beer barrels, allowing Walsingham to read everything. When Thomas Babingdon wrote to Mary with a plan to assassinate Elizabeth and give her the crown Mary wrote back with her approval; the spymaster's trap had worked perfectly, and he had ensnared his unwitting prey.

Walsingham leapt into action and ordered the conspirators' execution. Elizabeth had always been reluctant to execute her cousin, but she agreed she would have to stand trial. It was no surprise when the court decided that Mary should be put to death. Elizabeth grieved for Mary, or at least lamented her death. The man who had delivered the warrant was imprisoned and stripped of his title.

Elizabeth was always reluctant to sign a death warrant - or at least she was reluctant to be seen to sign it. We can't know how much of Elizabeth's grief was genuine, but she bitterly resented the circumstances of Mary's execution.

"Elizabeth was reluctant to be seen to execute first the senior nobleman in England, in Norfolk, and then a fellow queen, in Mary," says de Lisle: "That is not

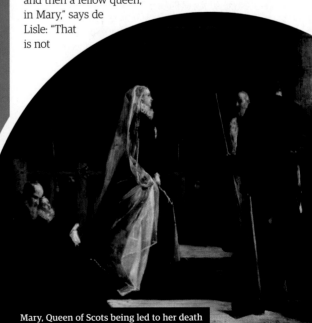

Mary, Queen of Scots being led to her death

The Spanish Armada is put into disarray by English fireships on 8 August 1588

The gun-crew on an Elizabethan ship - she funded the journeys of numerous privateers

to say she regretted their deaths. She would have preferred to have Mary murdered, for example, as she made very clear.

It is also notable that she was quite ruthless in ordering the deaths of traitors of humble birth - the 900 or so executed after the Northern Rebellion testifies to that. This was three times the numbers Henry VIII had executed after the far more serious Pilgrimage of Grace, and ten times the numbers Mary executed after Wyatt's revolt."

Mary's execution provided Philip II with the reason he needed to declare war and his Spanish Armada co-ordinated with the Duke of Parma's forces in the Netherlands, with the two forces meeting before sailing on England.

They launched on 12 July 1588, their forces possessing more than twice the number of English ships, but the English ships did have some advantages; they were smaller, faster, and designed to carry guns rather than men. The English ships could outmanoeuvre the Spanish fleet in open water and began to engage them in small skirmishes. It was at this point that Elizabeth rode out to meet her troops. With the threat of a Catholic force at their doorstep, the queen rallied the spirit

"The queen rallied the spirit of the English troops by declaring that she would fight by their side"

Did England become a nation to be feared?

Elizabeth's foreign policy was decidedly more cautious than expansive. She was desperate to avoid conflict because it was expensive and the outcome always uncertain. However, she had a spirit that could easily be won over by the idea of adventure. She delighted in the expeditions of John Hawkins and Francis Drake, which could be seen to be aggravating the King of Spain without actually declaring open conflict. In 1562, she agreed to a military expedition in Calais, which was crushed by Catherine de' Medici's forces, and this failure would influence her military decisions for the rest of her reign.

"There was no glory in it for Elizabeth as there was for a male monarch," Leanda de Lisle reveals. "She understood the truth of the adage of Mary of Hungary: that war made it impossible for a woman to rule effectively, 'all she can do is shoulder responsibility for mistakes committed by others.'"

Her ally and enemy lines were drawn by religion. France and Spain were clearly opposed to England on these grounds, which is why her courtiers were so anxious that Elizabeth marry an eligible man from either country. Even after the St Bartholomew's Day Massacre in 1572, Elizabeth was reluctant to be drawn into open war. The piecemeal way in which she gave the Dutch her assistance shows her reluctance to engage in open conflict of any kind, first offering financial support to the Dutch troops, then the Duke of Anjou, before finally agreeing to send an English force when there was no other option. Her cautious attitude towards foreign policy doubtless saved the kingdom a lot of money. However, it was taken out of her hands when the Spanish Armada sailed on England."

Verdict

The victory against the Armada was a shining moment but for the most part Elizabeth kept out of foreign conflict. When she didn't, she regularly suffered defeats.

Why did the Armada fail?

King Philip amassed his Armada and sent them to the Netherlands to join up with his ground troops, led by the Duke of Parma. The English outposts saw the ships coming and alerted the admiralty. The weather was against the Spanish, as they were blown off course. While they outnumbered the British fleet by two to one, the Spanish ships were enormous, built to carry troops that could board enemy vessels. Their crescent formation was famous, but it did little against the smaller English ships. When the English sent fireships into the Spanish fleet, the enemy panicked and scattered. They managed to regroup for one confrontation, and lost. The Spanish retreated, with many ships crashing on the rocks of the English and Irish coastline.

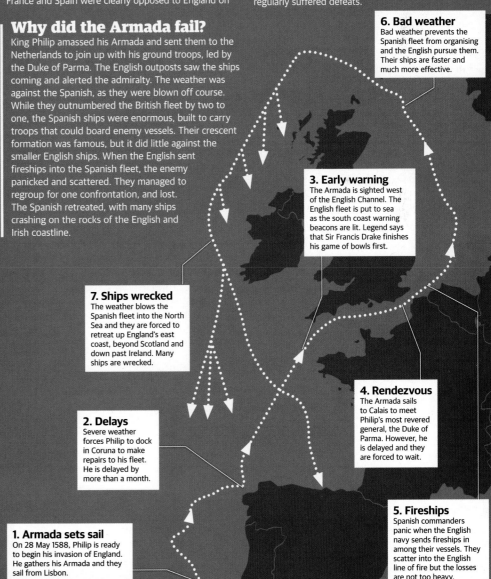

6. Bad weather
Bad weather prevents the Spanish fleet from organising and the English pursue them. Their ships are faster and much more effective.

3. Early warning
The Armada is sighted west of the English Channel. The English fleet is put to sea as the south coast warning beacons are lit. Legend says that Sir Francis Drake finishes his game of bowls first.

7. Ships wrecked
The weather blows the Spanish fleet into the North Sea and they are forced to retreat up England's east coast, beyond Scotland and down past Ireland. Many ships are wrecked.

4. Rendezvous
The Armada sails to Calais to meet Philip's most revered general, the Duke of Parma. However, he is delayed and they are forced to wait.

2. Delays
Severe weather forces Philip to dock in Coruna to make repairs to his fleet. He is delayed by more than a month.

5. Fireships
Spanish commanders panic when the English navy sends fireships in among their vessels. They scatter into the English line of fire but the losses are not too heavy.

1. Armada sets sail
On 28 May 1588, Philip is ready to begin his invasion of England. He gathers his Armada and they sail from Lisbon.

---

of the English troops by declaring that she would fight by their side to repel anyone who dared to set foot on their land.

This grandstanding was impressive and may have gone down in history's annals but was ultimately unnecessary. The Spanish Armada failed and Elizabeth's victory was the seal on her status. 'The Golden Age' had begun, where art and literature flowered. With England a visibly powerful state, the aristocracy began to patronise the arts with great abandon.

The famous playwrights of the age enjoyed patronage, albeit with some caveats. When Shakespeare wrote Richard II he was encouraged to remove a scene suggesting the ageing monarch should step aside. "Elizabeth did not care for plays," confirms de Lisle: "All too often they were used to lecture her on this or that."

Her crown may have been safe for now, but she received devastating blows with the deaths of two of her most trusted advisors, Dudley and Walsingham. Dudley was replaced at court by his handsome stepson, the Earl of Essex, and the young flatterer quickly became her favourite.

"Robert Dudley's death in 1588 signalled the passing of the old order, but Elizabeth still hoped she could continue ruling according to her motto, 'Semper Eadem' ('Always the same')" explains de Lisle. "As the years began to pass and her servants died she either did not replace them or find a near-equivalent to the servant she had lost." It's a sign of how much she leaned on her old guard that she continued to place her trust in William

Cecil, even though he was almost entirely deaf and increasingly ill. It was only when he died in 1598 that Elizabeth finally agreed to appoint Robert Cecil to his father's old post. When it became known that the Spanish were attempting to rebuild their fleet, Essex led a fleet on Cadiz and decimated their forces in port. The success gave Essex fame, something Elizabeth was taken aback by. She tried to curb him, aware that her standing among the people was her greatest asset, but Essex continued to promote his own celebrity. She became more and more frustrated with his outrageous behaviour at court, which came to a dramatic head when he half-drew his sword on her in a fit of pique.

The arts and literature may have been flourishing, but those who subscribe to this being a golden age in England's history often forget that even after the defeat of the Spanish Armada, other uprisings, such as the 1598 Irish rebellion, occurred. The country had long been a problem for Tudor England, which had attempted to impose English values and had seen the Irish as tenants on English territory. Now, with a Spanish-backed uprising, Elizabeth needed to take decisive action.

She sent her army at the start of 1599, led by Essex, who was looking to prove himself once more. He was a disaster. Rather than confronting Tyrone on the battlefield, he met him in secret and returned to England having made a treaty without the queen's authority.

When Essex thought Cecil was plotting against him, he rushed to plead his case. Assuming he was still the queen's favourite, he burst into her bedchamber while she was preparing for the day. He had seen Elizabeth without her make-up and regal dressing; not as a queen but as an old woman. She could not afford to be seen like this. The queen dismissed him before summoning him later to confront him with his failures and strip him of power. Rather than accepting his fate, Essex attempted rebellion. He assumed Londoners would back the popular war hero, but Elizabeth proclaimed him a traitor and sent her troops to meet him. The rebellion was a failure and Essex was executed as a traitor.

Although the later years of Elizabeth's reign were far from golden, she could still rally her people when needed. The war in Ireland was expensive and unsuccessful, while overcrowding and failed harvests caused agitation. When Parliament publicly condemned her for granting monopolies to her favourite courtiers, which had led to price-fixing, Elizabeth was forced to address them in 1601. She agreed to put a stop to the monopolies and she reaffirmed her love for England. She won over Parliament, there was a good harvest, and a truce was reached in Ireland and Spain. "Elizabeth, old and ill, did lose some of her former grip, but never entirely," states de Lisle. "She had followed Mary I's example in wooing the common people from the beginning of her reign, and they continued to support her."

Having seen off another uprising, the 50-year-old monarch's health was failing and after an all-too-rare period of good health, Elizabeth grew sickly. She was desperately frustrated by Cecil's growing

"She wooed her people with smiles, words of love and great showmanship, and so won their hearts"

Did peace reign in England?

The early years of Elizabeth's reign were extremely unstable. The Catholics regarded her as a heretical bastard without a just claim to the throne, and she had to prove to her people that she was capable of ruling alone. Conspiracies at home and abroad plotted to remove her from the throne, and when Mary, Queen of Scots took refuge in England, her Catholic enemies finally had someone to rally around. 1569 saw her face the first real uprising with the Northern Rebellion. The Earls of Westmorland and Northumberland rallied the rebel aristocracy around them, but they were not prepared for the force of her reprisal.

In her later years she saw rebellion rear its head again as Essex overstepped his bounds. With famine and overcrowded of cities, Elizabeth's position became unstable once again. "Imagine if Elizabeth had died in October 1562 when she had smallpox," asks de Lisle: "Elizabeth had been on the throne almost four years: only a year short of her sister's reign. If she died, as many feared she would, how would her reign have been remembered? Elizabeth's religious settlement was not viewed as settled by anyone save the Queen. One of her own bishops called it 'a leaden mediocrity'. In military matters, while Mary I's loss of Calais is still remembered, Elizabeth's failed efforts to recover Calais by taking Le Havre and using it as a bargaining tool are completely forgotten. The campaign had ended that August 1562, with the huge loss of 2,000 men."

Verdict

Elizabeth's reign featured numerous rebellions and uprisings, but this was not unusual for a Tudor monarch, and given the religious uncertainty in the country at the time, she handled the uprisings quickly and decisively.

Rebellions against Elizabeth

When Elizabeth ascended to the throne she immediately faced the threat of rebellion from the Catholic nobility, who resented the fact that she was turning away from the changes made by her sister Mary. The first great uprising came in 1569, when the northern noblemen took advantage of the return of Mary, Queen of Scots to England, and attempted to overthrow her. The Duke of Norfolk, unhappy with being sidelined by the Earl of Dudley, entertained a marriage plot with Mary, while the northern Earls mounted rebellion. It was summarily crushed and hundreds were executed.

The Earl of Essex, Elizabeth's great favourite, attempted a rebellion in 1601 after he was stripped of his powers in an attempt to gain power. In line with his apparently oversized ego, he overestimated his personal popularity, the people's dissatisfaction with their monarch and his Queen's capacity for forgiveness for one of her former favourites. When Elizabeth was confronted with open defiance she rarely hesitated to crush it. She understood when to be brutal and when to charm. With the rebellions against her she was unforgiving and generally unsparing, meting out punishments swiftly and unsparingly to rebels and traitors.

Elizabeth's golden moments

2. 1566
Elizabeth announces to a Parliament desperate to see her choose a husband that she is married to England.

5. 1587
Elizabeth is forced to execute Mary, Queen of Scots, which is the final straw for Catholic Spain.

7. 1601
Following famine and controversy over her granting monopolies to her favourites, Elizabeth gives her 'Golden Speech' to a furious Parliament and wins them over.

1550	1555	1560	1565	1570	1575	1580	1585	1590	1595	1600	1605

1. 1559
Elizabeth is crowned Queen of England. Everyone watches to see if she displays a Protestant leaning but the ceremony is ambiguous.

3. 1569
The Northern Rebellion is crushed. Elizabeth brutally punishes those responsible and sends a shocking reminder to anyone who would challenge her.

4. 1577
Francis Drake circumnavigates the globe and returns with boats filled with riches stolen from the King of Spain.

6. 1588
The Spanish Armada sails for England, but is decisively defeated. Elizabeth delivers her famous Tilbury speech from horseback, which becomes legend.

The deathbed of Queen Elizabeth in 1603

power over her and refused to go to bed as she realised that the end was coming soon. Elizabeth finally died on 23 March 1603. Although she had struggled to change with the times in the face of younger, ambitious advisors, she had been a formidable political operator. She had still shown the cunning and cleverness to understand her situation, and had never lost the image of a queen loved by her people.

"That image was not created for her," explains de Lisle. "Elizabeth never forgot the events of 1553 when the ordinary people had backed the Tudor sisters, while the political elite had supported Jane Grey. Nor did she forget how in 1554, Mary had made a speech at the Guildhall that roused London in her defence against the Wyatt rebellion. Mary had spoken of her marriage to her kingdom, describing her coronation ring as a wedding band, and her love of her subjects as that of a mother for her children. These were the phrases and motifs Elizabeth would use repeatedly and would become absolutely central to her reign.

In addition, Elizabeth also had an instinct for the crowd's demands. Even her enemies would admit she had 'the power of enchantment'. She wooed her people with smiles, words of love and great showmanship, and so won their hearts. Elizabeth's people would never forget her. When she died and James I become king, people hugely missed the Tudor theatre of reciprocal love, of which Elizabeth had been the last and brightest star."

Elizabeth's reign was not the golden age that legend so often depicts; she faced serious uprisings, both internal and external, during her reign. She was capable of heartlessness and ruthlessness, and could be indecisive and impetuous. During the course of her rule, England saw famine, rebellion and war. However, there's no mistaking her dedication to her country and her determination to listen to what the people wanted from her - and then give it to them. She walked a political tightrope for most of her life, and the fact that she died peacefully in her bed as queen was a major triumph in itself. The English people loved her, and she, in turn, loved them. In the hearts and minds of many of her subjects, she was - and will always be - Britain's golden monarch.

1555 – 1605
Naresuan the Great

A national hero in his native Thailand, Naresuan the Great single-handedly conquered Southeast Asia in the 16th Century

It says something that the 2007 film *The Legend Of King Naresuan* is the most expensive film in the history of Thailand. The action-packed, five-part historical epic, which celebrates the larger-than-life conquests of Somdet Phra Naresuan Maharat — otherwise known as Naresuan the Great — cost £13.2 million ($21.7 million) to produce. With financial backing from the Thai royal family, the film chronicled how Naresuan, a 16th Century warrior king, threw off the shackles of Burmese rule and established the Thai kingdom of Ayutthaya as political and military force in Southeast Asia. Imagine George Washington if the American general ditched his horse for a battle elephant.

To understand the importance of Naresuan to Thai history, you first need to understand the political dynamics of 16th Century Southeast Asia. First of all, the country we know as Thailand didn't exist until the 20th Century. For hundreds of years, the region was ruled by a series of Thai kingdoms known in the West as Siam. In 1555, Naresuan was born to King Maha Thammarachathirat, ruler of Ayutthaya, the dominant Thai kingdom of the age.

Naresuan's father ruled a kingdom literally surrounded by enemies: Burma to the north-east, Cambodia and the Khmer to the south-east, and disparate tribal states (Shan, Mon and others) to the west and north. Burma was by far the most potent threat. In 1548, Naresuan's father repelled a formidable Burmese attack, but the Burmese King Bayinnaung returned with an even larger force — including hundreds of Portuguese mercenaries — and Ayutthaya surrendered.

The Thai kingdom was now under Burmese control. King Bayinnaung allowed Naresuan's father to remain on the throne as a puppet vassal to Burma. As a pledge of his allegiance, the Thai leader was forced to send his two sons — Naresuan, age nine, and his younger brother, Ekathotsarot — to be raised in the Burmese capital of Pegu.

For seven years, Naresuan and his brother lived in the Burmese court while his father reigned over a neutered state. Because the Burmese restricted the Thai kingdom to a small military force, Ayutthaya fell victim to a string of crippling attacks from the Khmer in Cambodia. Meanwhile, Naresuan became a student of Buddhist philosophy and ethics, as well as an avid pupil of Burmese and Portuguese military tactics and hand-to-hand combat. One of his childhood sparring partners was Minchit Sra, grandson to the Burmese king, who would grow up to face Naresuan in the most famous duel in Thai history.

When Naresuan turned 16, King Bayinnaung of Burma allowed the Thai prince to return home in exchange for his sister's hand in marriage. Young Naresuan was put in charge of the northern Thai city of Phitsanulok as the Uparat, or presumptive heir to the Thai throne. As you can imagine,

Much like the vast majority of ancient and modern Thai people, Naresuan was a practising Theravada Buddhist

NARESUAN

Siam, 1555 – 1605

Brief Bio

This action-hero king rose from the position of a hostage at a rival court to reclaiming the throne that was rightfully his, in the process becoming a national hero. Siam, now Thailand, is still gripped by his powerful legacy. He returned home-rule to the nation as well as being the warrior-king that storytellers dream of.

"When Naresuan turned 16, King Bayinnaung of Burma allowed the Thai prince to return home in exchange for his sister's hand in marriage"

The Elephant Duel of Nong Sarai

An hour-and-a-half's drive outside of Bangkok is the province of Suphan Buri, home to one of the most popular tourist attractions in Thailand, a towering statue of a battle elephant bearing King Naresuan. The monument is believed to have been built over the exact site of the battlefield of Nong Sarai, where Naresuan fought the most famous duel in Thai history.

The year was 1593 and the Burmese army, under the direction of King Nanda Bayin's son, crown prince Minchit Sra, was marching toward the Thai capital of Ayutthaya. Naresuan and his troops marched west from Ayutthaya and met Minchit Sra's forces outside the small village of Nong Sarai. As the armies of thousands clashed, Naresuan's battle elephant panicked and ran into the middle of the fray. Naresuan spotted Minchit Sra on his own elephant and famously challenged the crown prince to a duel. "Let us fight the elephant battle for the honour of our kingdoms!" Legend has it that the two armies paused their fighting and circled around the two elephants and their royal riders. The duel lasted only a few minutes, but is recorded in dozens of paintings and even re-enacted in Thai action movies. As the two elephants converged, Minchit Sra slashed at Naresuan with his long-handled war scythe, but only nicked the king's hat. When Minchit Sra extended his scythe, he left his body exposed, giving Naresuan just enough room to deliver the fatal blow. Their prince killed, the Burmese army scattered.

Naresuan was in an unusual political position. Raised in Burma as a prisoner-prince, he both resented and respected the Thai people's feudal overlords. If he had early dreams of rebellion he hid them well, biding his time and pledging his continued loyalty to the Burmese throne.

Ironically, it was during a show of this loyalty that Naresuan aroused the deadly jealousy of Burma's new king, Nanda Bayin, who succeeded his father in 1581. Naresuan was sent by his father to pay homage to Nanda Bayin and express the Thai kingdom's unwavering allegiance to Burma. To test this allegiance, Nanda Bayin recruited Naresuan and his Thai army to help quash a rebellion in the Shan states to the north. When Nanda Bayin and his Burmese troops failed to take a key city, Naresuan swept in to conquer it. Instead of encouraging Nanda Bayin, the act embarrassed and enraged him. The ensuing decades of war between Burma and the Thai kingdom were as much personal as political – the anger of a native Burmese king against an adoptive and rebellious prince.

Naresuan returned to his home base of Phitsanulok, but he was quickly summoned by Nanda Bayin to help to help put down yet another rebellion. Dutifully, Naresuan assembled his troops, but not without his suspicions. Word had reached him that the Burmese were constructing a road to the Thai capital city of Ayutthaya, a sign that the foreign king was looking to further tighten his grip on the Thai kingdom. As Naresuan marched toward the Burmese capital of Pegu, he was

> In 1990, a college in Phitsanulok was renamed Naresuan University to celebrate his ascension to the throne

intercepted by two Mon princes, childhood friends from his days in the Burmese court. They warned him of Nanda Bayin's secret plan to ambush and kill Naresuan.

Naresuan had played the loyal puppet for long enough; the time had come to become the leader that his people needed. Naresuan publicly renounced his allegiance to Burma in 1584, and with his army at his back – plus the respective armies of the two Mon princes – he marched on the Burmese stronghold of Pegu, determined to win his people's independence.

The Thai offensive was repelled by Minchit Sra, Naresuan's childhood sparring partner and son of King Nanda Bayin. As Naresuan and his army fled over the Sitang River, Naresuan turned his battle elephant to face the attacking army. Legend has it that Naresuan asked for a Portuguese musket, a weapon useful for raining a volley of musket balls on an enemy, not sharpshooting an individual target. Nevertheless, Naresuan raised the musket, took aim at the Burmese general leading the charge, and shot a single ball across the Sitang River, striking the general dead. The fabled 'Royal Shot Across the Sitang River' gave the Thai army a chance to retreat back to the capital city of Ayutthaya and prepare for all-out war.

In the late 16th Century, Ayutthaya was one of the biggest and most culturally and technologically advanced cities in the world. It was the Venice of the East, a walled city of intersecting canals that floated as a fortified 'island' in between three converging rivers. Its walls and rivers defended Ayutthaya against attack while its interior culture flourished, producing remarkable Buddhist-themed architecture borrowed from the ancient temples of Angkor in Cambodia, as well as art and music influenced by both East and West. Fertile rice fields surrounded the city and Ayutthaya grew rich exporting rice to European traders and to China, the reigning superpower of the region.

When Naresuan arrived in Ayutthaya, his father the king entrusted him with the city's protection and with building an army ready to answer the full strength and anger of the Burmese. Naresuan capitalised on widespread disaffection with

Defining moment
Exile in Burma
1564-1571
After the Burmese conquered the Thai kingdom, they placed Naresuan's father as a vassal over Ayutthaya and took Naresuan and his brother as hostages. Many legends surround the seven years Naresuan lived among the Burmese royal court in Pegu. There's much talk of martial arts training and a budding rivalry between Naresuan and the king's grandson Minchit Sra, but that might be nothing more than a convenient backstory for their fateful duel decades later. Some accounts say that young Naresuan grew to love King Bayinnaung like a second father, adding to the sting of the betrayal by Bayinnaung's successor Nanda Bayin.

Timeline

1555

● **Noble Birth**
Naresuan was born Prince Naret. Royalty came through his mother, the queen, although his father was a high-ranking nobleman of Sukhothai heritage. Expectations were high for their first-born son.
1555

● **Declaration of Independence**
When the Burmese plot to assassinate Naresuan was exposed, the Thai prince had no further reason to feign loyalty to Nanda Bayin. He performed a ceremony formally declaring an end to the Burmese tributary and, informally, declaring war on Burma.
1584

● **Naresuan the King**
Although Naresuan's father was king of Ayutthaya, he was viewed by many as a traitor, nothing more than a puppet for the Burmese. Naresuan, on the other hand, assumed the throne as a proven military leader and political revolutionary.
1590

"Naresuan had played the puppet for long enough; the time had come to become the leader that his people needed"

Burmese bullying in the region, recruiting troops from the Shan and Mon states to reinforce the Thai ranks. King Nanda Bayin of Burma wasted no time answering Naresuan's rebellion. He sent his army against Ayutthaya less than a year after Naresuan's failed invasion of Pegu. Naresuan repelled the first attack easily, as with a second and third Burmese attempt in the years that followed. Even the Khmer tried their luck, hoping to capitalise on Thai entanglements with Burma. Incredibly, Naresuan not only held off the Cambodian offensive, but pursued his attackers all the way back to the walls of Lovek, the Khmer capital.

In 1590, King Maha Thammarachathirat died, making Naresuan the sovereign ruler of Ayutthaya. Naresuan devoted some of his energy to centralising political power and reforming the traditional patronage system enjoyed by princes. He also sidelined as a diplomat and ambassador, signing trade agreements with the Portuguese and Spanish. But Naresuan's greatest talents were as a savvy military strategist and cunning warrior.

Naresuan's greatest moment came during the fifth attempt by the

Burmese army to crush the rebellious Ayutthaya state. Thai spies sent word that Nanda Bayin's army was one the move yet again, lead by Naresuan's old foe Minchit Sra. Rather than hunker down behind the city walls, Naresuan marched his army westward to intercept Minchit Sra as his forces descended from Three Pagodas Pass. The two armies met near the small village of Nong Sarai and engaged in a bloody and drawn out battle that initially favoured the Burmese. The tide turned when Naresuan, mounted on his battle elephant, personally challenged Minchit Sra to a duel for the honour of their kingdoms. The two men faced off atop their elephants, armed with razor-sharp war scythes and surrounded by their battle-weary armies. Dodging an errant joust by Minchit Sra, Naresuan quickly dispatched his childhood rival with a mortal slash. In the ensuing chaos, the Burmese fled in retreat, but the Thai army pursued them, inflicting massive casualties.

The battle proved a critical turning point in the Burmese-Thai conflict. After his victory at Nong Sarai, Naresuan sent generals to take port cities in the coastal Burmese region of Tenasserim, winning unrestricted military and trade access to the Indian Ocean. Emboldened, Naresuan invaded Cambodia, toppling the Khmer king and returning to Ayutthaya with thousands of prisoners of war to repopulate Northern Thailand. Before his death in 1605 from a skin infection, Naresuan led military campaigns deep into a greatly weakened Burma, through the now-ruined capital of Pegu and north to Toungoo.

Naresuan was only 49 when he died, but his heroics on the battlefield cemented the Thai kingdom as the undisputed power in Southeast Asia for the next century. The legend of Naresuan the Great is more than a great action-movie plot; it's the story of a people's first taste of freedom and power in the modern age.

> Naresuan was close with his brother Ekathotsarot. Naresuan, the first-born, was known as the Black Prince

Defining moment
Chinese Chess
1592

The Ming Dynasty was the superpower of 16th Century Asia, and Naresuan courted a favourable relationship with the Chinese. The island kingdom of Japan, however, had its sights set on greatness. In 1592, Japanese naval forces sailed to the Korean peninsula and conquered it. But Korea was just a stepping stone on the way to toppling the Ming Dynasty. Naresuan received word of clashes between Japanese and Chinese forces and sent an emissary to the Forbidden City in Beijing offering Thai military support. He likely knew that the offer would be refused – which it was – but it was a strategic show of loyalty, one that would assure China's protection of lucrative Thai trade routes.

Life in the time of Naresuan

East Meets West
Portuguese explorer Vasco de Gama, one of the most successful explorers of the Age of Discovery, became the first European to sail a sea route to India in 1498, landing in Calicut. Successions of Portuguese armadas established a lucrative spice route and a colony in India. Naresuan wisely nurtured healthy trade relations with Portugal as well as the Spanish Philippines to the benefit of his own nation and its peoples.

Crown of Thai Civilisation
The city of Ayutthaya flourished from the 14th-18th Century and at its height was one of the world's largest and most technologically advanced cities with a population far greater then any other metropolis of its age. The island city was protected by three rivers and saved from floods with a remarkably innovative hydraulic system.

Ayutthaya Architecture
When the Burmese sacked and burned Ayutthaya in 1767 during the Burmese–Siamese War which started in 1765, they left only the ruins of a few Buddhist monasteries. These otherworldly stone towers and intricately carved bas relief sculptures have been designated a UNESCO World Heritage Site. The Ayutthaya historical park is the ruins of the former capital of the Kingdom of Siam.

Gun Power
The Chinese invented gunpowder in the 9th Century and crafted the first crude firearms or 'hand cannons' shortly after, but it was the Portuguese musket that was widely adopted by Japanese, Korean and Southeast Asian armies in the 16th Century. They became a cornerstone of the Ming army only after the Ming conquest of China, giving Ming armies a distinct advantage over their neighbours'.

Ming Superpower
The Ming Dynasty, also the Empire of the Great Ming, ruled China from 1368 to 1644 and extended its borders from Outer Mongolia to the north down to Vietnam in the south. China exuded tremendous political and military influence in the region during Naresuan's rule. At its zenith the empire's standing army exceeded one million troops.

1605

Birth of a Nation
After his victory in the epic elephant duel at Nong Sarai, Naresuan ordered that a pagoda be built over the very spot on which the battle took place, a version of which exists today. 25 January is also celebrated as Thailand's National Armed Forces Day.
25 January 1593

Collapse of Burma
Naresuan's highest goal was to march triumphantly into Pegu and personally drag Nanda Bayin to his execution. Ultimately, he failed to take the city while the king was alive, but witnessed the dissolution of the Burmese empire after Nanda Bayin's death.
1599

Death
For a decorated war hero, Naresuan eventually died a commoner's death, a victim of a deeply infected carbuncle on his face, or what might have actually been smallpox.
1605

© Jay Wong, Thinkstock

1566 – 1625
James I

James I, King of England and Scotland, struggled throughout his reign to create a united and prosperous realm of Great Britain under a Stuart dynasty

I t was widely hoped by English courtiers that King James VI of Scotland represented a safe pair of hands for the English monarchy in 1603. Elizabeth I had died after nearly 45 years on the throne and had left no clues as to who should succeed her. As far as the English court was concerned James was the natural choice even if he was the son of that notorious Catholic, Mary Queen of Scots. Unlike his mother, he was a Protestant. He had also reigned in Scotland successfully for 36 years. Secret meetings between James and members of Elizabeth's inner circle had been conducted to see if he would be interested in the job; as far as the English were concerned, his credentials were excellent.

James' disruptive and unstable childhood had forced him to become adaptable in dangerous situations, something that served him well when he became King of England. His mother had been forced to abdicate the Scottish throne in 1567 by a Protestant uprising, after which he was placed in the charge of her enemies to be raised as a Protestant. Not long into his adult reign as King of Scotland, he was kidnapped by a group of nobles and was compelled to rule through their influence for a year. These were dangerous times for James; he had been little more than a child and at the mercy of men who wanted

> After the events of the Gunpowder Plot, James became paranoid, and would, in public, wear a padded doublet as a type of armour

> James believed in the divine right of Kings, that he was placed on the throne by God and it was his heavenly duty to rule

nothing more than to claim the power behind the throne for themselves.

It was an unforgiving and impoverished life, his strict Protestant teachings made for a bland existence that consisted of rules and punishments. The sober education James received in his early years along with the impoverishment of the Scottish crown meant that when he journeyed south in 1603 he was astonished at the comparative abundance of the English realm. He quickly took to enjoying his new-found wealth by lavishing English gifts on his Scottish courtiers controversially from the English treasury.

His court became one of the most extravagant and audacious institutions in England, James did not care for studying documents or enacting laws. He'd rather go hunting, hawking or hosting his infamously drunken banquets. He was a man enjoying his new-found freedom away from the cold monotony of ruling Scotland and he did not want to make a new prison for himself by trying too hard to rule England. He left it up to his courtiers to do the day-to-day business, namely an old trusted advisor, Robert Cecil, who died nine years later from exhaustion.

While James' new-found extravagance irritated those who paid the bills, it was instead his religious beliefs that caused the most controversy.

JAMES I
British, 1566 - 1625

Brief Bio
Ascending to the throne of Scotland in 1567, James became the king of a unified Scottish and English kingdom after the death of his cousin, Elizabeth I. He struggled to continue her legacy and became increasingly unpopular with his Catholic subjects in particular, who made an attempt on his life in 1605.

James was the first monarch who argued for a union between England and Scotland. It was rejected by both countries

The sexuality of the King has long been the subject of enquiry; it is widely thought that James had relationships with men

The last King of Scotland

James was the last Scottish monarch to rule a fully independent Scotland without governing by proxy from other kingdoms. A Scottish King needed to be strong-willed and able to adapt quickly especially when dealing with the touchy and volatile clan system. James proved himself to be an able negotiator and a strong leader in this regard; he stopped the country tearing itself apart with religious violence and gained universal respect from the numerous clan-based factions within the Scottish court. Perhaps his greatest achievement was the book he authored called *The True Law of Free Monarchies*. In it he outlined a theory of absolute monarchy by which the King, granted his prerogative powers from God, could create laws and enact commands without consulting privy counsellors or Parliaments. This was a radical and explosive idea in the British Isles, where the power of Parliament governing in partnership with the monarchy was a long-respected institution. In Scotland the Parliamentary system was easier to manage because it was smaller and relied on business being conducted personally with the King. When James journeyed south to claim his English throne he quickly found that the English Parliament was not only far larger but also more vocal in its criticism of the monarch.

On 5 November 1605, a group of conspirators connected to the Catholic Jesuit community in England acted on a plot to assassinate James by attempting to blow up Parliament. The conspirators were appalled at James' overtly Protestant beliefs, so they decided to kill him in order to install his nine-year-old daughter Elizabeth as Queen in the hopes that she would become a pro-Catholic monarch. The plan on the face of it made sense: rather than just kill James they planned to kill his entire Protestant party at the opening of Parliament and thus create enough chaos for a pro-Catholic monarch to be installed in its wake. James was not in the Parliament building when a suspicious attendant discovered Guy Fawkes guarding barrels of gunpowder in the cellars.

When news of the conspiracy reached James, he acted decisively. He was no stranger to intrigue of this kind and knew what had to be done. He ordered Fawkes to be interrogated using the 'gentler tortures' which included racking, where Fawkes was tied to a device and stretched until his bones were forced out of their sockets. In keeping with his style of dealing with matters on a personal level, he journeyed down to the tower and interrogated Fawkes himself, asking him how he could conspire 'such a hideous a treason'. Fawkes replied: 'A dangerous disease required a desperate remedy.' James was appalled but he admired Fawkes' spirit, noting later that he put on a 'Roman resolution.' Eventually the King's torturers broke Fawkes: he gave up his fellow conspirators and they all suffered a traitor's death. While James had not

been physically harmed during the whole affair, mentally it affected him greatly. He had always known that he'd had English enemies and now some of them had tried to kill him. From then on he didn't travel without guards, he wore an extra-thick doublet and carried a knife at all times for additional protection.

Four days after the Gunpowder Plot on 9 November, James addressed the first session of Parliament with the following preamble, "it may well be called a roaring, nay a firing sin from fire and brimstone, from the which God hath so miraculously delivered as all." The sitting MPs heartily agreed. Unfortunately for James it would be about the only thing him and his Parliament would agree on for the next 20 years. They argued incessantly over money, religion and taxation. James was furious. It was his view that a monarch be unquestioned by their subjects, that ruling was his business and not theirs. After a particularly difficult session, he commented, "I will not thank where I feel no thanks due... I am not of such a stock as to praise fools... I wish you would make use of your liberty with more modesty in times to come."

Parliament held on to its liberty and refused James' proposal for a standard lump sum of money to be given to him to run the country, known as the 'Great Contract' of 1610. The MPs felt James simply couldn't be trusted with such a lucrative proposition. James blamed the insolence of the members of the house and listened to his favourites in court who sneered at what they saw as common

> James suffered from weak knees and later developed crippling arthritis in his knee joints; he was seen hobbling in later years

Timeline

1566

● **Birth of James**
James is born to Mary Queen of Scots on 19 June 1566. James is Mary's only son and while this secures the line of succession, his mother is deeply unpopular in Scotland.
19 June 1566

● **Crowned King of Scotland**
The nobles ensure that James is crowned King of Scotland while he is still in his minority so they can influence his upbringing and stop him from becoming a Catholic like his mother.
29 July 1567

● **Marriage to Anne of Denmark**
James marries Anne of Denmark by proxy to strengthen the ties of Protestant monarchies within Europe. The couple would go on to have seven children.
August 1589

● **Journey south**
After the death of Elizabeth I it is decided that James has the strongest claim to the throne of England and is invited south. He takes his household and courtiers with him.
5 April 1603

● **Flight of Mary Queen of Scots**
After facing a Protestant uprising from her nobles, Mary is forced to abdicate and flees south into England leaving the young James at the mercy of her enemies.
24 July 1567

Defining moment
Crowned King of England
25 July 1603
James had ruled Scotland as the sixth king of his name for 36 years when his cousin Elizabeth I died. Despite the family tension between the houses of Tudor and Stuart, he was the closest living relative of the unmarried, childless queen and became, by default, her heir. Ascending to the Scottish throne as a child, he becomes somewhat of a puppet prince for the Protestant nobles who support his rule. They ensure that he too adopts the Protestant faith, and this is a factor in his claim to the throne of England when Elizabeth dies. He becomes England's first King James at the age of 37.

upstarts impoverishing the crown. In the end he refused to call another Parliament for four years, only trying again in 1614 but ending with the same unhappy results. With no Parliament, there was no money, and James could not champion the Protestant cause abroad nor could he put his mind to building his kingdom at home. Deeply resentful, he retired to his court, allowed his ministers to run the country and became increasingly distracted with his own personal life.

James' sexuality had always been a subject of court gossip, but by 1620 it was actively destroying the trust between him and his courtiers. It was widely believed by the men closest to James that patronage and influence could only be obtained if you were male and the King took an interest in you. The situation was inflamed by men like George Villiers, the Earl of Buckingham, who was rumoured to be in a sexual relationship with the King. A handsome man from minor gentry, Villiers had risen from a knight of a small county to the second most powerful man in the Kingdom thanks to James, who once commented, '[I] confess to loving those dear to me... I love the Earl of Buckingham more than anyone else... Christ had his John and I have my George.' Whether sexual in nature or not, their relationship grew over the years; James called himself George's 'sweet husband' and George was James' 'wife', among other pet names. As James' marriage to Anne of Denmark resulted in seven children, the question of whether James was openly attracted to men as well as/instead of women is still a matter of debate.

The problem by 1620, at the age of 53, was that he had allowed the men he associated with to cloud his judgement. The astute negotiating skills he possessed in Scotland had abandoned him and he was now surrounded by less competent men like Villiers who gave poor advice to the aging King. It was this poor advice that made James continue to hope for a Spanish match in the closing years of his reign. A marriage between his son, Charles, and the Spanish Infanta Maria Anna would be a prestigious prize for James, so in 1623 Charles and Villiers boarded a ship bound for the Spanish mainland with James' blessing so Charles could attempt to woo the Infanta in person.

As soon as they stepped off the boat and introduced themselves to the Spanish court, they were arrested and held as 'guests'. James waited in England in anxious anticipation; a Spanish match would solve all of his financial troubles through the Infanta's dowry. When he received news that his favourite and his only son had been arrested by the Spanish court, he was furious. After some tentative negotiations, Charles and Villiers were released and returned to England with their tails between their legs. The Spanish had caused great offence in arresting Charles and now he was demanding war. Neither James nor the country was in any state to wage a war with Spain to save Charles' honour, and with deteriorating health after a bad case of dysentery James died 27 March 1625. He passed away deeply unhappy; his dream of a united and prosperous Britain with strong foreign allies and a humble Parliament hadn't been fulfilled. He would later be known as the 'wisest fool in all of Christendom', extremely able but counselled badly. He left behind an England that had become deeply suspicious of the monarchy and its role in governing the country.

> James had an overly large tongue, which was commented on negatively at the time by certain members of the English court

Religious intolerance
England at the time of James' reign was deeply intolerant of the Catholic minority that existed within the Kingdom. Catholicism or 'Popery' as it was more commonly referred to was seen to be in league with the devil and many of James' subjects feared a clandestine Catholic conspiracy to take over the country.

The rights of Parliament
After the end of the Tudor dynasty, Parliament had become more powerful through its ability to grant money to an increasingly impoverished monarchy. Often Parliaments granting the crown money was dependent on Parliament being bought off with new laws favourable to representatives in the chamber.

The King's court
The King's court was made up of the nobility of the realm and it acted as another organ of state that the King could use to govern the country. During James' reign the court became even more important because he used the presence of both English and Scottish courtiers to rule both his Kingdoms.

Troubles abroad
The prejudice the Protestant population had for Catholics in England was inflamed by the outright hostility experienced by Protestants from Catholic countries in Europe. England remained largely untouched by the fighting, however the influence of events abroad had a dramatic effect on religious prejudices and mental attitudes.

The New World
The first permanent settlements in America were established during James' reign starting with Jamestown, Virginia, founded in 1607. The allure of making a fortune in a new world free from religious persecution was an attractive prospect to many of James' subjects.

Defining moment
The Gunpowder Plot
5 November 1604
A plot to kill James while he attends the opening of Parliament is thwarted when guards search the cellars of the Parliament building and find Guy Fawkes guarding barrels of gunpowder. The plan was to ignite the gunpowder when James entered Parliament and destroy the English government. Fawkes and his fellow conspirators are all arrested, tortured and sentenced to a traitor's death. As a result of the plot, anti-Catholic violence increases throughout the country. James continues to call for religious moderation but has to allow a certain amount of anti-Catholic behaviour to stay popular with his subjects.

Defining moment
The Spanish match
March 1623
James had always dreamt of an alliance between England and the most powerful country in Europe - Spain. While the difference in religion was seen to be insurmountable, England being Protestant while Spain was Catholic, James insisted on pursing a match with his son Charles and the Spanish Infanta, Maria Anna. Charles travelled to Spain but was arrested and held temporarily in custody, with his travelling companion George Villiers.

1625

Jamestown established
The first permanent English settlement in America is established on the coast of Virginia, the settlers name it Jamestown after the King of England and battle to keep the settlement alive.
24 May 1607

The Great Contract
A plan to get the crown out of debt through Parliament giving James an annual subsidy is overturned by the members of the house because they don't trust James with the money.
February 1610

Dissolved Parliament
After wrestling with Parliament for more money to prop up his out-of-control spending, James dissolves the house and does not call another session for four years.
31 December 1610

King James Bible
The King James Bible is published by James and his bishops to bring a universal Protestant faith to the British Isles. It is still used as the basis for global Protestantism today.
January 1611

Investigation of monopolies
In an effort to break up the monopoly of businesses that are strangling commerce in London, James calls Parliament to take action but his sour relationship with the house prevents any progress.
December 1620

Death of a Stuart
James dies aged 58 after his health deteriorates. He leaves behind an uneasy and reformist England that his son Charles struggles to control.
27 March 1625

1594 – 1632

Gustavus Adolphus

A peerless statesman and fearless soldier, Gustavus defied an empire and carved his legacy in the battlefields of early modern Europe

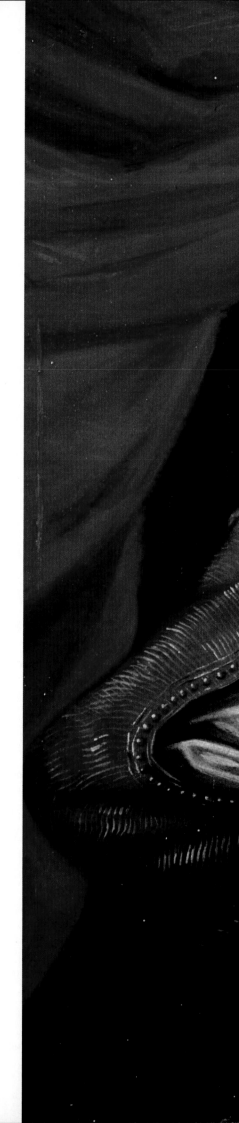

On 6 November 1632, a cold mist hung thick over the field at Lutzen, Germany, mixing with the choking gunpowder smoke to cover the battlefield in a foreboding veil that obscured the opposing sides from each another. Three horsemen, spotting a high-ranking enemy officer wounded in the field and lying separated from his main force, rode out to discover his identity. They found a nobleman, not of small stature, bleeding heavily into the earth. They demanded the dying man's name. "I am the King of Sweden," came the reply. Gustavus Adolphus, the champion of the Protestant cause who in two years had defied and humbled the entire Holy Roman Empire, had finally met his end.

The King of Sweden's campaign in Germany, which marked a turning point in the Thirty Years War, had gradually been gathering momentum and spreading hope throughout the Protestant nations of Europe that the Catholic powers could be resisted. However, his end, still today the stuff of legend, is only the poignant final line of a life that had stamped its mark on the continent forever. From the very beginning of his reign, when he was only 16, Gustavus had always known war. In 1611, when his father Charles IX died, the young prince inherited the throne of Sweden and with it a state wracked by debt and beset on by three separate conflicts. The war with Denmark was the most pressing of these, as the Danes had advanced even as far as the Stockholm archipelago and had completely cut the country off from western Europe.

Not even the young king's crown was guaranteed, as the Swedish Estate immediately demanded back certain powers that Charles IX had taken from them. For this reason it was agreed that Gustavus would not come into his majority until several years after the death of his father, and he wasn't officially crowned until the age of 23.

Even in this short period the young king was able to prove himself to be a formidable ruler who was destined for great things, typified in his speech to the crowd at his coronation: 'Trust in God, and that power which derives from the loyalty of Swedish men.'

> Gustavus inherited the Swedish throne from his father, Charles IX, at the age of 17 and ruled for 21 years

> He could speak several different languages including German, Dutch, French, Italian, Latin, as well as some English and Spanish

GUSTAVUS ADOLPHUS
Sweden, 1594-1632

Brief Bio

Remembered as Sweden's greatest king and known to his contemporaries as 'the Golden King', Gustavus Adolphus acceded to the throne as a teenager although wasn't officially crowned until he reached the age of 23. He is remembered for a decisive battle against Catholic forces, but despite Sweden's win Gustavus died on the battlefield, making it a somewhat Pyrrhic victory.

Gustavus was known as 'The Golden King' due to his bright blonde hair and fearless, chivalrous character

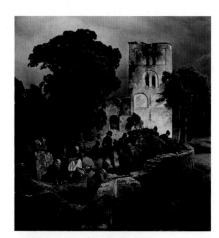

The Thirty Years War 1618-1648

Starting in 1618 with the Bohemian Rebellion, the Thirty Years War was a lengthy and brutal conflict that claimed the lives of over a quarter of the population of the German states. After the rapid spread of the Protestant Reformation throughout Europe during the 16th century, the Catholic powers (predominantly under Spain and the Holy Roman Empire) made decisive movements to produce their own Counter-Reformation. In an attempt to protect their religious freedoms, the German states formed their own Protestant Union, which found allies in Denmark, Sweden, Holland and even anti-Habsburg France. The Catholic League was formed in opposition, setting the stage for decades of bloody war across the continent. Though for a time the imperial Catholic forces prevailed, including the defeat of the invading Danish King Christian IV in 1627, the initially successful intervention of Sweden and Gustavus Adolphus proved to be a turning point for the Protestant cause.

Though the Swedish king ultimately lost his life in the campaign, which eventually waned, it presented the first real successes of the Protestant cause and eventually led to the end of the war in 1648. Gustavus' only issue, Christina, became queen after his death and continued his efforts to support the resistance of the Catholic Counter-Reformation.

Johan Schroderus, a wise and worldly man, primarily educated the young Gustavus, teaching the prince about the intricacies of court and undoubtedly how to fight. From a young age the prince showed a flair for learning languages, of which he spoke at least seven, and also demonstrated great adeptness in managing his own duchy. However, it was during the war with Denmark, which was brought to a swift if compromising peace, as well as with Russia and Poland, that Gustavus learned about both the balance of power in the Baltic region and the art of war. The Polish war was particularly poignant for Gustavus' development as a general - it was during this conflict that he conquered Livonia and fought his first pitched battle, and victory, at Walhof.

Though there were degrees of both victories and losses in his campaigns during the 1620s, Gustavus had succeeded in securing stability both for his throne and for Sweden. The country now benefited from strategic strongholds in Prussia and controlled most of the main ports of the Baltic Sea. However, his greatest challenge still lay ahead and it would see him risk his throne, his country and, yet again, his life.

In 1626, the Danish King Christian IV intervened in the Thirty Years War to defend the Protestant cause, with some support from England and Holland. Though Gustavus was unwilling to join the expedition, as he was pursuing his campaigns in Poland, when the Danes eventually were driven out of Germany later that same year he was left with the prospect of facing the threat of the Holy Roman Emperor, Ferdinand II, alone.

In 1630 the decision was made to take Sweden into the Thirty Years War. The hope, no doubt, was that the Protestant states could unite, casting

> He brushed with death several times during his reign, including nearly drowning when his horse fell through thin ice

aside their rivalries and fears, to face the Emperor together. Even as he announced his decision, the king seemed auspiciously fatalistic about the part he would play in the war: 'For me there remains henceforth no more rest, but the eternal,' he declared, almost as though he knew he was marching for the last time.

As well as his life, Gustavus was risking his country by leaving behind such a strong position that he had fought hard to gain. He was also leaving behind his only surviving child, Christina, who was four years old, as well as his wife, Maria Eleonora of Brandenburg, who had often been so grief-stricken when he left that she had previously accompanied him on his campaigns. This time, however, she would not travel with the king on his path into Germany, and she would never see him alive again.

As Gustavus' ships landed at Usedom, on the northern German coast, the king purportedly fell to his knees in prayer, before setting about digging defensive trenches with his men. He had brought with him around 15,000 men, only of which 3,000 were cavalry - a paltry number compared to the 40,000 Imperial troops that were operating in the area at the time.

On hearing of the arrival of the Swedish expedition, the Emperor Ferdinand is reported to have commented: 'So, we have got another kingling on our hands.' However, there was more to this kingling than met the eye. Though his force was small, Gustavus had several aces up his sleeve, including a good proportion of experienced and battle-hardened soldiers bred in the harsh climate of northern Europe.

His senior officers too were all infinitely experienced and capable leaders in their own right, for the most part trained by the king himself: 'All

"His greatest challenge still lay ahead and it would see him risk his throne, his country and, yet again, his life"

The Treaty of Stolbova
At the outbreak of Another war, this time with Russia, is concluded with advantageous gains for Sweden.
27 February 1617

Timeline

1594

The heir apparent
Gustavus is born in Stockholm castle, the first son of Christina of Holstein-Gottorp and Duke Charles Vasa who would later become Charles IX of Sweden.
9 December 1594

Ascending the throne
Just over a month before his 17th birthday, Gustavus' father Charles IX dies and he inherits the throne, but isn't crowned until he is 23.
30 October 1611

The Peace of Knared
The war with Denmark is brought to an end. It's agreed that a ransom will be paid to the Danes for their occupation of the fortress of Alvsborg.
21 January 1613

Future Queen
Maria Eleonora of Brandenburg, Gustavus' wife, gives birth. The baby girl, named Christina, was the only surviving issue from the royal couple and would inherit the crown on Gustavus' death.
8 December 1626

Wounded at Danzig
During a siege at Danzig, the King is severely wounded by a musket shot to the chest. It's likely this is the wound that made it so uncomfortable for him to wear armour in later life.
25 May 1627

A setback
The king is defeated by the Polish general Koniecpolski at Stuhm, northern Poland, at the end of a series of long and bloody encounters.
29 June 1629

these are captains, and fit to command armies,' Gustavus had once declared to a French envoy.

However, the Swedes also carried with them a healthy number of artillery units, which Gustavus would use to great effect in his overwhelming defeat of Johann Tserclaes, Count of Tilly, at the Battle of Breitenfeld, near Leipzig. Now commanding a force of around 40,000, including a newly arrived force of Saxons, Gustavus was able to fully utilise his innovative battlefield strategy. By combining his resources into self-supporting, co-ordinated attacks, bringing together cavalry, infantry and artillery, he was able to outmanoeuvre Tilly and entirely destroy his 30,000-strong army. Gustavus had effectively codified this new deployment of gunpowder units, which were still primitive at the time, moving them around the battlefield in a flexible manner to respond to the enemy's movements.

For a short time it seemed as though fate was finally smiling on the Protestant cause. In the King of Sweden, those opposed to the Catholic powers had finally found their champion who, unlike Christian of Denmark, could deliver victory. History, however, tells a different story.

Ever since he received his wounds on the battlefields of the 1620s, the King had declined to wear his full armour in the field, and the morning of 6 November 1631 was no different. 'God is my armour,' Gustavus declared with characteristic zeal and indifference to the perils that lay ahead. The Swedish army now faced the mighty imperial general Wallenstein - a gifted strategist and the Emperor Ferdinand II's ruthless Catholic enforcer - at the Battle of Lutzen. At around midday Gustavus lead a cavalry charge against Wallenstein's left flank, in an attempt to break it and divert pressure away from his infantry's attack in the centre.

However, in the confusion of the lingering mist and gunpowder smoke, the King and his escort became separated from the main force. Gustavus, already severely wounded in the arm by a pistol shot, turned to a member of his entourage and said: 'Lead me out of the tumult, for I am hurt.' As the group attempted to return to their lines, the King was shot in the back and he fell from his horse, which abandoned him. His luck had finally run out and he had earned the heroic death that he had seemingly so desired.

Gustavus' body was eventually found stripped, mutilated and left lying in the cold mud. Though many soldiers panicked on seeing the King's horse fleeing rider-less, the Swedish captains, whom Gustavus had put such faith in, were able to rally them and the battle was won, though in reality this victory was hollow. The Swedes had lost their chief and the Protestant cause had lost its champion. During his relatively short reign, Gustavus had made Sweden a great power in Europe and had single-handedly turned the tide of the 30 Years War that, arguably, may only have been half this length had he lived.

His brilliant tactical acumen and leadership even earned him recognition from Napoleon some 200 years later, who placed him among the greatest generals the world had seen - in the company of Alexander the Great, Hannibal and Julius Caesar - and undoubtedly there is no fitter place for Gustavus Adolphus.

> He is revered among Swedish society as their greatest leader and the day of his death, is commemorated by a holiday

Life in the time of Gustavus Adolphus

The Reformation
Sparking in the early 16th Century, instigated by Martin Luther and others, the Protestant Reformation saw a major split from the central doctrine of the Catholic church in Rome. Spanning well into the 17th Century and beyond, Protestantism permeated many northern European states, including Holland and England, creating widespread conflict with those still loyal to the pope.

Denmark
Denmark was Sweden's bitter rival throughout and beyond this period. Though technically they were fellow Protestant states, both with Viking roots, the two country's proximity to each other was the source of endless disputes over land, trade and so on.

The Swedish Vasa dynasty
Charles IX Vasa, Gustavus' father, had usurped the throne of Sweden from his Catholic nephew, Sigismund Vasa, who was de facto king of both Poland and Sweden. Charles had been a harsh ruler, restricting many of the freedoms the aristocracy had traditionally enjoyed, meaning Gustavus was initially forced to make drastic concessions to the Swedish Estates.

The Holy Roman Empire
The main power within Europe at the time was the Holy Roman Empire, led during the Thirty Years War by Ferdinand II. A staunch Catholic, Ferdinand led the Counter-Reformation against Protestantism in his realm and beyond, with the support of Spain and the Catholic League of German princes.

The Protestant Union
In an attempt to protect themselves from the threat of the Holy Roman Empire, several of the German states formed into a collective known as the Protestant Union in the early years of the 17th century. This union aimed to protect religious freedoms, with the backing, in theory, of military support.

Defining moment
The battle of Breitenfeld
17 September 1631
The battle of Breitenfeld is not just notable for being the first major Protestant victory of the Thirty Years War, but also for the innovative military tactics that the Protestant force employed. Commanding over 40,000 men, Adolphus was able to utilise a combined arms approach in his tactics, using his infantry, cavalry and superior artillery in self-supporting movements. This added flexibility enabled the Swedes, at times led by the King himself, to outmanoeuvre the Imperial army of over 30,000, which was almost entirely decimated.

Defining moment
A hero's death
6 November 1632
The Battle of Lutzen was fought between Gustavus' Swedish force of around 20,000 and Albrecht von Wallenstein's Imperial force of around 22,000. Though victory eventually went to the Swedes, it was dearly paid for in the loss of over 5,000 men, as well as the King of Sweden himself, whose body was later found shot and stabbed several times. This engagement signifies the end of the first major Swedish entry into the Thirty Years War and the loss of Gustavus was felt throughout the continent.

1632

● A final peace
The Treaty of Altmark saw the end of Sweden's series of campaigns against Poland. Though they left most of Prussia, the Swedes maintained control over crucial port towns.
25 September 1629

● Event: Entering a new war
The King lands at Usedom, northern Germany, with a small force of around 15,000 men, including many mercenaries, some of which had travelled from Scotland.
6 July 1630

1600 – 1649

Charles I

How Charles I lost his head - the King of England became the first British monarch in history to be tried and convicted of treason

On 20 January 1649, Charles I stood where no English monarch had been before him. He faced charges levelled by his own subjects, who accused him of treason against the country he claimed to rule. If Charles was found guilty, the penalty was death. He faced a rigged court made up of hand-picked enemies of the crown who demanded that he answer for the crime of being a "tyrant, traitor and murderer; and a public and implacable enemy to the Commonwealth of England."

However, Charles had never made a habit of listening to Parliament. Even as he faced the men who were waiting to pass their verdict, in his mind they had no power to do so. He was the King, after all, and the King answered to no one. "I am no less confident," he told the court, "that no learned lawyer will affirm that an impeachment can lie against the King, they all going in his name: and one of their maxims is, that the King can do no wrong." The assembled men before him saw things differently.

Charles's refusal to acknowledge the authority of Parliament wasn't just a final gesture of defiance; it was a hallmark of his reign which he had inherited from his father and one of the principal causes of the English Civil War. Frustrated by the fact that the House of Commons constantly

> Charles I was a great lover of the arts and spent large sums of money on paintings, which plunged England further into debt

> He married Henrietta Maria of France, who was a Catholic, by proxy. His choice of bride greatly angered Parliament

attempted to put a stop to his lavish spending, criticised his favourites at court and continued to raise questions about his increasingly Catholic leaning, Charles decided to take them out of the equation. Parliament was called by the King and Charles saw a simple solution to his problem. In 1629, beginning what would come to be known as the 11 Years' Tyranny, the King refused to call Parliament to session. During this time he levied increasingly extreme taxes and introduced unpopular measures to the Church of England that moved it away from Calvinism, such as appointing the despised Anglican William Laud as Archbishop of Canterbury. His opponents, who were already disgusted by his marriage to the catholic Henrietta Maria of France, believed that he was reintroducing Papal traditions to England. But as long as Charles didn't need Parliament there was nothing that they could do to stop him.

Everything changed when Charles attempted to introduce his new English prayer book to Scotland in 1637. Discord spread and Charles refused to negotiate as rebellion brewed until The Bishops' War finally began in 1639. Still the King was reluctant to call Parliament and attempted to put down the uprising himself, only to suffer a humiliating defeat. He was faced with the grim reality that, if he wanted to raise enough

CHARLES I
British, 1600 - 1649

Brief Bio

The art-loving Charles presided over a decadent Baroque court and was married to a French Catholic. This caused a schism with the increasingly Puritan Protestant majority, eventually leading to the political uprising and Civil War that tore the country apart and saw Charles put to death for treason against Parliament.

From 1647 onwards Charles refused to allow anyone to shave his face, possibly out of fear of assassination

"The final line was crossed when Charles was refused entry to the garrison at Kingston upon Hull"

The Divine Right of Kings

Charles I was unwilling to even consider negotiating with Parliament because he believed absolutely in the divine right of monarchs. The concept that Kings and Queens had been chosen by God Almighty to rule their kingdoms had been around for some time in various guises, but it was brought to the forefront during the reign of Charles's father James I. He wrote that "The state of monarchy is the supreme thing on Earth... As to dispute what God may do is blasphemy, so is it treason in subjects to dispute what a king may do... A good king will frame his actions according to the law, yet he is not bound thereto but of his own goodwill." Needless to say, this point of view was not popular in Parliament, who began proceedings to wrench power back from the hands of the King.

money for a force capable of crushing these rebels, he needed Parliament's help. It was with great reluctance that he ended his 11 years of independence on 13 May 1640, but when they began to criticise the King for his spending rather than answering his call for money, he dissolved Parliament in a fit of rage.

Meanwhile, the Scottish rebels continued to advance south. Charles would have to set his pride and his anger to one side. He needed Parliament, and the members knew it. The Long Parliament was called to session in November 1640 and, as Charles watched and listened, Parliament aired their grievances from their years spent in the cold. They passed a law that ensured that they would have to be called at least every three years, they made sure that any tax that the King wanted to impose needed to be approved by Parliament, and they passed a law saying that the King could not dissolve Parliament without their agreement. Charles's unpopular friends and appointments also came under scrutiny, but the issue becoming clear

> As a small child Charles suffered from rickets. He was unable to walk until age four, from which point he wore reinforced boots

was that Scottish rebels were not the only ones worried about Charles' drift towards Catholicism.

After nearly two years, the King had had enough. He identified the five main troublemakers in the House of Commons, John Hampden, Arthur Haselrig, Denzil Holles, John Pym and William Strode and marched into the House on 4 January 1642 to arrest them. Humiliatingly, the five men had heard the news and had escaped before his arrival. "I see the birds have flown," he told the assembled members. He fled London himself shortly afterwards. He could read the signs. War was imminent.

The final line was crossed when Charles was refused entry to the garrison at Kingston upon Hull. Enraged, he laid siege to the city but was defeated. All that was left now was a formal declaration of war, which Charles delivered on the 22 August when he raised his standard at Nottingham. It was a challenge to all those who would oppose him and the Parliamentarians accepted. Led by Robert Devereaux, the Earl of Essex, the Roundheads gathered their troops to meet Charles's Cavaliers before he reached London. After a skirmish at Worcester, the first open battle took place on 23 October at Edgehill with both sides claiming victory. Bragging aside, actual victories went back and forth. Charles was forced to take up residence in Oxford and lost his general, but the Royalists claimed victory at several battles. When Charles declared a ceasefire in Ireland, more troops were able to join his cause and the Royalist troops gained much needed numbers.

Things looked bleak for the Roundheads but when the Puritanical Oliver Cromwell and his cavalry won the Battle of Marston Moor on 2 July 1644, Parliament found a second wind. In 1645 they passed the Self-Denying Ordinance, which meant that anyone serving in the Civil War could not also serve in Parliament, and won conclusive battles at Naseby and Langport. In 1646, Charles was captured and handed over to Parliament.

The King was down, but not out. He may have lost the war but he was still the man chosen by God to rule these people. When he promised the Scots Presbyterian church reform in December 1647 they agreed to back his counter-revolution. Royalist uprisings began all over the country, with

Cromwell at the Battle of Dunbar, 1650, where Parlimentary forces were victorious

Timeline

Oliver Cromwell depicted imprisoning Charles I as painted by Alexander Christie

be allowed back onto the throne, word got out that Parliament was trying to negotiate with Charles.

The army that had fought so bitterly against their monarch could not and would not stand the idea of negotiation. Instead, they marched into Parliament and kept members out who were deemed to be sympathetic to Charles's cause. This was known as Pride's Purge, after the ringleader Colonel Thomas Pride. 145 men were not allowed into Parliament, and a further 45 were arrested. The 75 members who were allowed in were guaranteed to follow the army's agenda and voted that the King should be tried. The House of Lords refused to agree to pass the bill but Parliament continued.

There weren't any laws, any guidelines for how to deal with this kind of situation. Of the 135 judges chosen, only 68 were present at the trial. Charles refused to acknowledge the authority of the court and did not defend himself for the three days of evidence and depositions. The first British monarch to stand trial for treason was found guilty. It was only at this point that Charles, perhaps finally realising what had happened and what was going to happen to him, tried to speak. He was told that he could not. He would not be allowed to speak publicly again until his execution.

Charles I was beheaded on 30 January 1649. The death warrant was signed by the man who would take his power, if not his title: Oliver Cromwell. Standing on the scaffold, he caused many to take note of his calm and dignified demeanour as he delivered his final address. "I have delivered to my conscience; I pray God you do take those courses that are best for the good of the kingdom and your own salvation I go from a corruptible to an incorruptible crown where no disturbance can be."

> Like his father James I, Charles I loathed tobacco. It was forbidden to smoke in the presence of the King

a rebellion in South Wales looking like a real threat until Cromwell's cavalry arrived. Sir Thomas Fairfax put down a Royalist force in Kent, but was forced into a lengthy siege at Colchester. Charles may have been more desperate but the momentum was with the Roundheads and, perhaps more importantly, a large number of nobles who had fought for Charles during the first Civil War refused to rejoin him having pledged their allegiance to Parliament. After losing Cumberland, the Royalists were forced to march south through Carlisle and meet Cromwell's forces at Preston. The Roundhead forces overwhelmed them and they were forced to flee, finally surrendering to Fairfax and ending the Second Civil War.

There was no way for Charles to disguise what he had done. He had negotiated with the Scots to overthrow the rule of Parliament. He had connived and concealed with another nation, and by his actions he had caused the deaths of tens of thousands of men. But Parliament itself didn't know what to do with him. Clearly he had committed treason against them, but what was the solution? While they tried to decide whether or not he could

● **The King is dead**
After being found guilty of high treason, Charles I is beheaded. His manner was described as dignified and he impressed many who came to see him die. He becomes the first British monarch to be executed for treason.
30 January 1649

A crowd watches the execution of Charles I. Many were impressed with the dignified manner with which he went to his death

Portrait of Oliver Cromwell, Lord Protector of the Commonwealth of Britain

The life of Oliver Cromwell

A Puritan and a politician
With the excesses of Charles I's reign the stuff of legend, Oliver Cromwell was a sober, puritanical figure whose fierce beliefs propelled him to the forefront of the English Civil War. He came to prominence during the Short and Long Parliament in which he represented Cambridge with his unshakeable moral code.

A politician and a soldier
Cromwell came to prominence by leading the Roundhead cavalry and proving himself to be a formidable military leader, and assisted in the creation of a separate Parlimentary army with the New Model Army. He won crucial victories at Marston Moor and crushed the rebellion in South Wales.

Off with his head
Although it wasn't Cromwell who made sure that the Parliament that decided whether or not to executed Charles was rigged, he was one of the main driving forces behind the King's trial and signed his death warrant in 1649. His name is visible on the warrant.

No kingship for Cromwell
He was hungry for power but faced opposition after Charles's death. Still, Cromwell became Lord Protector and managed to keep hold of power so successfully that he was offered Kingship in 1657, despite cancelling Christmas. He refused, and died on 3 September 1658 following the death of his daughter.

Respect for the dead
When Charles II took the throne in 1661 the Royalists needed to make an example of those who had stood against them. Cromwell's body was exhumed, tried and hung from a gallows at Tyburn, while his head was stuck on a spike at Westminster.

1660

● **The King plots a rebellion**
While Parliament tries to decide what to do with him, Charles reaches out to the Scots and promises their Presbyterian church independence in exchange for their military support.
December 1647

● **The Second Civil War ends**
Parliament begins to negotiate Charles's surrender after crushing his forces. The King is imprisoned but, while the members decide what to do with him, he plots his escape.
15 September 1648

● **Pride's Purge hits Parliament**
Army troops march into Parliament and remove anyone sympathetic to Charles's cause under the leadership of Colonel Thomas Pride. 45 members are imprisoned and the Rump Parliament begins.
7 December 1648

● **Long live the King**
11 years after the death of his father, Charles II is crowned King of England on his 30th birthday. He orders the deaths of nine men associated with Charles's execution and symbolically executes Cromwell's corpse.
29 May 1660

1609 – 1672

John II Casimir Vasa

How the reign of the last of the Vasas signalled the beginning of the fall of the Polish-Lithuanian Commonwealth, one of most powerful countries of the 16th and 17th Centuries

The year is 1648, and against all odds, John Casimir Vasa is about to be elected to succeed his recently deceased half-brother Władysław IV Waza to the Polish throne. After living in his brother's shadow for most of his life, John Casimir will soon become ruler of one of the largest and most populous countries of the 16th and 17th Centuries, an area covering a huge 390,000 square miles: The Polish-Lithuanian Commonwealth. At the age of 39, his chance to be king had come.

Ironically, one of the main reasons John Casimir is said to have been regarded as an unpleasant man among the Polish nobility throughout his life was his blatant disregard and contempt for Polish culture - not the ideal attitude for a noble, nevermind a future Polish king. Unlike his older half-brother Władysław IV Waza, who has historically been remembered as outgoing, friendly, humorous and optimistic; John Casimir was known for being unfriendly and secretive, dividing his time between the lavish partying that could be afforded by his rank and quieter moments of religious contemplation, something that would become increasingly important to him at several points throughout his life. Most crucially, John Casimir had a dislike for politics, which resulted in him having a weak

> John Casimir lived in his brother's shadow for much of his life, even marrying his brother's widow in 1648

power base and very little influence at the Polish court.

Meanwhile, Władysław IV Waza became increasingly well known for his ability to charm whoever he met. He had had his own prince court from the age of ten, spoke and wrote in German, Italian and Latin, and had gained an international reputation for being a 'defender of the Christian faith' from his bravery in the many battles and campaigns he had fought seeking personal glory. When it came to being crowned king during the elections of 1632, John Casimir's much beloved brother had no serious contenders.

However, there was a darker side to the newly appointed king. Władysław was addicted to an extravagant lifestyle and known for spending more money than his royal court treasury could afford, as well as having several mistresses – even while he was married. Władysław was also a man with a very short temper, and he was obsessed with the idea of reclaiming the Swedish throne: a title his and John Casimir's father, Sigismund III Vasa, had for seven years before being deposed by their uncle in 1599. This had resulted in a long-standing feud, with the Polish kings of the House of Vasa demanding the rights to the Swedish throne ever since - a claim which led to decades of war.

> He was obsessed with reclaiming the throne of Sweden for the Polish-Lithuanian Commonwealth

JOHN II CASIMIR VASA
Poland-Lithuania, 1609-1672

Brief Bio

As a younger sibling constantly overshadowed by his brother, John did not expect to take the throne. A distinguished soldier, he proved his worth in the Smolensk and Thirty Years' Wars. Captured and imprisoned by the French, he became a monk on his release and after a relatively brief kingship, abdicated and retired once more to a life of spiritual contemplation as an abbot.

The Queen Regent of Poland

Marie Louise Gonzaga was a unique woman in history, having been queen consort to two Polish kings throughout her life. Marie was born in France in 1611 and spent her childhood with her mother. From a young age, it was planned for her to marry Gaston d'Orléans, the third son of King Henry IV of France and his wife Marie de Medici, but Henry IV's successor, his other son Louis XIII, strongly opposed the marriage and when Marie was only 16-years-old, imprisoned her in the Vicennes fortress then later in a convent.

The first proposal that she marry the King of Poland, Władysław IV Vasa, was made in 1634, but Władysław eventually married Cecilia Renata of Austria. Then, after Cecilia Renata died in 1944, Marie Louise Gonzaga married Władysław IV by proxy only a year later, with John Casimir himself representing his brother. She was now Queen of Poland.

However, it was only three years after her first marriage that Marie Louise Gonzaga was left alone once again, this time a widow after the death of Władysław in 1648 before marrying John Casimir the following year. Amongst the Polish nobility, she was hardly more popular than her new husband. They were scandalised by her active interest in politics, even though she later played an instrumental role leading the Polish troops to repulse the Swedish army during the Deluge.

It was in war, though, that John Casimir distinguished himself. Much like his brother Władysław, who successfully defended Poland against foreign invasions during his reign, Casimir was a very talented military commander. At only 15 years old, he had taken part in the Smolensk War against Muscovy in 1633 and later even unexpectedly joined the army of the Holy Roman Empire to fight against the French during the Thirty Years War in 1635, one of the longest and most destructive conflicts in European history; all when he was initially supposed to be going on a diplomatic mission to prepare for another war in Vienna. During Casimir's years at war, the new King Władysław unsuccessfully tried to enhance his brother's influence by negotiating a marriage for Casimir to Swedish and Italian nobilty, though upon John Casimir's return to the Polish-Lithuanian Commonwealth it was clear that Casimir had other plans. He had fallen in love with Baroness Guldentern, but his hope to marry her was thwarted by his regnant brother.

The repentant Władysław then tried to reconcile with his brother by attempting to make him the sovereign of Courland instead, but this was also vetoed, this time by the Commonwealth parliament, and an angry and offended John Casimir abruptly left his hated home country once again in 1638. His voyage was to Spain, set on becoming Viceroy of Portugal. Little did he know that he would never reach his destination.

On his way to Spain, John Casimir was captured by French agents and imprisoned by order of

Cardinal Richelieu until 1640, when he was freed by a diplomatic mission. His two long years as a prisoner changed his life, and Casimir, who had spent many years living lavishly at various European courts as well as leading a successful military life on the battlefield, was now set on dedicating his life to religion as a Jesuit novice. Once again, he left the Polish-Lithuanian Commonwealth for Italy to join the Jesuits in 1643.

Though King Władysław was famously tolerant of religious differences throughout his reign despite his being a Catholic, John Casimir's decision was one Władysław was very vocally opposed to - causing a diplomatic rift between the Commonwealth and the pope. Regardless of the opposition from the King, John Casimir continued to live his life as a Jesuit and had even become a Cardinal. Yet, only a few years after he had first started, Casimir found himself unsuited to ecclesiastical life and returned to Poland.

For King Władysław, the next few years marked the last of his life. On the 9 August 1647, his young son and only legitimate heir, then only seven years old, fell ill and died, a major blow to the king. Only a year later, while hunting in early 1648, Władysław suffered from a gallstone or kidney stone, a condition that worsened due to incorrect medication. At 2am on 20 May, the King was dead.

John II Casimir Vasa had since resigned as cardinal to stand in elections for the Polish throne, and that same year was elected to succeed his half brother. His reign would be monopolised by almost

> After imprisonment in France, he (temporarily) turned his back on royal life and became a monk

---

Defining moment
Attempted Betrothals
1632
Though generally disliked amongst the Polish nobility due to his open dislike of Polish Culture and politics, John Casimir had proven himself to be very talented as a military commander and had seen battlefields since he was a teenager.

With John Casimir now in his 20s, his regnant brother Władysław IV Vasa attempts to arrange marriages for John Casimir to Christina, Queen of Sweden, who was Queen regnant from 1633 to 1654. When this failed, Władysław then tried to negotiate a marriage between John Casimir and an Italian princess, which was also unsuccessful.

Defining moment
Life as a Prisoner
1638
In 1636, after his brother Władysław had thwarted John Casimir's plans to marry Baroness Guldentern after falling in love with her, an angry and offended John Casimir abruptly left his hated home country once again. His voyage was to Spain, set on becoming Viceroy of Portugal. On his way to Spain, however, John Casimir was captured by French agents and imprisoned by order of Cardinal Richelieu until 1640, when he was freed by a diplomatic mission. Casimir had previously joined the army of the Holy Roman Empire to fight against the French during the Thirty Years War in 1637.

Timeline

1599

The Loss of the Swedish Throne
John II Casimir's father, Sigismund III Vasa, had succeeded his own father to the Swedish throne only to be deposed by his uncle in 1599. Ever since, he had claimed the Swedish throne as rightfully his.
1599

John Casimir is born
John II Casimir Vasa is born on 22 March 1609 to Sigismund III Vasa (1566-1632) and Constance of Austria (1588-1631). His older brother, Władysław IV Vasa, is predecessor to the throne.
1609

Joining the Jesuits
Now in his early 30s, John Casimir decides to become a Jesuit and leaves the Polish-Lithuanian Commonwealth again, despite vocal opposition from King Władysław.
1642

Becoming a Cardinal
During the 1640s John Casimir lived in Italy where he was made a cardinal, but reportedly returned to Poland a few years later after finding himself unsuited to ecclesiastical life.
1646

constant war, and he would be the last of the Vasas in the Polish-Lithuanian Commonwealth.

John Casimir soon even married his brother's widow queen Marie Louise Gonzaga, a woman he had met years before when he acted as a proxy in the place of Władysław during their wedding itself, for his brother could not be present. Casimir's reign was one filled with war, from the Russo-Polish War between 1654 and 1667 to The Swedish Deluge from 1655 to 1660, representing the climax of a series of wars that had taken place in Poland-Lithuania in the mid-17th Century, which ultimately resulted in the Commonwealth losing an estimated 40 per cent of its population and arguably its status as a great power within Europe. Perhaps unsurprisingly, it was also because of the once-lost Swedish throne so desperately desired by Casimir's father that the foundations of such a devastating war were ever even built. The Swedish Empire had become one of the strongest nations in the world and boasted a huge army. King John Casimir continued to be regarded as a weak, 'Jesuit' king, lacking support from the Commonwealth nobility because of his disdain for their culture; The Polish-Lithuanian Commonwealth was already weakened, preoccupied with sustaining its other wars such as the Russo-Polish War to the east. The time was ripe to invade from the west.

Most of Poland was overrun by the Swedish army without much resistance, and the damages to Casimir's homeland were more extensive than even the destruction it later sustained during World War II. In Warsaw, the capital of the Polish-Lithuanian Commonwealth, only 2,000 people remained from a pre-war population of 20,000. In 1660, after five long years of war, John Casimir was forced to renounce his claim to the Swedish throne and acknowledge Swedish sovereignty over Livonia and the city of Riga. Then, in 1667, Casimir was dealt a final blow. His queen Marie Louise Gonzaga, who had always been an important source of support to King Casimir and a crucial individual when it had come to driving out Swedish forces during the Deluge, had just died. They left no surviving children.

Tired of external warfare and still mourning the death of his wife, John Casimir abdicated the Polish-Lithuanian throne on 16 September 1668, and returned to a society he had been a part of before he had ever become the ruler of so much: the Jesuits. After 20 years as king, he returned to France, where he took on the role of titular abbot of the Saint-Germain-des-Prés in Paris. Though his time as a monarch had been cursed by war, like King Władysław before him John Casimir had been a great patron of the arts. When he retired to France, most of his paintings went with him, and we have him to thank for the careful early conservation of works by Rembrandt, Rubens and Brueghel among many others that are still admired today. It was here, living the quiet existence of an abbot in the country that he had once been imprisoned in, that the man who was once a king spent the last years of his life in peace.

After an unhappy kingship, he abdicated and retreated into the church once more, becoming a Jesuit abbot

Defining moment
Resigning
1647

In October 1647, John Casimir resigns as cardinal to be able to stand in elections for the Polish throne, even attempting to gain the support of the Habsburgs and marry an Austrian princess.

His brother, King Władysław, had lost his son and only legitimate heir at only seven years old, due to illness. Only a year later, while hunting in early 1648, Władysław suffered from a gallstone or kidney stone, a condition that worsened due to incorrect medication. At 2am on 20 May, the king was dead.

Forced to abdicate
The Swedes were forced to retreat. The Peace of Andrusovo in 1667 ended the war with Muscovy, but the King faced stiff internal opposition and even armed uprisings.
1667

Life in the time of John Casimir

The Power of Poland-Lithuania
The Polish-Lithuanian Commonwealth was a joint state of Poland and Lithuania that was ruled by a common monarch. It was one of the largest and most populous countries of 16th- and 17th-Century Europe and had a multi-ethnic population of 11 million at its peak.

The Start of the Decline
The reign of John Casimir was a watershed in Polish-Lithuanian history, representing the separation of a time of greatness and an era of slow decline and eventual collapse. Decades of unresolved problems, overly ambitious territorial expansion and economic decline finally caught up with the Commonwealth in the form of the Deluge.

The Great War
The Deluge saw Cossack, Russian and Swedish forces alike take swarms across the borders of Poland-Lithuania to conquer almost all the land with strikingly little resistance. King Casimir and the nobles had failed to avert these catastrophic forces, with the King's personality and policies making it difficult for many to work with him in parliament.

The Swedish Throne
What became known as the Vasa King's traditional insistence on regaining the Swedish throne was one of the elements that first started the disaster. After John Casimir's father Sigismund III Vasa, was deposed from the Swedisth throne by his uncle in 1599, Sigismund spent much of the rest of his life trying to reclaim it.

Defeating Armies
Despite the devastation of The Deluge, it was the strength of the Polish-Lithuanian state that allowed it to survive, defeating the Swedes and fighting both the Cossack and Russian armies to a standstill. The period of invasions and civil wars that plagued the Cossack state after it seceded from Poland-Lithuania is still known to Ukrainians as the Ruin.

1672

King John
John Casimir is elected to succeed his half brother on the Polish throne, and eventually marries Władysław's widow, Marie Louise Gonzaga, a year later.
1648

Russo-Polish War
John Casimir's reign was marked by disastrous wars, first with the Cossack rebel Bohdan Khmelnytsky and then against the Cossack and Muscovite forces.
1654

The Deluge
The Swedes invade, facing very little opposition. John Casimir lacks support among the Commonwealth nobility, and the ensuing invasion adds to the Commonwealth losing an estimated 40 per cent of its power.
1655

Death of Marie
The Queen, who was always a great supporter of John Casimir, dies, and the dispirited John Casimir abdicates the throne and leaves for France.
1667

Joining the Jesuits Again
John Casimir dies at the age of 63, after having lived as a Jesuit and become abbot of Abbey of Sain-Germain-des-Prés in Paris since his abdication of the Polish throne.
1672

© Getty

1638 – 1715

Louis XIV of France

Louis XIV fought rebellions, civil wars and foreign conquests to become the greatest king to ever ascend to the French throne

With the resources of an imperial power behind him, King Louis XIV of France made it his life's work to turn himself from a mere king of a country into a semi-divine entity sent down from heaven to rule an empire. He dispensed with the traditional symbols of the French court and invoked his own; the emblem of the sun itself. In explaining this radical break from tradition, he announced to his court on his ascension to the French throne, 'I chose to assume the form of the sun, because the light it imparts to other stars, the good it does in every place, ceaselessly producing joy, assuredly the most vivid and beautiful image of a great monarch.'

The 'Sun King', as Louis would later be known, had a childhood that was anything but bright, yet the darkness and uncertainty he experienced as a young man served as an excellent education when he ascended to the French throne. As soon as he was born he was placed under guard to make sure the queen and her Spanish relatives did not gain undue influence over him. His mother ignored this challenge to her authority, refusing to surrender her prominent rule in his life. Men of ambition began to ingratiate themselves with her, like Cardinal Mazarin, who became so powerful that it was suspected that he and the Queen were having a relationship. The offspring of this union, according to the great

> If he was the Sun King he had become adept at blocking out its radiant light with the fog of blood-stained war

French political writer Voltaire, was thrown into the Bastille and encased in a mask of iron, becoming the famous 'man in the iron mask.' When Louis XIII died in 1643 after protracted health problems, Louis was finally crowned Louis XIV. A courtier said to the young king, "as a living god, the honours of the realm render honour and respect to yourself as to a visible divinity." Yet he was dominated by his mother and her cardinal, who presided over a regency government until he came of age. As Louis grew older he grated underneath this power, but he loved his mother and the cardinal, who tutored Louis on every aspect of kingship.

The love Louis extended to Mazarin was almost unconditional, but France hated the man, who was seen to be using the king as a puppet. In 1649, the French parlement - the principle judiciary of the government - rebelled against Mazarin, and the regency lost control of Paris. To make matters worse, the Spanish took advantage by invading, and the royal family was forced to flee. Parlement, acting on the direction of noblemen who hated Mazarin, demanded freedom of the individual rules on how much taxes could be raised and principles of democratic government. It took the presence of a royal army under French war hero Louis de Bourbon, acting in Louis' name, to bring the rebels to heel. The victory was short-lived, however, as Mazarin and the queen conspired to

LOUIS XIV
France, 1638-1715

Brief Bio

France's famous Sun King presided over a glitteringly decadent court. Basing his personal image on Apollo, god of the sun, his extravagant spending can best be seen in the construction of Versailles, a Baroque palace par excellence. Louis' reign wasn't all sparkle, though; he struggled with civil wars as well as international ones, notably with The Netherlands, over his bride's dowry.

Louis receiving Louis Bourbon, the grand condé who rebelled against the crown during the War of the Princes

Life with Louis

Health problems

Despite his self-aggrandisement as the embodiment of the Greek god Apollo, Louis suffered from serious health problems throughout his life, including diabetes, rheumatism, malaria, gout and persistent boils on his skin. He ultimately died through complications brought on by the onset of gangrene.

Powerful family

Louis' extended family included other monarchies in Europe, which in turn had the effect of increasing his already substantial influence abroad. His mother, Anne of Austria, was the older sister of King Philip IV of Spain (a connection Louis used for his claim over the country), and he was the first cousin of King Charles II of England.

Religious fanatic

Louis grew up a devout Catholic due to his strict religious education under his chief minister and trusted confidant, Cardinal Mazarin. These beliefs ultimately led him to persecute his Protestant subjects by revoking the 1598 Edict of Nantes, effectively banning French Protestants from worshipping and giving pastors 15 days to leave the country.

Architect of empire

Louis also expanded the French overseas empire during his reign. His explorers discovered the Mississippi river in 1673, as well as discovering the Mississippi basin, in which the colony of Louisiana was established. The old Franco-Ottoman alliance was also revived, as well as diplomatic relations being established with Siam (Thailand) and China.

Unfaithful husband

The political marriage between Louis and Maria Theresa of Spain was not a happy one. Of their six children, only one survived to adulthood, and Louis was repeatedly unfaithful, taking numerous mistresses which resulted in 14 illegitimate children. After her death in 1683, he went on to marry Françoise d'Aubigné in secret in the same year.

"Louis had sacrificed hundreds of thousands of his own countrymen by the end of the conflict"

The Sun King

For Louis, an absolutist monarch was the equivalent of a god sent down from heaven to rule his subjects with the splendour and glory associated with a divine figure embodied within the king. He truly believed in his heavenly role on Earth, and styled himself on the classical image of the Greek god Apollo, the champion of the hunt and associated with the light of the sun. Louis ordered his image to be painted with the sun as his emblem, he wore clothing which illustrated its glorious light and ordered his trusted courtiers to do the same. In his newly built palace at Versailles, murals of Apollo were stationed within the great halls, along with pictures of Louis portrayed in the role of a conquering hero in grand landscape paintings. He ordered that wherever he went music should be played so that his subjects would think of him as an awe-inspiring figure. In a ballet performed in 1653 he was portrayed as the rising sun; the giver of life. All of these grand gestures were designed to show the world that Louis was the greatest monarch on Earth and his role as God's representative was "grand, noble and delightful."

destroy Bourbon's career on the grounds that he was getting too popular, and another civil war subsequently broke out between the regency and courtiers who sided with Bourbon and his army.

The civil wars shook Louis to his core. Paris was in rebel hands, and the young king and his family were obliged to sleep in tents in the French countryside; it was a dangerous time for kings everywhere, as emphasised by Charles I of England's execution. His mother quietly told Louis that the axe falling on Charles' head was "a blow to make kings tremble." Louis heeded this warning, and decided that military strength through absolute power was the only way to avoid the same fate. When he marched back into Paris, he surrounded himself with Swiss mercenary guards; he no longer trusted his fellow countrymen with his life. He then decided to base himself at the Louvre, since "private houses without moats [for defence] were not for him." The crowds cheered: the young king had come of age and had been born again in the fires of civil war.

On 9 March 1661, Mazarin, died and with it his influence and power over the French throne. Louis' court was alive with excitement, as one official put it, "women with a claim to beauty flattered themselves that they would hold sway over the

> Stories abounded of courtiers dabbling in witchcraft. Louis' mistress was implicated as the ringleader of an underground cult

22-year-old prince, young courtiers believed that they would revive the rule of favourites." They were all to be disappointed, as nothing short of a revolution was taking place in the Louvre, where Louis proclaimed to his ministers, "I have been pleased to leave the government of my affairs to the late cardinal. It is time for me to govern them myself. You will assist me with your advice when I ask for it." It was unheard of for a French king to rule without the aid of a chief minister to handle affairs of state. It was to be dubbed later the start of 'a dictatorship by divine right'. Louis had turned himself from a king in charge of a government to a king who *was* the government. He wanted to be "informed about everything, the numbers and qualities of my troops and unceasingly giving my instructions to every requirement."

As a dictator sent down from heaven to rule his subjects, Louis felt he needed a role model to style himself on. The late cardinal and his mother did not fit the bill, nor did any of his minister lackeys; they were too normal, and his social inferiors, besides. He settled on nothing less than a god: Apollo, whose masculine qualities and awe-inspiring power suited his attitude towards kingship. Apollo was the god of the hunt as well as a warrior, matching Louis' ideal of glorious warfare. He was often observed "in the company of his musketeers, instructing them in discipline."

His first target for conquest was his old enemy, the Spanish, whose invasion of France was a humiliation that Louis was determined to avenge.

Defining moment
Coronation
1654

Despite the rebellion, Louis manages to hold on to his authority, as does Mazarin. Louis finally comes of age after 11 years of watching others make decisions for him, and at the age of 15 is officially crowned king of France in the Cathedral of Reims, with what was then regarded as the crown of Charlemagne. Although this ceremony didn't grant him any judicial powers, its religious value was great, elevating his status above the rest of his populace.

Timeline

1638

Birth of the Sun King
Louis is born in St Germain-en-Laye France to Anne of Austria and Louis XIII, king of France. The French kingdom is deeply divided, creating a dangerous political atmosphere.
1638

Start of minority
Louis XIII dies after a protracted illness and Louis is crowned king of France. He is still a child and his kingdom is run through a regency by his mother and his father's most trusted advisor, Cardinal Mazarin.
1643

The peace of Westphalia
Mazarin concludes the peace of Westphalia in, gaining recognition of French possessions won in the Thirty Years War and formalising the concept of the sovereign state.
1648

The Fronde rebellion
The French parlement refuses to ratify taxes demanded by Mazarin. Rioting breaks out in Paris, which is put down by the army.
1649

War of the Princes
Another rebellion breaks out, led by Louis de Bourbon, better known as the grand Condé, the man who helped Louis put down parlement the year previously.
1650

He saw a crumbling and feeble idiot in the Spanish king, Philip, and decided to show him what he was made of by invading the Spanish Netherlands - modern-day Belgium - on the pretext that his wife had dynastic claims to Spanish land. His battle-hardened royal troops decimated the dilapidated Spanish, the war serving as a grievous blow to their pride. Then, in a bizarre twist of events, in 1668 the Dutch - with Swedish and English backing - called for a truce. Louis saw it as a great betrayal; he had 'liberated' Dutch land from the Spanish, and now they were forcing him to relinquish it. He saw it as "ingratitude, bad faith and insupportable vanity."

Louis swore revenge and launched an invasion against the Netherlands. He paid off the English with gold, and butchered thousands of Dutch soldiers before his troops were finally cut off when dykes were flooded around the royal army. Louis was forced yet again to accept terms, but under the Treaty of Nijmegen of 1678 he was awarded new territories for his tenacity. His power had become almost unending, the portraits he had commissioned of himself as a god-like figure with his vast legions around him stirring his ambition further. In his final great war, he risked everything by going up against a grand alliance of major European powers to influence the Spanish succession and gain power on the continent. The French fought valiantly, but Louis' strength had been depleted, the Battle of Blenheim in 1704 destroying any hopes of influencing Spain. Louis had sacrificed hundreds of thousands of his own countrymen by the end

of the conflict, and if he was the Sun King, he had blocked its light with the fog of blood-stained war.

With the ceaseless slaughter in Europe costing thousands of lives and buckling the economy, the French court continued to bask in the glory of Louis' divinity. He commissioned the ruinously expensive palace of Versailles, continued to spend money on personal projects at the expense of the nation, and insisted that his will be obeyed without question. His court became increasingly detached from the nation, exhibiting the decadence and excess that would lend fire to the revolution of 1789. Scandalous stories abounded of courtiers dabbling in witchcraft and sorcery, and Louis' own mistress, Françoise Athénaïs, was implicated as the ringleader of a Parisian cult that worshipped fortune tellers in 1677. To quash these rumours, Louis ordered his court to be "pious in all things" and dismissed Athénaïs, but the gossip continued, to the detriment of his popularity.

By 1715 France, was suffering from a bitter famine after food supplies were diverted to the military. Louis, rarely leaving his palace, was dying of gangrene. On 1 September 1715 he finally passed away, his reign having lasted 72 years. France stood at the brink of greatness, and as a result of his zeal the country had become Europe's dominant force. Louis was France's Caesar, but when his body was moved to the Basilica of St Denis for burial, the people jeered and booed. The power Louis sought was for him alone; the people were merely a means to his ambitions. Ultimately, it was them who suffered under the Sun King's light.

> When he returned to Paris, he surrounded himself with Swiss mercenary guards; he no longer trusted his countrymen

Life in the time of Louis XIV

Absolutism versus constitutionalism
In the wake of the English Civil War, absolutist monarchies - where the monarch had complete control - had to reassess their roles. The governed demanded firm laws and civil rights enshrined in constitutions that no one could break or change.

Hereditary wars
Louis' family connections extended throughout Europe, causing massive upheaval. He demanded privilege in foreign lands that had rulers related to him, but this was extremely unpopular in countries like Spain, where anti-French sentiment was rife. In the end, the two countries went to war with each other, in the process engulfing all of Europe in conflict.

French patronage
In order for Louis to remain the most powerful individual in France, he maintained a patronage system that granted offices and money to people he could trust in return for their loyalty. The system worked so long as Louis could keep the most competent people in charge - which was something he couldn't always rely on.

Expanding world
By the time Louis ascended to the throne, explorers had discovered many new lands in the Americas, and were expanding European influence in the Far East. This enabled many opportunities for trade and diplomacy in distant lands. Louis began funding expeditions into China and the Philippines in search of power and gold.

Art of diplomacy
Exploration, trade and war had made it increasingly important for countries to form allegiances and treaties for mutual defence during the 17th Century. Europe was no longer made up of feudal kingdoms going to war on the whims of their lords, and diplomacy was becoming an art, as demonstrated by the peace of Westphalia.

Defining moment
Death of Cardinal Mazarin
1661
The death of Cardinal Mazarin, the man who had been the power behind Louis' throne, is met with joy from the French populace. The unpopularity of Mazarin and the authority released by the power vacuum caused by his death convinces Louis to demand complete control of the country through his personal will; he is unwilling to sit on the sidelines again. He tells his chief ministers, "I request and order you to seal no orders except by my command." This marks the beginning of the absolutist rule of the Sun King.

● **invasion of the Netherlands**
Louis' anger at the Dutch does not lose its venom, and in 1672 he launches an invasion of the Netherlands. The fighting is finally brought to an end with the Treaty of Nijmegen, which awards France new territory.
1672

● **Invades Spanish Netherlands**
Louis invades the Spanish Netherlands in what becomes known as the War of Devolution. The pretext of this bloody campaign is found in the marriage dowry of Louis' wife Maria Theresa of Spain, which he claims was never paid. Louis leads a lightning campaign, capturing huge swathes of land.
1667

● **Retreat**
A peace treaty is signed after the Dutch, Swedes and English threaten to go to war with France, which has the effect of forcing Louis to relinquish control of much of the conquered territory that he has previously captured.
1668

● **Court moves to Versailles**
Louis' self-depiction as a prince of the heavens is made manifest with the construction of Versailles - at the cost of wrecking the economy.
1682

● **Revoke of Edict of Nantes**
With his power abroad waning, Louis seeks to consolidate his domestic power by revoking the Edict of Nantes, which guaranteed Protestants' religious freedom.
1685

1715

● **Death of the Sun King**
Louis dies after suffering from a severe onset of gangrene aged 76. The populace jeer as his body is laid to rest because of the hardships he forced the country to endure.
1715

"The king's penchant for patriotic remarks and foreign war, along with him being English-born, played well to the masses"

GEORGE III
England, 1738-1820

Brief Bio

Famous in history and popular tales as 'Mad King George', the king was probably suffering from a disorder known as porphyria, which manifests with severe neurological problems. Despite this, for much of his reign George was loved by his people thanks to his British birth, and knack of saying the right patriotic thing at exactly the right time. His reign saw British achievements grow.

1738 – 1820

King George III

The first British-born king of England since James II, King George III was patriot and mad meddler in equal measure, leading to a reign arguably plagued by instability and financial mismanagement

George III was the King of the United Kingdom of Great Britain during one of the most tumultuous and disruptive periods in the power's history, with his reign witnessing the collapse of British control in the Americas, political instability in the British Parliament and near national bankruptcy. Despite this damning legacy however, for much of his reign George was well thought of among the commoners, with the king's penchant for patriotic remarks and foreign war, along with him being English-born, playing well to the masses. Even the king's famous 'madness', which grew more and more severe throughout his life did not seem to dent this view, with, as late as 1810 - near to the height of his insanity - the king popular among the people.

As one would expect however, George III was not as well thought of by the ruling political classes of England, with his reign leaving a disastrous legacy of political interference. Indeed, during his time as monarch, which began

George had nine sons and six daughters, including Edward Augustus, the father of England's future Queen Victoria

after his father Frederick, Prince of Wales died early from a lung injury and the crown passed from his Grandfather George II directly to him, George directly or indirectly caused the dissolution of the British government more than three times, with the most famous being the case of 1784, where George - dissatisfied with a bill setting forth the passage of powers in India from the East India Company to some of his parliamentary enemies - sent a message to the House of Lords that any member who voted for its passage would be considered 'his enemy'. The bill was rejected by the House of Lords and three days later the ministry was also dismissed. The subsequent election saw the then monarch-friendly William Pitt the Younger instigated as Prime Minister. This typified George III's attitude towards the elected parliament of his country during his reign, with the monarch frequently acting in his own interests or in the interest of the monarchy and overruling them. For example, during the tenure of William Pitt the

George used many titles throughout his reign, changing with the times and the countries he ruled

Younger as Prime Minister, George helped maintain his influence by creating an unprecedented number of new peers in the House of Lords, all of which – indebted to him as benefactor – voted in his favour whenever called upon. This not only disrupted the political establishment but, especially in the case of the American War of Independence, left Britain poorer financially and with less power overall on the world stage. Prior to the American War of Independence, Britain had been the leading military force worldwide, with its main rivals of France and Spain recently defeated in warfare and its cultural influence stretching throughout the Americas, Africa and even India. Thanks to George however, maintaining this at all cost would almost cripple the country.

In fact, with the American Revolutionary War, George III famously ignored the advice of his own ministers and voted repeatedly to keep Britain at war with the revolutionaries, even despite the fact that it was leading the country into a financial hole. According to the Victorian commentator George Trevelyan, George apparently wished to 'keep the

> During his reign Great Britain partook in the Seven Years' War, the American Revolution and the Napoleonic Wars

rebels harassed, anxious and poor by the indefinite prolongation of a war which promised to be eternal.' Of course, this kind of jingoistic flag-waving was often portrayed as merely the king being patriotic to the wider country, with public opinion staying firmly on his side right up until the early 1780s, when the desperate state of the country's finances began to become all too evident.

Indeed, George's financial mismanagement and lust for war meant that throughout the 1770s the national debt of the country rose to a level where it required an annual revenue of £4 million to service it and the king became famous for raiding the treasury to cover spiralling royal debts. This vast financial burden came courtesy primarily due to the costs of garrisoning and administering the large expansion of territory that control of the American colonies brought, a series of on-off wars with France and Spain, and huge annual loans payable to the East India Company to control Britain's interests in India. The country couldn't cope and eventually independence was won.

This loss of the American colonies hit George III badly and after the resignation of the then Prime Minister Frederick North he even considered abdication, with George bitterly resigned to the separation and loss of territory. While abdication

never came, the anxiety of losing the war seemed to place a great strain on George and throughout the following decades became increasingly ill, with bouts of his 'illness' making his appearances in public and participation in British politics more and more restrained. By the time he had a massive mental collapse in 1789 he was beginning to go blind and deaf and after relapses into illness in 1801 and 1804, was largely unfit to rule the country.

George's illness and decline reached a head in 1810, when after the untimely death of his youngest daughter, he mentally collapsed entirely and became completely deranged. As he was no longer fit to rule, the British Parliament passed the Regency Act of 1811 thereby allowing his son, the Prince of Wales George IV, to rule in his place.

> George III lived for 81 years and 239 days, while he reigned as monarch for 59 years and 96 days

For the last ten years of his life George III was largely confined to the interior and grounds of Windsor Castle, with his madness only punctuated by tiny moments of lucidity. His son George ruled the country in his place – albeit with none of the popularity that he had done during most of his years – the American revolutionaries established the young country of the United States of America – indicating that George was a tyrant in their Declaration of Independence – and, following his eventual death on 29 January 1820, views of his reign in Britain slowly altered from a stoic pillar of patriotic tradition in an age of unwanted revolution, to one wholly more negative.

Interestingly, today however, despite George III being largely remembered for just his madness, financial ineptitude and hunger for war, academically George's reign is increasingly being seen with a different, more positive perspective, one that highlights his learning and culture. In fact, it is true that George III was not only one of the most cultured English monarchs of all time, studying science throughout his childhood and

George (right) as a boy with his brother and tutor

"George's reign is increasingly being seen with a different, more positive perspective"

Timeline

1738

Born to rule
On the 4th of June George William Frederick is born in London at Norfolk House two months prematurely. He was thought unlikely to survive however was baptised and lived.
1738

Marries Charlotte Sophia
After succeeding to the throne in October 1760, almost a year later George III marries Charlotte Sophia of Mecklenburg-Strelitz. He is crowned King of England 17 days later.
1761

Signs of madness?
Unhappy with the then Prime Minister's – George Grenville – continuous attempts to reduce the King's prerogatives, George III dismisses him after falling ill for a brief period.
1765

George's tea party
Following decades of meddling, including introducing the grossly unpopular Stamp Act, the British government begins to lose its grip on the American Colonies starting with the Boston Tea Party
1773

A cartoon from 1786 depicting George III and Queen Charlotte raiding the national treasury to cover royal debts. The Prime Minister, William Pitt the Elder, is seen handing him another money bag

early adult life – he collected scientific instruments too, many of which can be seen in the London Science Museum today, and possessed his vary own observatory – but also taking a keen interest in the arts and agriculture. Indeed, it was George III who founded and paid the initial costs of the British Royal Academy of Arts and it was also George III who funded the construction and maintenance of famous astronomer William Herschel's ground-breaking 40-foot telescope. He was, rather cruelly, also comically referred to as 'Farmer George' by his opponents due to his keen interest and love of agriculture, writing numerous articles under a pseudonym in agricultural texts and pamphlets.

In fact, George's learning became rather quite famous in contrast to many earlier kings – and especially so in light of his stupid and unlearned son – with him accruing a royal collection of books that numbered the tens of thousands and opening his collection freely to learned scholars who wished to gain the knowledge held within. 65,000 of these books were later donated to the British Museum and now form the heart of its collection.

Whether or not this contribution to the arts and sciences can be seen as redeeming features capable of permanently redressing the perception of George III's reign is open to debate, however there is one thing that all commentators, both modern and historical alike, agree on and that is that his rule was no where near as bad as his son's, with George VI acting throughout his short reign with a wanton disregard for Britain and its people, while bringing the monarchy to an historical low. Writing in his diary, contemporary of George VI Charles Greville said of the king that, 'He only wishes to be powerful in order to exercise the most puerile caprices, gratify ridiculous resentments, indulge vulgar prejudices, and amass or squander money; not one great object connected with national glory or prosperity ever enters his brain.'

> George's reign is now seen as a very positive time for British arts and sciences, which flourished under his aegis

The mad monarch

Today, as in the 18th century, why George III regressed into madness is not fully understood, with records from the time of his 'illness' vague or nonexistent. Obviously, in the 18th and early 19th Century, mental illness was nowhere near as understood as it is today, with those affected typically just locked up. One thing is clear though, the recurring nature of George's illness – with the first record of it coming as early as 1765 – does seem to indicate it was more mental than physical.

A few hypotheses have since been postulated by historians, the most prominent being that the king suffered from the blood disease porphyria, a rare inherited series of enzyme disorders that can often lead to neurological problems. This cannot be confirmed however for sure, albeit with records of his madness and later dementia tallying well with the hypothesis. An analysis of a few surviving strands of George's hair in 2004 also revealed a high level of arsenic, which is also known to precipitate attacks of porphyria.

Arguably the worst recorded case of George's madness was the relapse that led to his death. Starting at Christmas 1819, George spoke nonsense for 58 hours straight before falling exhausted into a coma. He never recovered consciousness and was dead within a month.

George chooses Pitt
George III causes Parliament to be dissolved due to a dispute over the India Bill, with the subsequent election giving his own monarch-friendly candidate, William Pitt the Younger, a solid mandate.
1784

Ministry of All the Talents
After George's long-time bete noire William Grenville had taken back control of Parliament after Pitt the Younger's death in 1806, setting up his famous Ministry of All the Talents, George once more causes Parliament to be dissolved.
1807

Amelia dies
After a decade of decline in the health of his youngest and favourite daughter Princess Amelia, she suddenly dies at the age of just 27, sending the near-blind George into 'scenes of distress and crying every day'.
1810

Prince Regent
George finally accepts the need for the Regency Act of 1811, allowing his son to take over the official duties of king as Prince Regent. He does so until George's death.
1811

Mad man of Windsor
Following the Regency Act of 1811, George became increasingly mad, confined at all times to Windsor Castle. In 1818 his wife dies and he is too insane to realise.
1818

58 hours of insanity
Following a bad bout of insanity where he talked nonsense for 58 hours, George III collapses and never recovers. He dies on 29 January 1820 and is buried in St George's Chapel, Windsor Castle.
1820

1820

1784 – 1833

Ferdinand VII

During one of the most turbulent periods of European history, Spain suffered under one of history's most inept kings

In the early years of the 19th Century, Spain was in utter turmoil. Occupied by an invading army and ravaged by the bloody Peninsular War, the country was divided both by its enemies and its internal politics. Ferdinand VII, the king of Spain and the latest in a long line of Bourbon monarchs in Europe, sat imprisoned in France, with his throne occupied by Joseph Bonaparte, Napoleon's brother. Ferdinand's reign, or reigns after his forced abdication and restoration, was one of the least popular in Spain's history and the king was often at odds with the majority of his subjects, including the growing number of progressive liberals.

A sickly youth, Ferdinand's early years were spent among the power struggles and bitter rivalries of the Spanish court, though he was almost entirely excluded from any decision-making or governance. Charles IV, his father, was at best heavily influenced and at worst totally dominated by his Prime Minister Manuel de Godoy, one of the most important figures in this period of Spanish history. Widely rumoured to be Queen Maria Louisa's lover, Godoy had risen through the ranks of the army to gain favour with the royal couple who, when they ascended the throne, elevated him further. However, his de facto rule was unpopular with many, including Juan Escoiquiz, Ferdinand's tutor, who turned the young prince's mind against

Godoy. It's against this backdrop that Ferdinand became embroiled in a plot to overthrow the Prime Minister in 1807 and to take the throne, but the conspiracy was swiftly revealed and the prince was forced to give up his fellow conspirators before being briefly imprisoned. Ferdinand's first wife, Maria Antonieta of Naples, was also embroiled in the plotting, as her family was vehemently against Godoy and France.

Though unsuccessful, Ferdinand's attempted coup came at a difficult time for Godoy, who was himself struggling to keep France at bay. He had failed to protect Louis XVI of France, another Bourbon king and distant cousin of Charles IV's, from being executed in 1893 and had allowed French troops to travel through Spain to confront a hostile Portugal. This fractious condition of the Spanish seat of power led Napoleon to strike for the heart of the country's government and in 1808 the French troops began to take up key positions in San Sebastian, Barcelona and Figueras. Later a popular uprising in Aranjuez, where Charles IV had been staying, forced the king to abdicate in favour of Ferdinand, who promptly entered Madrid in vainglorious and ignorant triumph.

Ferdinand was entirely blind to the realities of both his and the country's situation. Though at long last he had ascended the throne and Godoy

> He was the last Spanish monarch to hold claim to the absolute divine right of the monarch

FERDINAND VII
Spain, 1784-1833

Brief Bio

His father was widely reputed to be the puppet of his own Prime Minster Manuel de Godoy, and Ferdinand soon tried to overthrow the Svengali-ing statesman (who was also rumoured to be his mother's lover). Finally acceding to the throne, he spent much of his reign struggling with the risks of the Napoleonic Wars, which saw him imprisoned for six years as a rebel.

Ferdinand reigned in two separate periods: in 1808 before his forced abdication, then from 1814 until his death.

A portrait of Charles IV and his family, including his son and future king, Ferdinand. Painted by Francisco Goya

Life in the time of the felon king

Napoleon's Empire

Emerging from the chaotic French Revolution, and the ensuing wars, Napoleon had quenched the revolutionary anarchy threatening to spread throughout Europe and now led a larger, much stronger France, with himself as its emperor. France's neighbours, most with monarchs at their head, were in constant conflict with the new regime and in fear of its growing power, embodied in Napoleon's great military victories.

The Constitution of Cadiz

Named after the city it was written in, one of the few territories left in Spanish hands after the French occupation in 1808, the Constitution declared a radical shift in power from the centralised state to the people. It aimed to establish equal rights for all Spanish citizens and even extended certain rights to the growing Spanish colonies in the Americas.

The French Revolution

Between 1789-90, the Third Estate in France – the third class, or proletariat – rose up in arms against the nobility, overthrowing aristocratic rule and turning the established power structure on its head. This culminated in the execution of King Louis XVI in 1793 and the period that is known as the French Revolutionary Wars.

The Peninsula War

In an attempt to block it off from trading and aiding Britain, Napoleon launched a campaign against Portugal, seeking to reduce Britain's capacity to oppose him. He did this with the permission of Ferdinand's father, Charles IV, to march French troops through Spain. However, these troops swiftly became an occupying force and the ensuing war ravaged the Iberian Peninsula for several years.

Absolutist monarchs

With the growth of the middle class throughout the 18th and 19th Centuries, the need for greater democracy and the wider distribution of power became ever more prevalent in European society. However, this was at odds with many ruling monarchs, such as in France, who saw the rights of the monarch as pre-eminent above all others.

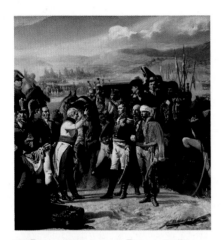

The Napoleonic Wars

The series of campaigns in Europe fought between the French Empire and numerous allied coalitions are collectively known as the Napoleonic Wars. Spreading out from the earlier French Revolutionary Wars from around 1793 onwards, the wars saw Napoleon Bonaparte dominate much of continental Europe before his final defeat at the Battle of Waterloo in 1815. As part of the campaigns against France, the Peninsular War ravaged the Iberian Peninsula from around 1807 until 1814. This conflict, in hindsight, proved extremely costly for Napoleon, who simultaneously had to deal with the British, Portuguese and Spanish guerrillas. Later he would track back his eventual demise to this war, which he called his 'fatal knot'. The Spanish people were by far the biggest losers in this conflict and it left a crisis within the country that would leave it scarred for decades to come.

Defining moment
The rise and fall 17 March 1808

The revolt of the town of the Aranjuez, south of the Spanish capital, triggers the forced abdication of Ferdinand's father, Charles IV. Ferdinand is placed on the throne by the rebels, many of whom favour the prince. However, the new king immediately comes under the grip of Napoleon I and his army stationed in Madrid. The Emperor of France summons the new king and forces him to give up his crown the following month. Before long the entire court is exiled and imprisoned in France.

had been taken prisoner, he failed to realise that the French, who occupied Madrid even as the new king returned to the capital, were far from his ally. Napoleon had by now taken nearly all of Spain without a single pitched battle. Despite widespread riots in opposition to the French occupation, Ferdinand was convinced that the Emperor was acting in his favour and travelled to talk with him personally the month after his accession. Of course, this was another grave mistake. Napoleon swiftly forced Ferdinand and his father to relinquish their claims to the throne and placed the prince under arrest at the castle of Valençay.

For the next six years Ferdinand sat imprisoned in France, while his country became ravaged by the Peninsular War and his subjects, for the most part, rebelled against the new king Joseph I Bonaparte, who had been placed on the throne by his brother Napoleon. For many, despite his severely poor judgement and leadership in his brief sojourn as king, Ferdinand became a symbol of Spanish resistance to the French occupiers. Along with the invading British forces under the Duke of Wellington, the Spanish guerrilla fighters sought to restore the Bourbon king to the throne, despite his apparent lack of competence to rule. In his absence, Spanish society was now without official governance and was split into a series of improvised juntas and localised councils. The most

> He married four times, each time to a close or distant relative, but was only able to leave two surviving children

important of these was at Cadiz, where the liberal Constitution of 1812 was written up. This paper would prove to be crucial for the remaining years of Ferdinand's reign, as once again he would prove to be at odds with the majority of his subjects.

After years of the Napoleonic wars raging far beyond the confines of his prison, Ferdinand was finally released by the French Emperor and returned to Madrid in March 1814. Before long he was seeking to establish his power, so on 4 May suspended the Constitution of 1812 and decreed the restoration of the absolutist monarchy. He followed this up by swiftly rounding up and arresting the liberal leaders in Madrid, as well as those Spaniards who had co-operated with Napoleon during the occupation. The hypocrisy of this action, clear to all who remembered Ferdinand's compliance with the French when he sought to take the crown from his father, made him deeply unpopular with many. While in captivity he had agreed to honour the Constitution, so this betrayal, along with his brutal suppression of the liberals who still had connections within the army and elsewhere, bred extreme distrust and outright hatred for him.

In the ensuing years there were a series of unsuccessful revolts and coups throughout Spain, as well as in Hispanic America, mainly from within the embittered army who resented serving overseas and was, by this point, far too large for purpose. Along with his rejection of the

On the third of May, 1808, a number of civilian uprisings against the French occupiers triggered a brutal reaction from the army, here immortalised by Francisco Goya

Timeline

1784

● **A Bourbon prince**
Ferdinand is born to Charles IV and Maria Louisa of Parma at the palace of La Granja de San Ildefonso, north of Madrid.
October 14 1784

● **A plot foiled**
Ferdinand is involved in a plot to topple Prime Minister Godoy and to take the Spanish throne for himself. The conspiracy is discovered, however, and the prince is thrown in jail.
29 November 1807

● **The rise and fall**
The revolt of the town of the Aranjuez, south of the Spanish capital, triggers the forced abdication of Ferdinand's father, Charles IV. Ferdinand is placed on the throne by the rebels, many of whom favour the prince. However, the new king immediately comes under the grip of Napoleon I and his army stationed in Madrid. The Emperor of France summons the new king and forces him to give up his crown the following month. Before long the entire court is exiled and imprisoned in France.
17 March 1808

● **Imprisoned**
Ferdinand, his family and the royal entourage are forced to leave Madrid. They are received by Charles Maurice de Talleyrand and held in Valençay castle.
10 May 1808

● **The usurping king**
Joseph Bonaparte, brother of the French emperor, is given the crown of Spain and enters Madrid in the midst of the Spanish War of Independence from France.
7 June 1808

Constitution, Ferdinand had also raised petty noblemen to high stations and many army officers saw this as a betrayal of their efforts and merit. This culminated in an outright military coup attempt led by Rafael del Riego, which eventually forced Ferdinand to agree to the Constitution, under duress, in March 1820. However, this time the liberals faltered, as they failed to form a stable form of government, hampered by pro-royalist revolts. Once again Ferdinand found himself at the centre of a crisis that, though he had in part created through poor judgement and misrule, he was completely incapable of rectifying. Before long another army of France, this time under the banner of the restored Bourbon dynasty in France, was marching into Spain to free the troubled king from his own people and to restore his full control. This army, popularly known as the Hundred Thousand Sons of St Louis, entered Spain in 1823, propping up the weak and unstable government of Ferdinand. The king of Spain had to reach out to any authority he could grasp at, as clearly the Spanish army would never totally support him and his series of successive governments, all of whom failed, weren't up to the task either.

Though the French army swiftly defeated the liberal rebels, it wasn't expected that it should remain in Spain. However, Ferdinand saw it as another opportunity to reinforce his position – spilling the blood of his own countrymen through the might of a foreign invader.

Though shameful to many, this tactic worked to a large extent and the liberal rebels capitulated under the agreement that their freedoms and lives would be guaranteed. Ferdinand again went back on this promise and proceeded to ruthlessly

Though he left an unstable succession, his great, great, great grandson is today the king of Spain

During Ferdinand's imprisonment in France, the improvised government set up in Cadiz wrote up the Constitution of 1812, which espoused Enlightenment ideals and a reduction in centralised power

imprison over a thousand liberal rebels, nearly all purely for political crimes.

He hanged the original instigator of the 1820 revolt, Rafael del Riego, on 7 November 1823 and quickly signed an agreement with the French army that it would remain in Spain until a secure government could be established. Though this also reduced the army by half, it extended its stay in the country by several months. For the following three years the king wrought vengeance on the revolutionaries that had opposed him.

Though there is great competition for exactly which period of his rule was the least successful and most disastrous, Ferdinand's final years do nothing to redeem him as a capable ruler, or virtuous king. Old, sick, bloated and still without a

secure succession - he had no male heir - the king married his fourth and final wife, Maria Christina, in 1829. When the royal couple only produced two daughters, Isabella and Luisa Fernanda, the king was forced to go to the very men he had suppressed so forcefully - the liberal party. Shamelessly, the king formed a liberal government in order to change the country's laws of succession to include Isabella. In reality, this was far too little, too late. When Ferdinand died in 1833, after a long period of illness, his daughter's succession was disputed by his brother Charles and the Carlist Wars began, which set a new flame to burn the whole of Spain once again. The hapless king had left his country in as much ruin and distress as he had ruled it.

"There is great competition for exactly which period of his rule was the most disastrous"

Defining moment
The Liberal revolt 10 March 1820
Col. Rafael del Riego, declaring his support for the Constitution of 1812, leads a popular revolt from within the army, using the widespread discontent with Ferdinand's rule. The rebellion leads Ferdinand to capitulate and the liberal rebels take possession of him. This revolution turned civil war ended when France intervened with an army named the Hundred Thousand Sons of St Louis, aiming to restore the Bourbon king to power. The revolution is quashed and Ferdinand exacts brutal vengeance of many of his liberal opponents, including del Riego, who is hanged in November 1823.

1833

Mexico rises
The Mexican War of Independence begins, which will see the country totally split from Spain in 11 years time. Gradually Spain begins to lose all of its lucrative American colonies.
16 September 1810

The return to Spain
As the allies of the sixth coalition begin to grind down the French, Napoleon decides to restore Ferdinand to the throne and withdraws remaining troops from Spain under the Treaty of Valençay.
24 March 1814

Rejecting the constitution
On returning to Spain, Ferdinand throws out the liberal Constitution of Cadiz, 1812, which features many enlightenment notions that seek to move the centre of power away from the monarchy.
4 May 1814

The future queen is born
Ferdinand's first daughter and surviving heir, Isabella, is born. Her reign is just as tumultuous as her father's and her accession is contested with an immediate war.
10 October 1830

Death
After a period of illness Ferdinand dies in the midst of the succession crisis of his daughter, Isabella. Her disputed claim to the throne leads to the Carlist Wars.
1833

1787 – 1828

Shaka, King of the Zulus

Through wisdom, courage and warrior strength Shaka, King of the Zulus, united the greatest African kingdom the world has ever seen

Shaka flexed his muscles and adopted a hunting posture as he looked down at the venomous snake in the long grass. The black mamba had just killed one of the prized bulls his chief and patron, Dingiswayo, had charged him to protect and now it had turned on Shaka. By allowing the snake to kill Dingiswayo's property Shaka had failed him, the man who had taken him in after he and his mother were cast out of his father's tribe; he had also brought shame on the dignity of his warriors. The snake hissed and made a warning gesture, Shaka had to best it in order to keep his place within the tribe. He was tall, fast and agile, but he knew the bite from the venomous pest would be fatal if he lost. The snake struck, Shaka side-stepped the lightning-fast strike and lunged with his spear, driving it into the snake's body. Dingiswayo had always lauded Shaka for his royal blood, it was one of the reasons he took him and his mother in when they were alone on the plains. As Shaka stood triumphant having revenged the death of the bull, he was now more than a political tool -

he was a fully fledged Zulu warrior with his first kill.

The victory over the snake was the first of many conquests won by Shaka as he rose through the ranks of Zulu society. His next success came when he joined the warrior fraternity of his tribe, the Impi regiment, in 1809. He found the kinship and acceptance of the soldier group a welcome relief from the constant taunting over his status as an outcast from the other boys in Dingiswayo's tribe. The children would shout, call him names and insult his beloved mother. Now he was a man who commanded respect from the other warriors and he quickly became a popular and able leader. His physical size and hunting ability stood him head and shoulders above the rest, but he was also known to be a man of original ideas. He found traditional forms of African combat, which often involved little more than small skirmishes with throwing spears, to be no test of a warrior's mettle. He introduced a short stabbing spear, the iklwa, and ordered them to be used in close combat with large shields in

> Shaka was noted for his strength and agility, however he was a poor public speaker and was often tripping over his own words

> Shaka's given name was actually Tshaka. Shaka literally means bastard and was used to taunt him as a child, but it stuck

SHAKA

Zulu Kingdom, 1787 – 1828

Brief Bio This powerful warrior rose through tribal ranks from decidedly humble beginnings. Proving himself in combat, he began unifying the tribes of the Natal region through brutal conquests. Power rapidly went to his head, however, and the king became increasingly power-crazed as his dominance in the region grew.

Zulu warrior charging with the iconic short stabbing spear, the iklwa

Life in the time of Shaka

The white settlers

During the time of Shaka white settlers began encroaching on the lands of the Africans in increasing numbers. The African tribes were forced to flee, fight or otherwise accommodate the settlers as best they could. Some tribes, like the Zulus, initially became allies and trade partners with the invaders.

The Mfecane

The Mfecane or 'crushing' came at the end of Shaka's reign and was a direct result of his constant warfare within the Natal region. Refugees and scattered tribes were forced out of the area and into the surrounding landscape, creating widespread famine and the scramble for crop-producing land formed a crush of thousands of people.

Climate change

It is widely thought that changes in the climate in south-eastern Africa caused the largely peaceful farming tribes that lived in the region, like the Nguni who became the Zulus, to become more volatile and militaristic as available farm land shrunk due to the weather becoming much drier.

Zulu rites

Zulu society was highly ritualised and based around codes of kinship. One of these kinships came in the tribe's military system, where males as a rite of passage would become a warrior with other males the same age. When Shaka took over as king he used this custom to expand his kingdom.

An oral tradition

Much of what we know about Shaka and his early years comes from the rich Zulu oral tradition, where history was repeated in stories passed down from generation to generation through word of mouth. It was only after explorers came into contact with the Zulus that their history was written down.

Shaka's tactics

Shaka completely revolutionised the way Zulus waged war during his reign as king. Tribal conflicts would never again amount to little more than small raids for cattle or posturing to display strength. Unlike the African armies of old, Shaka's military was designed to do one thing: crush opposition and grind rival tribes into the dust. He devised a new Impi system where all males would serve him for a fixed term in his army, which by 1820 numbered nearly 40,000 men.

He introduced the iklwa, or short stabbing spear, which suited Shaka's preference for leading his warriors into hand-to-hand combat with the enemy. Close combat required a heavier shield, so he introduced the cowhide-covered Impi shield, which was used with the stabbing spear to keep the warrior alive long enough for him to deal out death on the plains. The greatest innovation brought to the Zulu military doctrine was Shaka's bull-and-horns tactic. He would order his men to close in on the enemy, which was the bull charging in, and at the last moment order troops to sweep around onto the enemy flanks, creating the horns, crushing them in a pincer. With these developments, Shaka's kingdom swept through the South African plains like wild fire, carving out the Zulu kingdom.

order to devastate the enemy's position quickly and with deadly efficiently.

Dingiswayo was impressed by these reforms and the victories Shaka stacked up during his early years as a warrior. He had found a powerful ally and had been proven correct to welcome him into his village when no one else would accept him. As a way of showing his gratitude for his service, Dingiswayo helped Shaka return to his father's tribe as chief in 1816. The men who had insisted on his banishment shortly after his birth were quickly brought to heel by Shaka's fearsome Zulu warriors. Dingiswayo restored his honour and the honour of his mother and in return Shaka offered his undying loyalty. It was this loyalty that inspired Shaka to take action when Dingiswayo was killed by tribesmen of the Ndwandwe. Shaka was compelled to take revenge on his patron's killers and he quickly combined his tribe with Dingiswayo's to create a fledgling Zulu kingdom. He then launched a campaign of conquest against the Ndwandwe and their chief, Zwide. They met in battle near the Mhlatuse River, Shaka led the

charge and used his new bull-and-horns formation to completely destroy Zwide's forces. The survivors and their womenfolk were incorporated into the Zulu kingdom. In the space of three years Shaka had expanded a small village group into a nation to be feared across the continent.

With his new army behind him and the destruction of his immediate enemies complete, Shaka set about subjugating all the peoples within the Natal region, whether they were hostile or not. He organised his new kingdom along military lines – he had no intention of being cast out again or killed through weakness, so he built up his military prowess. All men within his domain were now eligible for military service. They were organised in their Impis according to age, with the rest of the kingdom providing the war machine with food and weapons. Conscription could last years and soldiers were housed within purpose-built barracks so their king could call on them whenever he needed military muscle to satisfy his whims. The Zulu nation had become a country completely dedicated to warfare and conquest under the leadership of Shaka.

> Shaka was born during a period of extreme famine in the south-eastern region of South Africa

"In three years Shaka had expanded a small village group into a nation to be feared"

Defining moment

Shaka crowned King of the Zulus 1818

After Dingiswayo is captured and killed by a neighbouring tribe, the Ndwandwe under the ferocious Zwide, Shaka makes a courageous bid to unite all of the Zulus under his rule. After a number of ritual displays of courage and with the presence of his loyal warriors behind him, Shaka manages to convince Dingiswayo's tribe that a united Zulu nation would conquer all of Africa and bring Dingiswayo's killers to justice. He is crowned King of the Zulus and quickly sets about reforming the military system in preparation to confront Zwide and the Ndwandwe across the Mhlatuse River.

Timeline

1787

Birth of a warrior
Shaka is born to the Zulu chief Senzangakhona kaJama and his lover Nandi. Despite his noble birth he is rejected by his father and he and his mother flee his father's court.
1787

First kill
Shaka is charged with guarding a prized bull by Dingiswayo, his new chief. A black mamba kills the bull so Shaka attacks the poisonous snake, dodges its venomous blows and kills it.
1800

Shaka joins his Impi
Shaka approaches manhood, joins his Impi or age regiment and becomes a warrior for Dingiswayo. His large size and reputation as an uncompromising and brave warrior quickly impresses his chief.
1809

Retakes his birthright
After 26 years of exile Shaka retakes the tribe he was born into by successfully beating his illegitimate half-brothers. He uses the military muscle of Dingiswayo to do this.
1816

Victory against Zwide
Shaka uses his superior fighting ability, as well as the new skills he has taught his Zulu warriors, to completely destroy the Ndwandwe war host assembled at the Mhlatuse River and bring the killers of his great patron to justice. The battle is unlike anything fought by warriors living in the region before. Rather than a small skirmish or a non-violent gesture to prove superior fighting ability, Shaka orders an all-out attack and his Zulu warriors quickly move into close combat using the bull-and-horns tactic to slaughter Zwide's men.
1819

As a champion fighter and king to his warriors, Shaka realised he had to expand his kingdom in order to keep his prestige high among the men that he led into battle. He needed more fertile land, more cattle, more everything to satisfy his people. What's more his warriors would soon become restless if they weren't fighting anything. He decided to launch raids into the regions north of Natal, killing off rival warriors, murdering or enslaving the women and children that were left undefended. This created a mass migration of refugees out of the area and into the tribal lands in what is today central South Africa, causing famine and starvation in the wake of Shaka's conquests. He had no idea he was causing such a huge humanitarian disaster, but the consequences of his relentless pursuit of warfare is remembered as the Mfecane or 'crushing' of the African people.

The mass migration of refugees and the tales of destruction they brought with them into the lands north and west of Natal did not go unnoticed by the other great power that was beginning to show dominance in the area: the British Empire. Word had spread to London of an African king with a fearsome reputation for conquest in the eastern reaches of the cape - it was said he was unbeatable in combat. The British were too weak in the area to challenge Shaka openly, so instead they sent a delegation to negotiate with him. Shaka was impressed by the men who saw him and offered generous trade agreements and peace with the British. He cared little for their firearms

Shaka's temper was legendary and one of the reasons he had a reputation as a blood-thirsty tyrant by the end of the 1820s

and technology, which he dismissed as useless against the agility and speed of the bull-and-horns formation of his Zulu warriors. He negotiated with the British on equal terms, his kingdom would need the trade and the British needed their eastern flank secured. Despite this seemingly amicable arrangement, Shaka could tell a predator when he saw one and knew the British would be back in greater numbers.

By 1827, Shaka had turned the Zulu Kingdom into one of the most powerful African dynasties in history. Yet his warriors had become weary of the constant demands for war. He had broken from tradition in making them fight hundreds of miles away from their homes and insisting that they remained celibate throughout their service in his army. He had also become ruthless in dealing with his adversaries - often a death sentence would be bestowed with a simple nod of his head while he sat on his throne. When his beloved mother died in 1827 he realised that he was now alone, he had never married and so the only thing that could hold any meaning in his life was his skill as a warrior and the kingdom he had built. He ordered his warriors to mourn his mother but when his

demoralised horde became less than enthusiastic about spending night after night performing ritual burial dances to someone who meant little or nothing to them, Shaka descended into a fit of rage. He ordered all the men not seen to be putting enough effort into the mourning executed. He then marched into selected Zulu villages and told his warriors to force every man, woman and child to grieve for his mother on pain of death.

After the brutal events of 1827, Shaka had become dangerously unpopular among the Zulus. He was no longer seen as a great warrior and noble leader, but a tyrant soaked in the blood of his own people. As he continued to insist on plunging his kingdom into war after war, his half-brother, Dingane, plotted to assassinate him. On 22 September 1828, Shaka's glorious rule came to an abrupt end when an iklwa was plunged into his back by Dingane and his bodyguard Mbopha. As Shaka lay dying outside of his barracks his last words were: "Are you stabbing me, kings of the Earth? You will come to an end through killing one another." He had fought as a warrior his whole life and could see nothing but warfare as he took his last breath on the African plains.

Since his death, Shaka has become a symbol of great pride for the people of the Zulu tribe who still live in South Africa today

Defining moment
Death of his mother
1827
Shaka's mother dies in 1827, which causes the warrior king to descend into a deep depression. As his only source of protection and strength during his early years, his mother was a strong influence on him and Shaka insists on elaborate mourning ceremonies that his entire kingdom, including his demoralised warriors, is forced to take part in. As the ceremonies get under way he goes into a psychotic rage when he thinks his people are not mourning hard enough and orders hundreds of his own men killed in front of their families to inspire more effort in honouring his mother's passing.

Annual raids
Beginning in the mid-1820s, Shaka begins to use his standing army to raid the population surrounding his kingdom inspiring fear and ensuring the overwhelming dominance of the Zulus.
1820

The British delegation
A British army officer, Lieutenant James King, visits Shaka and successfully negotiates trade agreements, including permission for the British to build a fort in Zulu territory.
1825

Attack on Delagoa Bay
After the events of the previous year, his soldiers become increasingly demoralised but Shaka presses ahead with building his kingdom, launching raids on the European slave hub at Delagoa Bay in the north of his lands.
1827

Starvation
Shaka's unrelenting quest for power devastates the surrounding region. The continuous warfare causes mass migration into already overpopulated lands and starvation. This becomes known as the Mfecane or 'crushing'.
1828

1828

Betrayal and death
Shaka becomes increasingly unpopular because of the devastation he has brought on the region and is murdered by his half-brother and bodyguard. He leaves behind a Zulu Kingdom that is feared by friend and foe alike.
22 September 1828

© Alamy; Getty

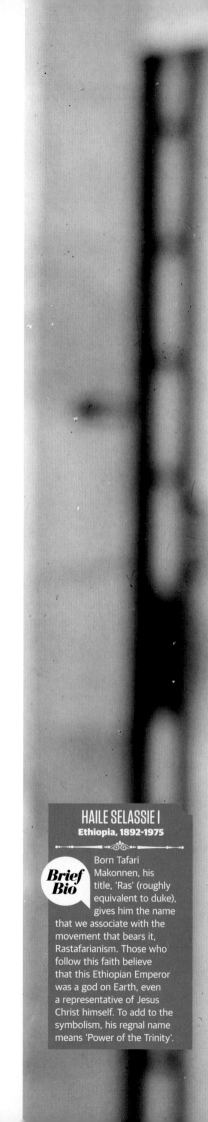

1892 – 1975
Haile Selassie I

Controversial for some, but an inspiration and even God for many others, the Lion of Judah is one of Africa's most important figures

The year is 1966, and a crowd of thousands is gathered at Palisadoes Airport in Kingston, Jamaica, anxiously awaiting the arrival of the one they call the King of Kings, the Lion of Judah, the Almighty One. Scores of devoted Rastafaris have travelled from across the country to catch a glimpse of the man they believe to be God on Earth, an African Emperor travelling thousands of miles across the ocean to visit this small Caribbean nation. A hum of drums and joyous singing rings through the air and as the long-awaited plane finally lands and crawls to a halt, a symbol of a lion blazoned on its side, the crowd surges to meet it. Officials appeal for calm from the crowd for some minutes before eventually a figure is spotted at the top of the plane's landing steps. An elderly man of small stature, wearing a military uniform that almost engulfs him, steps out to greet the ecstatic crowd - Haile Selassie has arrived.

Though in later life he would brush shoulders with state leaders and even be worshipped as God among men, Haile Selassie's surroundings at his birth, at least, were humble. He was born Tafari Makonnen in a simple mud hut, in Ejersa Gora, Ethiopia. His father, Ras Makonnen, was the governor of Harrar, an Ethiopian province, as well as a close advisor of Emperor Menelik II. After his father's death, Tafari became close with the Emperor, who saw great potential in the young

man who was made governor of Harrar when he was just 17.

The young Tafari's rise to power was quick and in 1913, at the age of just 21, he became regent and heir apparent to the late Emperor's daughter, Zauditu. During this period he struggled against the Empress' relative conservatism and resistance to modernisation, but he did successfully bring Ethiopia into the League of Nations, the international body set up in the aftermath of World War I, in 1923. His reforms of the country signalled further centralisation of power, removing many of the powers held by regional rulers. In 1930, Empress Zauditu died, and Tafiri was able to assume the throne. He took the name Haile Selasssie, meaning Power of the Trinity, as his official title, a name that would very shortly be known throughout the world.

Over his first few years as Emperor, Selassie sought to continue his education reforms, modernising education and placing his country further on the world stage. However, he couldn't have predicted the horrific crisis looming on the horizon that would devastate Ethiopia. The menace of Fascism had been gradually sprouting in Italy since the 1920s, and by the 1930s Benito Mussolini was in complete control of the country as dictator. Known as Il Duce or The Leader, Mussolini was seeking to build a new Roman Empire for himself, to restore Italian

> He was the last emperor of Ethiopia, which fell into turmoil after his deposition

> He was and still is revered by Rastafarians as a prophet from God and even a reincarnation of Jesus Christ

HAILE SELASSIE I
Ethiopia, 1892-1975

Brief Bio Born Tafari Makonnen, his title, 'Ras' (roughly equivalent to duke), gives him the name that we associate with the movement that bears it, Rastafarianism. Those who follow this faith believe that this Ethiopian Emperor was a god on Earth, even a representative of Jesus Christ himself. To add to the symbolism, his regnal name means 'Power of the Trinity'.

Like many of Ethiopia's traditional leaders, he drew his authority as a direct descendent of King Soloman

"Haile Selassie chose to flee Ethiopia as the inevitable conclusion to the war became apparent"

The Second Italo-Ethiopian War

On 3 October 1935 Italy invaded Ethiopia on the presupposition of retaliating against a cross-border attack. In reality, Mussolini was seeking to gain greater control over East Africa, as well as regain Italian pride after its defeat to the African nation in the 19th Century. Il Duce was also looking to exploit the rich mineral wealth that he believed lay in Ethiopia's earth. Selassie reacted to the aggression initially by withdrawing his troops away from the advancing Italian force, in a bid to display an unaggressive front and perhaps negotiate a peace. As the war continued and it became more likely that the invaders would win, Selassie chose to flee the country and began travelling to England. In his later speech to the League of Nations, Selassie spoke of how the Italians used chemical weapons on civilians, in order to terrorise the population into surrender, or even to wipe them out altogether. After five years of occupation, the Italian occupation came to an end when British forces, along with Ethiopian resistance fighters and their allies, expelled Mussolini's army. This came shortly after Fascist Italy allied itself with Hitler shortly after the outbreak of World War II. Selassie finally returned to his country in 1941.

pride and exploit the mineral wealth of Africa. Years earlier, at the end of the 19th Century, Italy had tried and failed to take Ethiopia in an embarrassing series of defeats by the army of Emperor Menelik II. By 1934 the European power was poised to strike once again, but this time with deadly efficiency. On 3 October 1935 the Italian army invaded and within a year the country had been conquered.

In a move that attracted much criticism from his opponents in later life, Selassie chose to flee Ethiopia as the inevitable conclusion to the war became apparent. He escaped through neighbouring French-held territories on his way to England. The full horrors of the war he left behind would not be fully revealed to the world until June of the same year when he addressed the 52 state members of the League of Nations. In his famous speech, he decried the inaction of the League, which he had expected to protect his vulnerable country, as was its mandate. He also spoke of the great atrocities that were committed by the Italian army as it pressed forward. "It is not only upon warriors that the Italian Government has made war," he said. "It has above all attacked populations far removed from hostilities, in order to terrorise and exterminate them." His accounts that Italy had been using chemical weapons - including noxious gases that had been

> In his speech to the League of Nations in 1936, he warned of a horror awaiting Europe, foreshadowing World War II

banned since the end of the First World War - were shocking. His ominous warning to the League is perhaps one of the most famous forewarnings of the impending world war: "I decided to come myself to bear witness against the crime perpetrated against my people and give Europe a warning of the doom that awaits it, if it should bow before the accomplished fact." Selassie spent the remainder of the 1930s in exile, in a small house near Bath, England and became a symbol of the resistance against the Italian invaders. Soon enough Europe slipped into war once again in 1939, and in 1940 Mussolini declared war on Britain and France, joining with Hitler. The Italian adventure in Africa came to a decisive close as British colonial forces and their allies drove the Italians out of most of Africa in what became known as the East African Campaign. A combined force of African, Ethiopian and British Commonwealth troops helped to free Ethiopia and in 1941 Selassie re-entered Addis Ababa to retake his throne.

After his return, Selassie was if anything more determined to centralise the country's power around himself, as well as further modernise its infrastructure, though this contradiction would later cost him dearly. In 1950 he founded the University of Addis Ababa and in 1955 released a

Defining moment
Appeal to the League of Nations
June 1936

Speaking in Geneva, Haile's famous speech to the League of Nations, denouncing the Italian invasion of his country, catapults him even further onto the world stage. As a member of the League, Ethiopia expected the support of the other countries and Haile even explained how this presupposed protection deterred him from preparing for the Italian threat. He decries the use of chemical weapons, including mustard gas and other noxious substances sprayed down by the Italian air force. These weapons had been prohibited since the First World War, where their use had been devastating. Haile calls upon the League to act in defence of his small nation and warns that a similar fate is awaiting the countries of Europe.

Timeline

1892

Born in Ejersa Goro
Haile is born Tafari Makonnen in a province of Ethiopia, in a mud hut. He is the only surviving legitimate heir of Ras Makonnen, the governor or Harrar and advisor to Emperor Menelik II.
23 July 1892

Becomes regent
Emperor Menelik II dies with no male heir and Tafari becomes regent, with the late Emperor's daughter Zauditu inheriting the position of Empress.
1913

Crowned Emperor
After Zauditu dies on 2 April, Tafari inherits the crown. He adopts the new title Haile Selassie, or 'power of the trinity', as his official name as Emperor.
2 November 1930

Mussolini invades
In a bid to expand its Imperial ambitions and extend its control over Africa, Italy invades Ethiopia. This brief war lasts until May 1936, when the Italian army enters Addis Ababa.
3 October 1935

Exile in England
After the Italian occupation, Haile flees to England, where he remains in exile. He buys Fairfield House near Bath, Somerset, where he spends the next five years.
2 May 1936

The East Africa Campaign
With the help of British and other forces, the Italian army is defeated in Ethiopia and the occupation comes to an end. Haile returns and reforms a government.
January 1941

new constitution for the country, extending voting rights further. However, he still maintained close control over the main facets of government, with all the key figures of authority, including the prime minister, acting almost as his royal court. These policies struck a peculiar balance - on the one side stretching out the hand of modernity and progress, while with the other maintaining a vice grip over all the executive power.

By the turn of the Sixties, Selassie was becoming an elderly man, but some of his most turbulent years still lay ahead of him. While the Emperor was on a state visit abroad, a group of disgruntled students, along with members of Selassie's own bodyguard, attempted to form a coup and take over the government. Though the plotters failed due to hopeless planning, it rocked the royal boat and gave the country a taste of mayhem to come. The very intelligentsia he had created through his reforms had turned against him.

Undeterred, Selassie continued to build his legacy, founding the Organisation of African Unity in 1963, a body designed to bring together the continent's nations and end colonisation, as well as making numerous state visits all over the world. He visited America several times, a country he greatly admired and relied on as an ally, but perhaps his defining and for many people most memorable visit was to Jamaica in 1966.

From the moment of his crowning as Emperor, from 1930 onwards, a sect of dedicated followers had formed in Jamaica, known as Rastafari. The religious sub-culture was and still is entirely based around Selassie himself, taking his name before

his coronation, Ras Tafiri, as its identity. The Rastafari worshipped Selassie as the living God on Earth, the promised descendant of Solomon, the African King. As the land ruled, Ethiopia was also considered sacred, and many Rastafari believed and still believe it to be their Zion, the holy land where they should return. His brief visit to Jamaica in 1966 was a poignant occasion for the movement, which swelled in numbers in later years after the emergence of and popularity of Bob Marley and reggae music.

If the Emperor's popularity abroad was on a high, it couldn't have been more different on his own soil. The seeds he had planted with his educational and structural reforms had by now taken root in the form of a progressive and leftist youth, impelled by the liberal Sixties and hungry for faster progression and greater freedoms than the old regime was willing to provide.

By 1974, the revolutionary aspects of the military, buoyed by new ideology and ambition, were ready to make their move on the government and forced the Emperor to step down in September of that year. Not long after, in August the following year, Selassie was declared dead while in the custody of the revolutionary government. Though his reign cannot be characterised as perfect, the Lion of Judah embodied the great changes that happened to his country and Africa as a whole throughout the 20th Century. Certainly, he occupies the unique position of being revered as a god, and it is for this, as well as remaining the enduring symbol of his nation and his people, that he is remembered.

> The word Rastafari actually derives from Selassie's former title and given name, Ras Tafari

Addis Ababa, Ethiopia. Haile Selassie, Emperor of Ethiopia, in his study

Life in the time of Haile Selassie

The League of Nations
Formed in the aftermath of the First World War, the League of Nations consisted of 52 member states. The League's aims included protecting its members from aggressive nations, as well as preventing illegal trafficking, though the outbreak of World War II is testament to its overall ineffectiveness.

Italian Colonialism
After his gradual rise to becoming the Fascist dictator of Italy in the 1920s, Mussolini sought to create his new Roman Empire, with himself at its head. As well as restoring hurt Italian pride, Il Duce also believed that by taking parts of mineral-rich Africa he could solve his country's economic woes.

The Rastafari Movement
Emerging around the 1930s, largely in Jamaica, the Rastafari movement mixes Zionist Christian theology with ritualistic cannabis use. Rastafarians consider Haile Selassie to be God on Earth, as they believe is prophesised in the Bible.

The Organisation of African Unity
The OAU was founded in Addis Abba, the capital of Ethiopia, by Haile Selassie. Its chief aim was to strengthen the bonds between the nations of the continent and to form a united front against external aggressors and colonialism in general. It was eventually disbanded in 2002.

Spread of Marxism
Communism and Marxism were the most influential political ideologies to emerge during the 20th century and reshaped the political landscapes of the world forever. Though they were slower to become popular in Ethiopia, left-wing, socialist and progressive ideals became more and more popular as the century wore on.

Defining moment
Visit to the Caribbean
21 April 1966
On landing in Kingston, Jamaica on a state visit, Haile is greeted by a frenzied crowd of thousands, many of whom are members of the Rastafari movement. Emerging during the 1930s, this religious and spiritual movement claimed that the Ethiopian Emperor was divine and even a reincarnation of Jesus Christ. During his brief visit, Haile addressed both houses of the Jamaican parliament and laid a wreath of remembrance at Kingston's war memorial. His presence causes utter chaos wherever he travels around the island, such is the devotion of those people who consider him to be God on Earth. It's debated whether Haile actually denied or supported the claims of his divinity.

1975

● **Silver jubilee**
Haile celebrates 25 years as Emperor and in the same year grants a new constitution giving greater freedoms to his subjects, without diminishing his own powers.
2 November 1955

● **A failed coup**
While on a visit abroad, groups of discontent students, in collaboration with members of the royal bodyguard and army, attempt to organise a coup to depose the Emperor.
14 December 1960

● **Deposed as Emperor**
By now advanced in age, the Emperor is no longer able to maintain the authority he once held and he is deposed by a socialist coup led by the military, beginning the Ethiopian Revolution.
13 September 1974

● **Death**
Haile Selassie dies while in the custody of the revolutionary military government at the age of 83. The circumstances of his death are still shrouded in suspicion.
27 August 1975

Edward VIII

Edward VIII shocked the world in 1936 when he announced to Britain and her empire that he was abdicating his throne for an American socialite named Wallis Simpson

In the late Thirties, Britain was facing its darkest hour. Hitler and his fascist thugs were rattling the sabre across Europe, quashing the rights of free men and women everywhere. Italy and Spain had fallen to the oppression of right-wing dictatorships and it wouldn't be long before war would sweep through the last free countries of the European continent. This was a time for stout hearts and stiff upper lips, for every British soul to look to the defence of the country and face these evil forces valiantly. Meanwhile Edward, Duke of Windsor, who until very recently had been King of Great Britain, sat in his villa in Antibes, France.

Edward's childhood and teenage years were a preparatory education to groom him for the day he would become King of Great Britain. He had one-to-one tuition with the best tutors in the land and attended renowned military schools - yet he was deeply unhappy. His father George, later to be crowned King George V, stood as a domineering and at times terrifying figure to Edward and his two siblings. George ran his household like a military operation, the children were forced to always be on time, to dress correctly and behave properly. Punishments included frightening confrontations with George in his study; a harsh prospect for Edward who was small and shy.

At just 12-years-old, Edward's father felt he needed a military education in order to prepare him for public life. He was sent to the naval college at Osborne on the Isle of Wight. Edward's

> According to his biographers Edward had an unhappy childhood; his nanny would deliberately hurt him

shy nature meant that he struggled to fit in with the other boys and bullying was an almost inevitable consequence. He did eventually find his feet and settled into this regimented life, passing the naval examination board for Dartmouth officer school in 1909. Edward continued to be a shy young man. During his cadet training, his parents threw a party for him at Buckingham Palace about which he recorded in his diary, 'I had to dance, a thing I hate, the whole thing was a great strain.' The 19-year-old Edward was still struggling to find his place in the world outside of the ritual of royal protocol.

It was clear that Edward lacked direction but World War I would see to it that all men of his age would be given a chance to prove themselves. Edward wanted to serve with the men of his army regiment on the frontline, he yearned to make a difference and war afforded him the opportunity. Unfortunately, the Secretary for War Lord Kitchener refused his request stating that it would be too dangerous for the young man. Edward continued to insist on being allowed to go and in the end toured the front regardless.

His admiration for the troops was shown in a correspondence he sent back to England, 'I'm very keen on the fighting troops being made as comfortable as possible always... the poor devils have a bloody enough time in the trenches... they are absolutely marvellous.' The war years had given Edward a sense of freedom he wouldn't normally have been permitted, he could meet other

"He continued to make horrendous errors in judgement, conducting a tour of Nazi Germany in 1937 and allowing himself to be photographed with Hitler"

During World War I Edward visited the trenches and saw first-hand the devastation and suffering caused by modern warfare

Wallis Simpson was the love of Edward's life, though it was known that he had other mistresses previously

EDWARD VIII
Britain, 1894 – 1972

Brief Bio Playboy prince Edward never really wanted to be king, but the death of his father forced it on him. The rigours of an unhappy childhood resulted in a man who pursued pleasure and he struggled to combine this with his royal duties as Prince of Wales. His affair with Wallis Simpson sounded the death knell for his kingship.

Edward VIII

173

A dark connection

The dark connection between Hitler and the British royal family in the Thirties begun in 1935 when the Fuhrer used Karl Eduard, the Duke of SaxeCoburg-Gotha as an informal ambassador of goodwill to the royal family. Eduard seemed to have succeeded in persuading Edward that Hitler was the only defence against communism. The connection grew stronger when Edward decided to visit Germany in 1937. A clandestine meeting between Edward and committed Nazis Rudolf Hess and Martin Bormann took place in Edward's hotel in Paris before the visit. An impression of the meeting written by Hess informed Hitler that, 'the Duke was proud of his German blood' and there was 'no need to lose a single German life in invading Britain. The Duke and his clever wife will deliver the goods.' Hess fully expected Edward to regain power in Britain and persuade the populace to seek peace. The visit to Germany then went ahead, Hitler was charming and Edward enjoyed his tour. As the war progressed, a secret memorandum to American president Roosevelt from J. Edgar Hoover claimed, 'that the Duke of Windsor entered into an agreement. If Germany was victorious [Herman Goering] would install the Duke of Windsor as King of England.' While it seems unlikely Edward did agree to this, he must have maintained links with the Nazis for this type of rumour to circulate.

men his own age under the guise of these tours and drop the cold protocol normally required of official visits.

After the armistice it was as if this new-found freedom had disappeared with the rifles and bayonets. He commented in 1919, ' I mixed with men... I found my manhood.' His father was quick to clip his new found self-confidence sternly informing him, 'don't think you act like other people.' He longed for the freedom given to him during the war and found his new life of state openings and formal banquets smothering. He drifted through his university career failing to make an impact academically and then went on an extended tour of the empire. While this should have offered him the adventure he yearned for, he quickly saw that he was just as much a prisoner abroad as he was at home. Every step he took was closely monitored, and he became frustrated and depressed. His frustration made him angry and he began to display the bigotry and dismissive nature inherited by many English aristocracy of the time. He was appalled by the Australian aborigines describing them as, 'the most revolting form of living creatures I've ever seen.' He also began to hate communism with unrelenting zeal.

It was during this unhappy time that in 1931 he met the woman that would change his life forever - Wallis Simpson. Edward had already had a number of affairs but they were fleeting. In Wallis he found something that he hadn't seen in other women, a strong independent character that knew

> Edward gained his pilot's licence and founded the 32 Royal squadron, used for royal flights to official engagements

her own mind and refused to stand on ceremony. He quickly became infatuated by her, it was said by observers that he lost 'all sense of reason' when he was around her. He lavished her with jewellery, gold or whatever she wanted, it seemed as if Edward had finally found someone to give his life meaning. There was however a complication as far as Edward's position as the Prince of Wales was concerned; Wallis was a married woman. When she became Edward's mistress she promised to give up her second husband for him but this wouldn't soothe the sensibilities of his family. To compound the issue she wasn't from a royal household, she was an American socialite from Baltimore. When it became obvious to Edward's father in 1934 that this wasn't another casual relationship he was furious; he angrily told him to get rid of her.

On 20 January 1936, George V died and the question of Wallis's status was immediately brought into question. Would she become queen? The short answer was absolutely not - she was twice divorced and unpopular with the British establishment. Absurd rumours circulated about the spell she had placed Edward under, her devious manipulation, her dark hold over the new king. The issue was becoming even more serious, especially considering that the country was edging ever closer to another world war. The nation needed leadership, not uncertainty, but Edward did not see the two issues as related. He wanted to marry Wallis, and everything else was of secondary importance. Besides, Adolf Hitler would defeat the

Defining moment
Tour of the empire
5 August 1919

After the war, Edward spends the next five years touring the empire and representing his father abroad. He does a number of public relation events including presenting the Prince of Wales cup to the Canadian hockey league and visiting the politically sensitive city of Quebec where he receives a warm welcome. His charm and good looks serve him well and he becomes a popular figure. Not all of his visits went so smoothly however; in a high-profile visit to Australia he wrote of the Aborigines, 'they are the most revolting form of living creatures I've ever seen'.

Defining moment
Royal family meet Wallis
November 1934

Edward's less than discreet affair with Wallis Simpson comes to a head in 1934 when Edward invites Simpson to an evening party at Buckingham Palace. Edward's father had originally struck her name out of the list of invitations but Edward invited her, regardless. When George finds out, he becomes outraged and shouts his disapproval. Simpson is subsequently frozen out of all royal family functions. This puts enormous strain on the relationship between Edward and his father, lending more fuel to the suspicion that Edward will abdicate when George dies.

Timeline

1894

● **A prince is born**
Edward Windsor is born at White Lodge, Richmond Park London to George and Mary, the Duke and Duchess of York. He is given the title His Highness Prince Edward of York.
23 June 1894

● **The Prince at Dartmouth**
On the wishes of his family, Edward joins the navy as an officer cadet at Dartmouth Navy College. He spends two years there before becoming a Midshipman.
September 1909

● **Prince of Wales and heir apparent**
On the death of Edward VII, Edward's father becomes the King of Britain and her empire. Edward is immediately invested as the Prince of Wales and is now next in line to the throne.
23 June 1910

● **War**
At the outbreak of World War I, Edward joins the Grenadier guards and asks to serve at the front. This request is refused by the Secretary of State for War Lord Kitchener.
28 July 1914

● **Time magazine story**
Time magazine publishes a story in which Edward is reported to have said that he would abdicate the throne. This is officially denied, but the story serves as an insight into his thoughts.
29 April 1929

communists and the world would be at peace - there was really nothing to worry about as far as he was concerned.

The fact that Edward was for the appeasement of Hitler was not unusual; many members of the British establishment were in the late Thirties. What was compounding the issue was the Nazi party was seen to be influencing the King through Wallis. Whether this was true or not is debatable but many influential people saw it so; the American ambassador commented, 'many people here suspect that Mrs Simpson is actually in German pay.' The situation was looking bad and as an illustration of the tense atmosphere, Edward suffered an assassination attempt when a lone gunman apparently working for an undisclosed foreign power tried to pull a gun on him. When Edward returned to Buckingham Palace the first sympathy call was from Hitler.

Then in November 1936 Edward told Prime Minister Stanley Baldwin that he was going to marry Wallis. Baldwin rejected the proposal, stating that it would be unacceptable to the British cabinet if the head of state married a twice-divorcee. Wallis herself expected full marriage, and Edward refused to give her up. He saw no option; on the 11 of December he announced to Britain and the empire, "I have found it impossible to carry the heavy burden of responsibility and to discharge my duties as King... without the help and support of the woman I love." He abdicated the throne, passing the duty to his brother Albert, the father of Queen Elizabeth II.

Edward and Wallis were now in limbo. They were granted official titles, the Duke and Duchess

> Edward was stanchly anti-communist and feared the communist takeover of Europe during the Thirties

of Windsor, but were frozen out of much of the public salary they should have received for the role. Once again Edward fell into a deep depression, he relied on the hospitality of friends abroad and used the Château de Candé in France to marry Wallis. He became an embittered and ungrateful guest, running up huge phone bills and refusing to pay for anything. He also continued to make horrendous errors in judgement, conducting a tour of Nazi Germany in 1937 and allowing himself to be photographed with Hitler.

In 1940, as a way of preventing any more embarrassment to the royal family, Winston Churchill gave the Duke a governorship in the Bahamas. Edward saw it for what it was - a way to get him out of the way. He conducted his duties, made inroads into improving the situations of the workers on the islands but hated his current position none the less. He had become increasingly estranged from his family.

By the time the war was over and the dust had settled over his relationship with Wallis, the Duke was content to live quietly. He established himself in France at the 4 Route du Champ d'Entraînement Paris, later to be known as Villa Windsor, where he spent the rest of his days in retirement. He had lived a privileged life but it was a life he did not want, in the end he gave up the power he inherited at birth for the woman he loved.

The British Empire

The British Empire still remained the single biggest empire on the face of the planet during the years leading up to the war. Many of its dominions like Canada, Australia and New Zealand governed their own affairs but still held political ties with Britain through the British monarchy. Other countries like Burma and India were governed directly as colonies.

An age of extremes

The huge social upheaval caused by the Great Depression created a credibility gap between liberal governments and their citizens in Europe. This gave rise to extremist governments from the communist left and fascist right. Adolf Hitler in particular was starting to make a name for himself as an uncompromising totalitarian leader.

Role of the monarchy

The role of the monarchy in Britain and throughout the Commonwealth was changing in the wake of the mass media. It was no longer enough for the monarch to simply open Parliament once a year, the Royal family was expected to set an example of British values in the country and take on a leadership role in times of national need.

Colonial unrest

The Thirties gave rise to independence movements in many imperial colonies. The most vocal of these movements came from India and Mahatma Gandhi's freedom group. While the British government doggedly hung on to its empire in India, the British people started to wonder if it was worth it

Britain, a waning power?

No-one could dispute that British influence throughout the globe remained strong during the Thirties, but the government's reluctance to rearm and prepare for war in the face of fascist and communist threats was said to be indicative of an waning power that no longer had the stomach for military commitments.

Edward preparing to inform the nation that he is abdicating the throne in 1936

● **Governor of the Bahamas**
In an effort to prevent Edward and Wallis, now Duke and Duchess of Windsor, from embarrassing the British government even more, Edward is given the governorship of the Bahamas.
18 August 1940

● **Retirement**
With the war won and the new world order establishing itself in Europe, France becomes safe again for British citizens. Edward and Wallis retire there comfortably.
November 1952

Defining moment
Abdication
10 December 1936

Edward makes it clear to Prime Minister Stanley Baldwin that he will not change his mind about marrying Wallis as soon as her second divorce is finalised. Baldwin informs Edward that the cabinet and the imperial parliaments will not accept his marriage to Wallis if he still wishes to be king. With Edward finding it impossible to reconcile his personal life with his duty as a future monarch, he finally decides to abdicate and signs the act at Fort Belvedere in the presence of his younger brother Albert the Duke of York who is next in line to the throne.

1972

● **Succession to the throne**
George V dies and Edward is immediately put forward for the succession. It also becomes known within the government that he intends to soon marry Wallis.
20 January 1936

● **Assassination attempt**
A man called George McMahon pulls a gun on Edward and is quickly set upon by police. He testifies that he was working for a foreign power although this is never proved.
16 July 1936

● **Marriage to Wallis**
Edward and Wallis marry at the Château de Candé in France. While the service is attended by a number of high-profile socialites, none of the royal family attends.
3 June 1937

● **Visit to Germany**
Against the advice of the British Government, Edward and Wallis visit Nazi Germany and are warmly welcomed by Adolf Hitler. It is reported that he almost gives a Nazi salute.
October 1937

● **Death of a Duke**
Edward dies peacefully in his sleep aged 77. His body is flown back to England and a funeral service is attended by Queen Elizabeth II. His body is buried at the royal burial ground at Frogmore.
28 May 1972

© Alamy

DISCOVER

The legend of Robin Hood
Discover the truth behind the world's most famous folk hero

ALL ABOUT HISTORY

10 DIRTIEST TRICKS OF WWII

THE TITANIC TRAGEDY
The full story of the ship they thought unsinkable

+
Battle of Marathon
Piazza di Spagna
Sp

About the magazine

All About History is the only history magazine that is accessible and entertaining to all, packed with world-leading features covering the most amazing real-life events.

* This offer entitles new UK Direct Debit subscribers to receive their first 3 issues for £5. After these issues, subscribers will then pay £17.95 every 6 issues. Subscribers can cancel this subscription at any time. New subscriptions will start from the next available issue. Offer code 'ZGGZINE' must be quoted to receive this special subscriptions price. Direct Debit guarantee available on request. This offer will expire 31 March 2015.

** This is a US subscription offer. The USA issue rate is based on an annual subscription price of £50 for 13 issues, which is equivalent to $78 at the time of writing compared with the newsstand price of $9.99 for 13 issues being $129.87. Your subscription will start from the next available issue. This offer expires 31 March 2015.

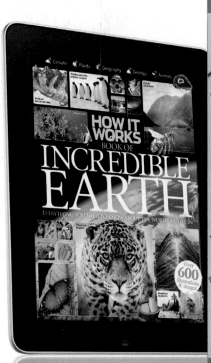
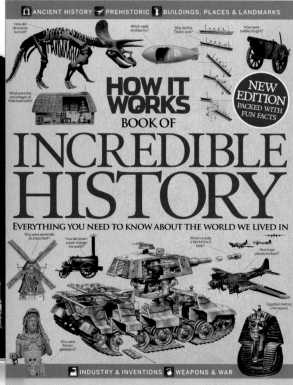
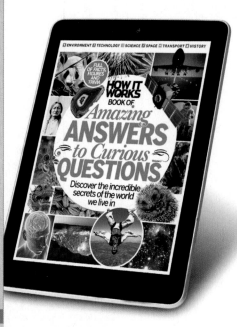